JOHN WILLIS is Professor of Law Emeritus, Dalhousie University

The Dalhousie Law School is the oldest common-law law school in Canada, the distinguished prototype for the entire system of Canadian legal education. In this volume, John Willis takes a warm and personal interest in the development of 'Dalhousie's Little Law School.' As he recreates the school's past, a past characterized both by problems and by triumphs, Willis places this famous institution's activities into perspective against the larger background of the many law schools in Canada.

Conducting the reader on a tour along the history of the school from its inception in 1883, Professor Willis brings to life the struggles for survival and growth of the British Empire's first professional common-law law school. From 1887 to 1945, we see the miniscule faculty and small student body at work as a closely knit family. The Dalhousie Law School has always generated loyalty and affection among its graduate students and faculty, this through the clearly defined goals of its first dean, Dean Weldon. Here were developed the school's unchanging concern with both the professional and the cultural approaches to the study of law, as well as its pride in being an active contributor to the national life of Canada, and the development of the nation's legal education system. John Willis shares with the reader the enthusiasm and pride of all associated with this ever-changing Canadian institution.

JOHN WILLIS

A
History of
Dalhousie
Law School

UNIVERSITY OF TORONTO PRESS
Toronto   Buffalo   London

© University of Toronto Press 1979
Toronto   Buffalo   London
Printed in Canada

Canadian Cataloguing in Publication Data

Willis, John.
A history of Dalhousie Law School

Includes index.
ISBN 0-8020-2337-1

1. Dalhousie University. Faculty of Law –
History.   I. Title.
KE322.D35w54   340'.07'1171622   C78-001572-X

PREFACE

This history is the work of two hands: it was begun by the late Dean Emeritus Horace E. Read and finished by me. Horace Read had conceived the idea of writing the School's history; he did most of the research and succeeded in completing what is best described as a rough preliminary first draft of the period 1883 to 1950. After he died in February 1975 I was asked to finish the project which was so dear to him and upon which he had spent so much time and trouble.

In order to qualify myself for the task I went back to the materials on which he had based his first draft – a process rendered rather difficult by the fact that the draft contained very few references to his sources – and supplemented them by some research of my own into matters he had not dealt with, e.g., developments in the curriculum and what was going on at other law schools. To enable me to cope with the period not covered by his draft, 1950 to 1976 – this history had to end somewhere, and I decided on 1976 – I had available to me various memoranda written by him on various subjects during the years 1950 to 1964 when he was dean; these too I supplemented by some researches of my own. On the period 1964 to 1976 he never, as he himself repeatedly said, intended to do anything, and here I have been entirely on my own; many thanks to colleagues, students, and others who helped me garner information about those eventful years.

Although this history is to the extent I have just described the work of two hands, the finished product is mine alone. Read's draft was little more than a detailed chronological record of 'events'; the arrangement, the shape, the tone, and, of course, the writing of what is now presented to the reader are all mine. Had Horace Read lived to finish what he began, the book would probably have been long, detailed, and, if I may dare to say so, a shade too boastful about the achievements of the School. I have deliberately kept it short, panoramic, and at a level where the reader will, I hope, be able to say, 'Willis has, as he should, told us about the problems as well as the triumphs of the School but always, always, in a voice of filial respect.'

It is said to be poor policy for an author to apologize for what he has written, but that is what I am now going to do. The book I should like to have written about Dalhousie Law School would be something very different from this: it is a history of Dalhousie Law School as an educational institution. Mine would, at one extreme, have been an essay in social history – an account of the part played by the graduates of the School in the development of the legal profession in the Atlantic and Prairie provinces. Or it would, at the other extreme, have been an intimate, rather sentimental account of what it felt like to be a student at the School in all of the years from 1883 to 1976, something along the lines of the reminiscences in the special issues of *Ansul*, January 1976 and December 1977. Both of these projects would, alas, have been beyond me and were in any event beyond my terms of reference, which were 'Finish What Horace Read Began.' And that is what I have tried to do to the best of my ability.

I have received so much help from so many people that all I can do is thank them generally and without naming them. A special word of thanks is due the Canadian Bar Association for their permission to reprint in Appendix I and Appendix III two articles from the *Canadian Bar Review*. A very special word of thanks is owed to Ronnie Macdonald, the present Dean of Dalhousie Law School, for the number of general ideas he injected into my thinking about the School and its history. And I owe much more than mere thanks to my wife, Dorothy, who has had to live with me – which meant living with 'the history' too – during the years in which I was so submerged in the ins and outs of Dalhousie Law School that only occasionally did I, as she expressed it, 'come up for air.'

JOHN WILLIS
Sandy Cove
Spring 1978

CONTENTS

A HISTORY OF DALHOUSIE LAW SCHOOL

INTRODUCTION

At the end of October 1983, Dalhousie Law School will be a hundred years old. In a country as young as Canada any institution which reaches such an age has for that reason alone earned the right to have its history written. But there are so many other reasons for putting together this book that the School has earned the right several times over. Here are a few of them.

What began in 1883 as a purely local venture in the eastern extremity of Canada had by its fiftieth birthday in 1933 succeeded in making, through those who had taught or had been students there, a signal impact on the national life. What was in its inception no more than a daring experiment with a new way of training students for the public profession of the law in Canada has become in the last twenty years the orthodox method, accepted right across the country. The triple tradition of high academic standards, public service, and an easy relationship between teacher and student which its first dean, Richard Chapman Weldon, is said to have started in the little School of long ago today (1976) inspires, under the name of 'the Weldon tradition,' the thirty-six full-time teachers and about four hundred and fifty students who might, were it not for Weldon and those who carried on what he began, be thinking of themselves as just another law school. To these reasons for writing the School's history must be added what is perhaps the most important one of all – the affection felt for it by so many of those who graduated from it when it was still 'Dalhousie's Little Law School,' and the need to remind those who work in the Weldon Building today of the past that they have inherited. However little interest others may have in the story that is going to be told, these men and women will want to listen.

It is to the devoted affection of one of those who graduated from and taught at the School when it was 'just like a little family' – the late Dean

Horace E. Read – that this book owes its existence. Right up to the time of his death in 1975 the School was always first in his thoughts. First a student and then a teacher during the years 1921 to 1933, a period we can now recognize as 'the Golden Age,' and subsequently Dean from 1950 to 1964, a period in which the School was slowly but surely changing into the very different kind of institution it is today, he embarked towards the end of his life on what to him was always a labour of love – writing what was to be its first complete history. He did not, unfortunately, live long enough to finish it. The word 'complete' is used because there were already in existence a.few 'capsule' histories prepared at various dates and for various special occasions, all of them, however, quite short and, what is worse, very difficult to find. Notable among them are: a short perceptive piece in the *Dalhousie Gazette* of 26 November 1929 written by Dr Charles Morse, the founding editor of the *Canadian Bar Review* and earlier a member of the class of 1885, the first class ever to graduate from the School, and entitled 'The Second of a Series of Articles on Dalhousie's Little Law School "the training school of a nation"'; and a longish, overpitched, but eminently readable article by David MacDonald, the journalist son of Dean Vincent MacDonald, in *Maclean's Magazine* of 1 March 1954 with the title 'The Brainiest School in the Country' and the subtitle 'So many prime ministers, provincial premiers, chief justices, M.P.'s and millionaires have been turned out by Dalhousie Law School that it's become famous as Nova Scotia's biggest Brain-export factory.' And in 1976 and 1977 there was published in two special issues of *Ansul*, the student periodical, a series of reminiscences by former students and teachers at the School, vignettes which are full of flavour and give, as no formal history can, the feeling of what it was like to be there. Alas, they cover no more than the relatively short period 1916-60.

In the writings collected at the end of this book under the headings 'The Weldon tradition' (Appendix II) and 'What Dalhousie Law School says about itself when it is on parade' (Appendix III) will be found reverberating three themes in which the School has always taken great pride: its contributions to the national life of Canada; its special place in the history of Canadian legal education; and the clearly defined goals which, under the name of the Weldon tradition, it tries to set for its students and teachers.

The impact of the little School on the national life of Canada was seen at its most striking in the early thirties, a date when it had, after fifty years of operation, produced no more than about seven hundred graduates. There was at that time a Dalhousie Law School graduate on every provincial Supreme Court in the country except in Prince Edward Island, Ontario, and Quebec; at the dinner celebrating the School's fiftieth birthday in 1933 Premiers L.P.D. Tilley of New Brunswick ('93) and Angus L. Macdonald of Nova Scotia ('21) were sitting at the head table and there was read a congratulatory letter from no less a person than the Prime Minister of Canada, R.B. Bennett ('93). Three years later Sir Lyman Duff, Chief Justice of Canada, had this to say in his address on behalf of the honorary graduates at a Dalhousie convocation:

the contribution of the Law School of Dalhousie to the education of the lawyers of Canada, to the elevation and maintenance of professional standards in point of mastery of legal principle, and otherwise, cannot be over-emphasized or exaggerated. There is hardly a province of Canada in which graduates of Dalhousie Law School are not to be found upon the Bench or among the leaders of the Bar. From the Pacific to the Atlantic the power of Dalhousie has been felt in all spheres of collective activity where lawyers are wont to exert preponderant or signal influence.

Going on to 'the men associated in some capacity with the Law School of Dalhousie, either as teachers or as graduates, who have distinguished themselves in Canadian life,' he continued:

I pass over the influence of Dalhousie upon the public and professional life of the Province of Nova Scotia. That is better known to you than it is to me. In careers pursued beyond the limits of the Province graduates of this School have won renown in public and professional life, and have exercised high influence upon the course of public affairs in critical periods.[1]

These thoughts were echoed by Vincent MacDonald, by then Mr Justice MacDonald of the Supreme Court of Nova Scotia, when in his convocation address at the opening of the Studley building in 1952 he said: 'In terms of service on the Bench, the record – relative to numbers – is probably unmatched in the whole country'; and 'In political leadership the record – again relative to numbers – is astoundingly high.' Mr Justice MacDonald filled out with some details the picture he was painting; for these details the reader is referred to his 'A national law school,' reproduced in Appendix III.

In more recent years the impact of the graduates of the School on the public and professional life of Canada has not been as great as it was in the early thirties, but it is still considerable. For several years in the seventies four out of the ten provincial premiers were graduates: Allan Blakeney of Saskatchewan ('47), Gerald Regan of Nova Scotia ('52), Richard B. Hatfield of New Brunswick ('56), and Alexander B. Campbell of Prince Edward Island ('58). An amusing by-product of 'the four premiers' is an article in the *Atlantic Advocate* for November 1971 with the provocative title 'Dalhousie Law School – Training Ground for Premiers?' and an equally provocative subtitle, 'How deliberate is Dalhousie Law School's policy to produce leading politicians?'

Dalhousie Law School was, as everyone knows, the first law school, and the first university law school, to be established in the common-law provinces of Canada. But, leaving entirely aside the distinction of having been first in the field, there are two even more noteworthy facets to the special position it holds in the history of Canadian legal education. The first facet is that as long ago as 1891 it had succeeded in achieving between itself and the Nova Scotia Barristers' Society that separation and co-ordination of functions in preparing people for admission to the practice of law which is today universally accepted right across the country: a period of full-time academic study in an independent law school, supplemented by a shorter period of apprenticeship in a law office. The second, and far more important, facet is that it was from its very beginning in 1883 a university law school with a liberal as well as a professional orientation – which is what all Canadian law schools are today.[2] All this was in striking contrast to the situation in what has always been by far the most populous common-law province, Ontario. Until as recently as 1957 the only law school there, Osgoode Hall Law School, was owned and operated by the profession, whose governing body, the Benchers of the Law Society of Upper Canada, regarded it as little more than an adjunct to what in their opinion really mattered, the time spent by a student in acquiring 'the nuts and bolts' as an apprentice in the 'real world' of a practising lawyer's office.

For a proper appreciation of what is meant by saying that Dalhousie Law School has been from the beginning an independent university law school the reader is referred to John Read's 'Fifty years of legal education at Dalhousie' and Vincent MacDonald's 'A national law school,' both reproduced in Appendix III. All that need be done here is to quote from them one or two telling passages. After referring to the importance of insuring 'an even balance between the cultural and professional sides of legal education,' John Read has this to say about the curriculum of 1883:

In its content, the curriculum was based upon the balancing of two principles. On the one hand, its scope was sufficiently extensive to give to the student an adequate foundation for his professional needs. On the other hand, the curriculum included the cultural elements in legal education. The relationship of law to the other elements in human knowledge and in life was not forgotten. It demonstrated that it was possible to make the study of law a liberal education and, at the same time, to place the student in a position where he could readily learn to cope with the difficulties of practice after his graduation.

On the same topic, but this time laying emphasis on the School's 'independence,' here is Vincent MacDonald:

In a life full of paradox, it is notable that in all matters pertaining to curriculum and admission to practice, the School has been subject to the control of the Nova Scotia Barristers' Society. Had that Society been possessed of a narrow vocational approach to a legal education, it could have aborted or warped the growth of the School. Fortunately it never sought to keep the School in thraldom to such an approach. On the contrary, it has been eagerly co-operative in the attempts of the School to provide a broadly based education which – without despising professional 'know-how' – sought to embrace knowledge of law in all its implications and particularly as an agency of government. In the result, the School has been able to pursue the true purposes of a University Law School ...

If, as indeed is the case, the Dalhousie model of an independent university law school has everywhere in Canada now prevailed over the Osgoode model of one tied to the profession, what part did Dalhousie Law School play in bringing that about? In Ontario it was Sidney Smith ('20), successively student, teacher, and dean at the Law School in the twenties and early thirties, who, as president of the University of Toronto, played a leading part in the events that culminated in 1957 in the abandonment by the Law Society of its monopoly over legal education and the subsequent establishment of several university law schools in that province. In each of the three western provinces of Saskatchewan, Alberta, and British Columbia, systematic instruction in law was first offered by the local law society, but that Osgoode model was later superseded, and here too with the assistance of graduates of Dalhousie Law School, by an independent law school run by the local university.[3] As to Alberta, so many Dalhousie graduates had gained positions of power in the legal profession there that one can say without doubt that it was their influence which, soon after the end of the First World War, brought about the change. In Saskatchewan, where the change came a little earlier than in Alberta, both the first dean of the College of Law at the University of Saskatchewan and his assistant were from Dalhousie: the dean, Arthur Moxon, was an Arts graduate who had done his law at Oxford as a Rhodes Scholar and his assistant, Ira MacKay, was a Law graduate of 1905. And in 1945 it was N.A.M. MacKenzie ('23) who, as president of the University of British Columbia, brought legal education in that province into the Dalhousie fold by starting a Faculty of Law and appointing as its first dean George Curtis, who had for the last eleven years prior to his appointment been teaching at Dalhousie Law School.

Coming now to the third theme in which the Law School takes pride, the Weldon tradition of 'high academic standards, public service and the ever-open door policy,' the reader is, once again, referred to Appendix II for a more detailed exposition of it. All there is room for here are a few comments from a historical point of view.

This inspirational slogan is, if the writer's memory serves him aright, a very modern invention. It was not in use when he taught at the School from 1933 to 1944 and the first time he ever heard it was when he came back there for three years in 1972. It was probably invented, and given currency, by Horace Read while he was dean. In any event the first use of the slogan in print occurs in Read's Report to the President, 1950-54, where, referring to the death of Angus L. Macdonald, he writes: 'In his professional and political life he completely fulfilled the Weldon Tradition – by devotion to legal scholarship and unselfish public service.' The fact that the slogan is often heard today is, he guesses, a product of the change that has taken place in the size and nature of the School since the move to the Weldon Building in 1966. A small intimate school staffed mainly by its own graduates – which is what the pre-1966 School was – does not talk about its traditions, still less express them in a slogan with a rather definite content. No such explicit guide to conduct was needed until the School became large, impersonal, and staffed preponderantly by 'outsiders,' as it did during the last ten years.

How correctly, as a matter of historical fact, does the slogan portray what went on in the past? Academic standards at the Law School have had their ups and downs – in the writer's personal experience, 1933-44 was a clear down and 1972-75 a clear up – but it is plainly incorrect to give to Weldon a credit which rightly belongs to MacRae. It was Donald MacRae, the much under-praised successor to Weldon, who made the School academically notable by raising admission standards, bringing the curriculum into the twentieth century, and inspiring his students and young colleagues (Sidney Smith, Vincent MacDonald, and Horace Read among them) with his own sense of legal scholarship.

Public service? In his unpublished 'Dalhousie Law School – Ideals and Traditions'[4] John Barnett ('07), a student of Weldon's subsequent to the period 1887-96 when Weldon had been, as we shall see, a member of Parliament, tells us that 'Quietly but constantly he [Weldon] preached the duties of lawyers to the state in all branches of public service. It was the duty of lawyers to take part in the political life of the country for whatever party they chose, but always to keep in mind the higher duty of cleansing and purifying it from within.' No doubt as a result of this, a very vital part of the Weldon tradition, Sidney Smith ('20) is able, twenty years later, to speak in a letter to Horace Read of 'that fine sense of citizenship (it is no less than that)' which he found at the Law School. And twenty years later still we find Gerald Regan ('52) saying that 'all students were made very much aware of the fact that Bennett, the former prime minister, and Angus L. Macdonald, who was Nova Scotia's premier, had gone through Dalhousie Law School.'[5]

'The ever-open door policy'? To quote again from John Barnett, 'The writer early heard, that quite a number of students were visitors to the Dean's [Weldon's] private office and that he loved to have them come ... These student visits must have broken into and added greatly to the burdens of administrative and lecture duties; but there was never any sign of this; the door was rarely closed to entry and the visits seldom hurried or curtailed.' The writer can testify from his own personal experience that by the thirties, and probably long before, Weldon's easy-going ways with students had hardened into the rigid rule that a teacher's door must always be physically open – even when a student's desire to do no more than 'chew the fat' conflicted with a teacher's need to prepare for his classes. In 1976, however, it must be admitted that, because of the large number of students and the pressure on teachers to write, the rule is less strictly observed than it once was.

There are other, and less high-sounding, themes which run through the story of the School and must be borne in mind by the reader as he goes through the more or less chronological record of events that this history, or any history, has to be. The following summary of what the succeeding chapters in this book will contain is a necessary prelude to saying what those themes are.

Part I, 'Beginning,' will relate the salient events in what is the only dramatic episode in the School's long history. Against a discouraging background – an attempt by some young lawyers in Halifax to bolster the faltering apprenticeship system of training law students by setting up a law school, which fails for lack of money, and a Dalhousie University which looks as if once more it will have to close its doors, also for lack of money – there begins in 1883 the first university law school in the common-law provinces of Canada and, indeed, in what was then the British Empire. It is an instant success. Headed by Weldon, a highly educated man with what today we should call a political science background, and staffed by an unusually distinguished group of practising lawyers, it strikes from the very beginning a balance which it will always maintain between the cultural and the practical aspects of law. It has only one full-time teacher, Weldon, but he is a man of high ideals and endearing personality and he will be its dean for thirty years. For almost fifty years it will normally graduate no more than a dozen students a year.

Part II, 'Dalhousie's Little Law School,' will be immensely long and divided into four sections. It will record the main events and the main trends in the nearly sixty years which elapsed between the move to the Forrest Building in 1887 and the end of the Second World War in 1945, a period in which there were never more than ninety students or more than four full-time teachers: Section One, '1887-1914,' the long Weldon period, in which Weldon and his old friend 'Benny' Russell, men of affairs as well as teachers, put their stamp on more generations of students than anyone else has since and in which so many graduates left the hard ground of the Maritimes to become 'success stories' elsewhere that it was not too much of an exaggeration for the *Dalhousie Gazette* to speak in 1929 of 'Dalhousie's Little Law School, the training ground of a nation'; Section Two, '1914-24,' the MacRae period, in which MacRae, an erstwhile classics professor, against whose appointment as dean Benny Russell had made strong representations, and until 1920 still the only full-time teacher, succeeded, as we said earlier, in making the School academically notable; Section Three, '1920-33: The Golden Age,' in which such 'names' as John Read, Sidney Smith, Angus L. Macdonald, Vincent MacDonald, and Horace Read were at various times full-time teachers at the School and which culminated in a bout of justifiable self-congratulation on the occasion of the School's silver jubilee in October 1933; and Section Four, '1933-45,' the frustrating but relatively stable years of the Great Depression and the Second World War.

Beginning with the return of the veterans at the end of that war and ending with the life-changing move in 1966 to its present home, the Weldon Building, the School is for many reasons – but chiefly because there is for the first time in its long life a little money available – changing so surely, though slowly, that this relatively short period has had to be given a part all to itself – Part III, 'Changing.' There are changes in size, in the make-up of the faculty, in the curriculum, in the library, and in 'plant,' each one of these changes foreshadowing even greater changes to come.

In the years 1966 to 1976 there are so many noteworthy events and the School – staff, students, curriculum, library, and building, each one of them – has by 1976 become so very different from what it has traditionally been that Part IV, 'In the Weldon Building,' has had to be set up a little differently from the previous parts. Section One, 'Significant Events,' emphasizes the events; Section Two, 'Significant Changes: Faculty, Students, and Curriculum,' puts emphasis on contrasting the then and the now. Gone forever is Dalhousie's Little Law School with its intimate atmosphere and its many problems. In its place is the institution described in *The Dalhousie Law School*, an illustrated brochure written by Professor George Nicholls and issued in 1975. It has: a faculty of thirty-six full-time teachers 'with an almost international flavour,' which writes as well as teaches; a student body of four hundred and fifty men and women which is only sixty per cent Nova Scotian in origin and now contributes as much to the public image of the School as the faculty does; a curriculum which is directed as much to policy-makers as it is to practising lawyers; a library which is, for the first time, worthy of the School's aspirations; and a building which is, again for the first time, at least adequate. What has not gone is the Weldon tradition; academic standards are the highest they have ever been; true to the ideal of public service, the students operate the Dalhousie Legal Aid Service and the faculty a continuing legal education program; and, despite the vast increase in numbers and the advent in the late sixties of student activism, what Benny Russell said in 1914 is as true today as it ever was: 'during the whole history of the law school ... there has never been a single instance of friction or misunderstanding between the faculty and the students.'[6]

Of the themes to be borne in mind by the reader of this history the first, and the most outstanding, is that the story is singularly uneventful; from the beginning the School knew what it was trying to do and has to this day continued to do it. It has none of the excitement to be found in the turbulent history of Osgoode Hall Law School, with its ever-present tension between the ideals of the liberal academic and the ideals of the hard-nosed practitioner.[7] Its hallmark is continuity and tradition. For more than thirty years the School's two co-founders, Weldon and Russell, will constitute its core faculty; for more than sixty years it will be housed in the same place, the north wing of the Forrest Building; for nearly seventy years the downtown practitioner will remain the vital member of the faculty that he was in the beginning; from the beginning until today the curriculum will be a mix of the cultural and the professional.

In this tradition-fraught institution two specific traditions call for special mention. The first is that the School is a small school with all that that implies of warm family atmosphere and a sense of loyalty to the institution on the part of its teachers and students. It was, as we have just said, a small school in fact until as late as 1945 and so strong is this tradition that the large institution of today has not wholly lost the 'feel' of the earlier small one. The second tradition is that the School is a Maritime school which aspires to be a 'national' one – an aspiration sometimes voiced by its deans on public occasions. Its Maritime complexion is evident in the fact that: every one of its eight deans has, by deliberate policy, been a Maritimer; until as late as 1966 nearly all its teachers have been its own old students; and, despite claims to the contrary, nearly all its students have, until a little earlier than 1966, been drawn from the Maritimes, a make-up which has been preserved by a Faculty ruling, made in the early seventies, that seventy-five per cent of the places in the first-year class are reserved for those coming from the Atlantic provinces. Regarding its aspirations to be a national school, it has from the beginning been national in the sense that a large proportion of its graduates have been forced to go elsewhere in Canada to find work ('this School must export or die') and also in the sense that it has never tied itself in its teaching to the law of any one province. It has never been, and is never likely to be, national in the sense that students come to it from right across the country because it is recognized as being 'first in the field,' as are some of the great schools in the United States. No law school in Canada has ever been, or is likely to be, a national one in this sense of the word.

Because the reader is going to find that the path of Dalhousie Law School has not always been an easy one, the second, and almost equally important, theme he or she should bear in mind is best stated in the form of a question. What are the difficulties with which the School has had to contend and how has it managed to surmount them? Its chief difficulty has been lack of money – a problem shared with all the other Canadian law schools. It was literally starved for money until 1945. Here are a few examples. In 1883 a first-rate librarian was secured, but in 1884 he had to be let go because there was no money to pay him; result – no librarian until seventy-five years later and then only because of the generosity of the Sir James Dunn Foundation. In 1922 a Law Building was built on the Studley campus but it had to be 'temporarily' occupied by the Arts Faculty until 1952, by which time it had become inadequate to the needs of the School; result – no adequate building until the move to its present home in the Weldon Building in 1966. In 1914 Donald MacRae, a classics professor who had turned to law in later life and was then just a year out of law school, was, to the enduring benefit of the School, appointed to succeed Weldon as dean because and only because he was the only man the Board could get at the price they were able to pay; he was a great success but in 1924 he left because the Board could not afford to meet what Osgoode Hall Law School was able to offer him. In the hungry thirties there was one year in which the School was given no library appropriation at all, so that Dean Vincent MacDonald had to write begging letters to old graduates – without, it should be said, much success.

Another difficulty – which has had, and still has, consequences of far-reaching importance – is the School's remoteness from the centres of population of Canada. For more than half a century after its foundation 'it provided intellectual leadership in the critical study of the common law in Canada,'[8] but the thousand miles separating it from Toronto effectually prevented it from having any effect in all those long years on the only law school of any size in the country, Osgoode Hall. For Dalhousie Law School itself, geographical remoteness meant, in a past without money for travel, that its faculty was intellectually isolated and today, when money is no longer the barrier it once was, it means that full-time teachers are hard to get and hard to keep; for the bright young man usually wants to be 'where the action is,' and that Halifax is not.

To offset these disheartening difficulties, the School has always had a number of things going for it. It has been fortunate in its deans – and, be it remembered, in the days of the small school the Dean *was* the School – Richard Weldon, Donald MacRae, John Read (later Judge Read of the International Court of Justice), Sidney Smith (later President of the University of Toronto), Vincent MacDonald (later Mr Justice MacDonald of the Supreme Court of Nova Scotia), and Horace Read (in one respect the best of all the deans: he was never looking over his shoulder for something else). It has also been fortunate, generally speaking, in its students, particularly those who came there as veterans of two world wars. Until 1950 the only law school of any consequence in the Maritimes,[9] it long had a virtual monopoly of every ambitious young Maritimer who wanted to 'get on' through law. The Bar of Nova Scotia has always actively supported it. From the beginning until 1920, it was a series of judges and distinguished practitioners from downtown Halifax, the so-called 'downtown lecturers,' who taught (with an occasional exception) *all* the 'professional' subjects; even after the establishment of a full-time faculty of four during the twenties it was they who came up and gave the 'nuts and bolts' courses such as Evidence, Procedure, and Shipping; it was not indeed until the mid-fifties that the downtown lecturer ceased to be the familiar figure he once was. Even more important perhaps than the active help given by these individuals has been the always sympathetic approach of the Nova Scotia Barristers' Society to what the School was, with all faults, trying to do. The University has always given, and given wholeheartedly, as much support as it could: in the beginning because the School was necessary for its own survival and in later years because it realized how much its own reputation depended on the reputation of the School; as a Calgary lawyer put it, a little two extremely, in 1935, 'if Dalhousie University is known beyond the Maritimes at all, it is because of the record of its law school and not the other faculties.'[10]

No less impelling than the tangible aids thus given to the School are the dreams that its students and teachers have had for it. A very early example is the dream George Patterson ('89) had for it in his Valedictory Address for the Graduates in Law 1889: 'is it too much to hope that Nova Scotia will soon, in legal matters, become the Massachusetts of Canada? That state owes her splendid, undisputed supremacy to the Law School at Harvard and surely we are not over confident in believing that the Law School at Dalhousie is destined to produce a like effect in Nova Scotia.'[11] Other later examples are: 'when I was attending the Law School [1916-1920] we had the feeling that the Dalhousie Law School was the Harvard Law School of Canada';[12] 'Oh heavens! What a chance [in 1929] to make Dal *the* Law School for the cream not the skim milk of Canada, a centre of creative legal thought';[13] and 'Dean MacDonald [at the end of the nineteen forties] ... continually sought ... to inculcate or 'program' us with the notion ... that his graduates were a little special and that more in the way of public service was expected of them than of law graduates generally.'[14]

The reader now knows how this history of Dalhousie Law School came to be written and why it was thought to be worth writing. He has been told of the three things in which the School, small as it was until after the end of the Second World War, takes most pride: of the impact it has had on the public life of Canada; of the example it has set for Canadian legal education; and of the tradition, 'the Weldon tradition,' that has for so long inspired it. He has been given a thumbnail sketch of its beginnings, of what happened to it during its long sojourn as Dalhousie's Little Law School in the north wing of the Forrest Building – at which time it was to the minds of many, including the writer's, the 'real' Dalhousie Law School – and of its transformation into the School as it is in the Weldon Building in 1976. He has been prepared against the moment when he may be tempted to say to himself 'this is not very exciting stuff, is it?' – continuity and tradition does not make for exciting reading – and he has had brought to his attention in a very general way the main problems with which it has had to contend and the main forces, human and spiritual, that have helped to sustain it. Armed with all this foreknowledge, he is now ready to turn to the record of uneventful events – uneventful, that is, after the 'experiment' of 1883 had, with the move to the Forrest Building in 1887, become an established institution – which constitute its history.

PART I

Beginning

Dalhousie Law School or, to give it its correct title, the Faculty of Law of Dalhousie University, was opened for students on 30 October 1883. The founding of it was an ambitious undertaking, a pioneer step not only in Canada but in what was then the British Empire. For the idea that a university, an institution dedicated to the giving of a liberal education, should train men to pursue the money-making craft of practising law was quite foreign to English thinking of the time. How did it come about that so daring an experiment in common-law legal education was made at that time in the thoroughly English little city of Halifax?

We know so little about the beginnings of the School that we can only guess at the answer to so fundamental a question, but our guess, made with some confidence and without too much strain on the imagination, is that it resulted from the combined effect of two factors. The first factor was something outside and beyond Nova Scotia, the 'law school idea' that was very much in the air in the England, the New England states of the United States, and the Canada of the eighteen seventies and eighties. The second, and more important, factor was a purely local one. A number of able young lawyers in Halifax wanted to strengthen the increasingly inadequate system of becoming a lawyer through apprenticeship by setting up a 'technical' school for law students, but couldn't find the necessary money. Dalhousie University wanted to raise itself above the ruck of the no less than five denominational colleges in a Nova Scotia of only half a million people by establishing professional schools, and was able, through the generosity of George Munro, to find the money for what could form the nucleus of a law school – an endowed chair in the liberal subjects of Constitutional and International Law. The lawyers with their technical aim and lack of money and the University with its liberal aim and George Munro's money – and, even more important, George Munro's nomination of a political scientist, Richard Chapman Weldon, to fill the chair – in effect joined forces, and in this way was born Dalhousie Law School with its then uniquely distinctive mix of the liberal and technical approaches to the teaching of law.

The last quarter of the nineteenth century was in each of the three countries just mentioned – and Nova Scotia lawyers would know something about what was going on in all of them – a time of ferment in legal education. Although more than a hundred years had elapsed since Blackstone had demonstrated in his celebrated *Commentaries* that the common law was no mere hodge-podge of unregulated regulation to be picked up by experience on the job but a reasoned system intended to promote the welfare of the people who lived within it, the English had only just begun to accept the notion that law was 'scientific' enough to be acceptable for study in a university: witness the establishment between 1852 and 1873 for the first time of law faculties at Oxford and Cambridge, and then only with a hesitation expressed in the revealing title of Albert Venn Dicey's inaugural lecture at All Souls College, Oxford, in 1883, 'Can English Law be Taught at the Universities?' But these English law faculties concentrated on teaching law as one of the liberal arts without much attention to its practical aspects; it was not, as they saw it, their function to prepare students for the legal profession. Such preparation as these students had consisted of an apprenticeship eked out by sporadic and unsystematic lectures, given by the governing bodies of the two arms into which the profession was, and still is, divided (the barristers and the solicitors) – a thoroughly unsatisfactory situation. From 1870 to 1875 an unsuccessful attempt to remedy it by establishing a 'General School of Law' for them in London resulted in a controversy, both inside and outside Parliament, which was widely publicized and was no doubt present in the minds of the young lawyers in Halifax who, as we shall see, tried to start the 'Halifax Law School' in 1874.[1]

With what was going on in legal education in the New England states most Nova Scotia lawyers of the time would be fairly familiar. For there were among them a number of graduates of the Harvard Law School, including, for example, one of those young lawyers who took part in the formation of the abortive Halifax Law School, one of those practising barristers who came up to Dalhousie Law School in its first year of operation to take Weldon's lectures on Constitutional Law and Mr Justice Thompson's lectures on Evidence and one who in 1886-87 was a part-time lecturer in Shipping. In striking contrast to England, distinguished universities such as Harvard, Yale, and Columbia were giving, and giving without any qualms, in their law schools what was – to make no bones about it – a superior kind of vocational education for intending lawyers. And even more important, Dean Christopher Columbus Langdell of the Harvard Law School was in the seventies pioneering, to the horror of many respectable Boston lawyers, a truly university approach to legal education which would later make Harvard the model for all law schools on the North American continent – trying to teach his students to think like lawyers instead of, as had traditionally been done, filling them up with legal information: for that is what Langdell's famous case method is really all about.

In Canada there were in the civil-law province of Quebec as many as three university law schools: at McGill (1848); at Laval (1854); and at a branch of Laval in Montreal (1878), now the University of Montreal; all three of them have remained in continuous operation ever since. For in accordance with a European tradition going back to the eleventh and twelfth centuries, in France, and therefore in Quebec, it has always been considered the natural thing that a young man coming to the practice of law should receive his academic training in a university. But our Nova Scotia lawyer of the seventies and eighties would know little – and care less – about what French-speaking civilians did. He would, however, have some knowledge of recent developments in Ontario. These were in a direction entirely opposite to the creation of a school connected with a university. Influenced, no doubt, by what was going on in England, the Law Society of Upper Canada had made up its mind that the academic side of preparing students for the practice of law should, if done at all, be done by the profession and as a minor adjunct to the work done by them in law offices as apprentices. It opened such a law school of its own in 1873, which collapsed after five years, and another in 1881, which also collapsed, and it was not until 1889, six years after the founding of Dalhousie Law School, that, after rejecting a suggested co-operative arrangement with the University of Toronto, it succeeded in putting its Osgoode Hall Law School on a permanent basis. For nearly seventy years Osgoode Hall Law School, with its hard-nosed practitioner's slant, stands in sharp contrast with Dalhousie Law School and its attempt to make the study of law a liberal as well as a technical pursuit.[2]

The training available to the young Nova Scotian preparing for the practice of law was, until the opening of Dalhousie Law School in 1883, limited to apprenticeship in a law office, unrelieved by any organized instruction in the principles of law upon which he had to pass examinations before he could be admitted to the Bar. What Beamish Murdoch, 'The Blackstone of Nova Scotia,' said in his *Epitome of the Laws of Nova Scotia* was still almost as true in 1883 as it had been in 1832: 'Students generally begin to serve their time from 16 to 18 years of age, and are admitted to the Bar at 22 or later. Many in the Colonies who are destined to the profession have cause to regret that they are first hurried from school to an office, and again hurried into practice by the force of circumstances, without having enjoyed the opportunity of sufficient time to mature their reading, so as to give them ease and satisfaction in their progress at the Bar.'[3] As late as 1864 indeed the examination system was as haphazard as the instruction. From a petition of that date from an organization called the Law Students' Society to the Nova Scotia Barristers' Society – which had been formed in 1825 to accumulate a library for the use of the judges and its members, and had been formally incorporated in 1858 but did not acquire until 1872 any responsibility for the training and admission of would-be lawyers – we learn that there were no 'definite Books or Branches of Law ... laid down to be read during Studentship as in England, Canada and elsewhere' and that there was one and one only final examination, covering the whole range of law, instead of 'the system in operation in England where there is [an] ... examination in certain books at the end of two years and a final one at the end of four years.'

Russell has left us an entertaining description of what the system of legal education used to be in Nova Scotia when he was a candidate for examination in 1872:

The young candidate and aspirant for professional honours and political distinction articled himself to a practising barrister. If his barrister happened to be a very busy one the chances were that he would have very little time indeed to give to his student, and if *per contra* it was a man who was blessed with ample leisure, well then, the chances were that his leisure was due to the fact that he was not fit for anything better than to sit and twiddle his thumbs, so that in either case, whichever way you choose to take it, the dilemma seemed to work out that the student had rather a poor chance. I quite well remember that the examination at the end of the term [of apprenticeship] used to be such as perhaps the student of one year in Dalhousie

College Law School at the present day would think a very trivial ordeal indeed for him to be called upon to pass.

The examination lasted a couple of hours. It was supposed to cover the whole range of English jurisprudence, and you can imagine how searching an inquiry might have been made in the course of two hours, if the poor candidate had gone over what was supposed to have been the work of three or four years' study. In fact I remember when I was approaching the ordeal myself, I was confidentially taken into his residence by a friend of mine who was also about undertaking the trying ordeal, and I was shown a washtub full of manuscripts. I asked him what these were, and I was told they were accumulated examination questions which had come down from generation to generation of law students, and by the diligent perusal of that washtub full of examination questions, or even half of them (because they followed one another in the ordinary accepted groove from generation to generation, I suppose from the time that we first had examiners in the Province of Nova Scotia) – by diligently perusing and preparing to answer these questions the candidate would invariably pass, and be very likely indeed to pass with high marks and to obtain first class distinction with honours.[4]

Some efforts were made by some lawyers to improve this dismal state of affairs. In 1872 the Nova Scotia Barristers' Society took over from the judges of the Supreme Court the responsibility for supervising the training and admission process – albeit with some reluctance on the part of some of its members and a later deliberate disregard of one of the specific duties newly imposed on it[5] – but it did not attempt, as the Law Society of Upper Canada did, to go one step further and give courses of instruction.

In 1874, however, a group of twelve lawyers, all but one of them under forty and most of them destined for distinguished careers in later life, took at least the first step towards filling this obvious gap by having themselves incorporated under the name of the Halifax Law School for the purpose of establishing a school of law in the City of Halifax. What kind of a school they had in mind we do not know, but it would almost certainly have been a technical or vocational one. What we do know is that as early as ten years before the opening of Dalhousie Law School this group of leading spirits among the lawyers in Halifax wanted *a* law school. What we also know is that four of them were later members of the original faculty of Dalhousie Law School and among those four were Robert Sedgewick, aged twenty-six, who was probably the principal energizing force behind the movement which led to its foundation, and Benjamin Russell, aged twenty-five, who was, with his friend Weldon, certainly the co-founder of Dalhousie Law School and taught there continuously from 1883 until as recently as 1921. The Halifax Law School never got any further than the Act incorporating it – the reason being, our safe guess is, that its sponsors could not raise the money necessary to operate it.

'The system for the training of lawyers now in vogue in this Province is too despicable to admit of criticism, and has succeeded in giving us a class from whom we can expect no reform in this matter and from whom we turn to other sources ... In connection with this College there can be no weighty objection urged against the establishment of a legal faculty.' So runs an editorial in the 18 February 1876 issue of the *Dalhousie Gazette*, the official organ of the student body of Dalhousie University. A just criticism and a fine aspiration, an aspiration no less fine and no less impractical than that voiced by the Reverend James Ross when in his inaugural address as Principal at the re-opening of Dalhousie College and University in November 1863 he had expressed the hope that the College would soon gather around it faculties of Law and Medicine and become a university in fact as well as in name. For in 1876 it looked as if Dalhousie, founded though it had been in 1820 and occupying as it still did the building then built for it on the Grand Parade where City Hall now stands, might once more have to close its doors. Like the lawyers who sponsored the Halifax Law School, Dalhousie College also wanted a law school and seemed to have just as little chance of getting one.

Odd as it seems to us today, Dalhousie, a non-sectarian college situated in the capital city and therefore ideally suited to become the only university in a little province of five hundred thousand people, was having an even harder struggle for existence than the five denominational colleges – Anglican King's at Windsor, Baptist Acadia at Wolfville, Methodist Mount Allison at Sackville on the New Brunswick – Nova Scotia border, and Roman Catholic St Francis Xavier at Antigonish, as well as St Mary's in Halifax. In a Nova Scotia torn by religious differences it did not have behind it the prayers and pockets of the faithful; it was indeed subjected to continuous political harassment by them. It had, after passing through many vicissitudes, been revived with high hopes in 1863 and three years later had sent forth its very first graduates, just two of them. But by 1879 its future was dark and uncertain. In all but two of the intervening years, the annual number of its BA graduates had been no more than a mere handful, between five and ten. Between 1867 and 1875 it had made its first experiment with a professional school, a medical faculty, but the experiment proved too costly and came to nothing. Worse still it was financially embarrassed and able to pay only meagre salaries. Arrears were constant and unfailing and it had only been kept alive during the early seventies by gifts collected from its friends and from 1876 on by a government grant of $3 000 a year, made as part of a plan by the government of the day to centralize all the colleges under a new university to be called the University of Halifax (which would fail) and was due to expire in 1881 (which it did).[6] At this dark moment appeared the Great Deliverer, George Munro.

At the instigation of his brother-in-law, Rev. John Forrest, a member of the Board of Governors, this Nova Scotian, who had made a fortune as a publisher in New York, began in 1879 a series of gifts for new chairs, exhibitions, bursaries, and tutorships on a princely scale which at that time was without parallel in Canada. He did not, as the typical benefactor likes to do, spend his money on buildings. He spent it on education – i.e., on students and teachers – and devoted most of it to endowing professorships at good salaries which would attract good men. In the course of the next few years he endowed five chairs at salaries varying from $2 000 to $2 500 – the salary of the premier of the province was then $2 400 – and nominated fine men to them: in Physics, J.G. MacGregor, later Professor of Physics at Edinburgh; in History and Political Economy, Rev. John Forrest, who would become in a year or two the President of Dalhousie for many years; in Metaphysics, Jacob Gould Schurman, destined to become President of Cornell; in English Literature, W.J. Alexander, who would later make his name at the University of Toronto; and in 1883 'he made possible the organization of the Faculty of Law by endowing a chair of Constitutional and International Law, to which he nominated Dr. Richard Chapman Weldon. Two years earlier the Board had obtained legislation authorizing them to establish such a Faculty; but it was Munro's liberality that enabled them to inaugurate it and his discernment that led them to choose a professor whose ability and character was to mould many generations of lawyers, judges and statesmen.'[7]

In his letter of 13 March 1883 to the Board offering to endow the chair Munro wrote: 'Professor Weldon of Sackville is recommended by competent judges as most suitable to be at the head of the Law Faculty.' What kind of a law faculty did Munro and his advisers have in mind? The writer has already given at the beginning of this chapter his all too confident answer to this question, but the truth is that we do not really know. And why was 'Professor

Weldon of Sackville,' more a political scientist than a lawyer, 'recommended' and who were the 'competent judges' who recommended him? In an article which has been reprinted in Appendix I Russell says that the idea of bringing him from Mount Allison to Halifax as Dean of the new faculty came from Robert Sedgewick and a number of associated Dalhousians who were interested in the then-current movement to consolidate the colleges, but that does not tell us what we really want to know. But details of this kind do not matter. What does matter is that with Weldon as its head Dalhousie Law School was from the beginning no mere vocational school.

When Richard Chapman Weldon left his post as Professor of Mathematics and Political Science at Mount Allison to come to Dalhousie, he was a tall, handsome, athletic man of thirty-four with an established academic reputation. He was born and brought up on a farm near Sussex, New Brunswick, but was cajoled by his father into going to college, at Mount Allison. While there he developed a close and enduring friendship with a fellow student named Benjamin Russell, who has written of him that 'he always stood at the head of his class and was the delight of his teachers. For him class recitations and examination papers had no terrors. He had no specialties. He took all knowledge for his province. As a mathematician he seemed to his fellow students to be a wonder. But history and economic science were his favourite fields at Sackville.'[8] After receiving his BA at the age of seventeen he taught in a country school for three years and then taught mathematics at Mount Allison for another two (taking at the same time his MA), until he had saved enough money to make it 'scantily possible' to pursue graduate studies at Yale. Two years of study and research in international and constitutional law under distinguished teachers there earned him a PHD; his thesis was in international law. In 1873 he became Professor of Mathematics and Political Science at Mount Allison, but a year later took a year's leave of absence to do still further graduate work, this time at Heidelberg under a professor with an international reputation in the field of public law. He then resumed his post at Sackville and while teaching there was admitted to the Bar of his native province of New Brunswick but never practised. So that when he came to Dalhousie in 1883 he was 'a person whose intellectual and ethical horizons had been broadened by intensive studies in American and European universities as well as at home. He brought to Halifax from the outside world an appreciation of international academic standards [and] an understanding of the importance of public law.'[9]

Even more important for Dalhousie than his academic equipment was the kind of man he was. Here is what a member of the first class ever to graduate from the School has said about him:

To sit at the feet of Richard Chapman Weldon was a priceless boon to a young man in serious quest of law learning. He was a born teacher, eager and able to communicate the fullness of his knowledge to the willing and receptive mind. Physically he was tall and of a commanding presence. To observe that, and then to note the fine moulding of his head and the mobile play of his eyes when elucidating some theme that engaged him at the moment, created for one an unforgettable mental portrait of the man. His words travelled fast upon his thought, but they were lucidity itself. No one was left in doubt as to his meaning. To his intellectual power as a teacher was added a charm of manner that invited approach from the shyest student. Kindliness clothed him as with a garment. Small wonder then, that such a man should be hailed as ['the great man'] throughout the institution over which he presided, and small wonder that the institution under his guidance should succeed from the start and that after his passing it should make his memory the very soul of its traditions.[10]

Weldon's first official act as Dean was to be a member of 'a committee appointed by the Governors to confer with some of the leading barristers of Halifax and to endeavour to secure their services in teaching the common law subjects.' The quotation is taken from the first entry in the Faculty minutes, dated March 1883. This stout, well-preserved book is still in existence and the entry is in Weldon's own handwriting, rounded, bold, clear, and eminently readable. The chairman of the committee was the Chairman of the Board of Governors, Sir William Young. Distinguished son of a distinguished father, he had been Chairman since 1848 and it was he who had thereafter been mainly responsible for Dalhousie's precarious survival and for its successful re-opening in 1863. He was furthermore a wealthy man with a long record of generous gifts to worthy public causes, had recently resigned as Chief Justice after a tenure of twenty years, and would shortly be the chief mover in, and chief contributor to, the erection of the Forrest Building in which the Law School was destined to spend more than sixty years. With his influence behind it – coupled with the ready co-operation of the Bench and Bar – the committee had no difficulty in getting together a faculty of 'volunteer,' that is to say unpaid, lecturers who were prepared to give some of their time and their talents to the creation of the new School. After only eight days there were five of them and before classes began there were two more.

Here is a list of the original faculty and the subjects assigned to them: Dean R.C. Weldon, MA, PHD, Constitutional History, Constitutional Law, International Law and Conflict of Laws; Mr Justice John Thompson, Evidence; Wallace Graham, BA, QC, Commercial Law; Benjamin Russell, MA, Contracts; John Y. Payzant, MA, QC, Torts; James Thomson QC, Conveyancing, Hon. S.L. Shannon, DCL, QC, Real Property, Crimes; and Robert Sedgewick, BA, QC, Equity. All of them, please note, except Mr Justice Thompson and possibly James Thomson, were college graduates; college graduates were rare in those days. And all of them, except Weldon and Russell, were QCs; to have a QC in those days meant you were an acknowledged leader of the Bar.

Mr Justice Thompson must, because of his later eminence, have a paragraph to himself. So must Robert Sedgewick, because, as we have suggested earlier, he was probably the spearhead in the movement that created Dalhousie Law School. And so must Benjamin Russell, because he will, as we shall see, earn the right to be called the co-founder, with Weldon, of the School.

John Thompson, a self-made man of humble origins, had by his own efforts turned himself into a learned lawyer and was in the process of drafting an act that would revolutionize court procedure, the Judicature Act of 1884; he would later, as Minister of Justice, sponsor in the Parliament of Canada the no less revolutionary Canadian Criminal Code. He was, together with his two friends, Robert Sedgewick and Wallace Graham, deeply interested in the law school 'experiment' as he called it and did not consider it beneath the dignity of the judicial office – which in those days was considerable – to help further the cause by addressing envelopes for circulars advertising it and by going around merchants' offices to beg money for the library. After lecturing for two years on the subject of Evidence, a 'natural' for him, this remarkable man was, as everyone knows, suddenly translated into a new career in Dominion politics and soon became Sir John Thompson and Prime Minister of Canada.[11]

Robert Sedgewick was a son of that famous 'old man eloquent,' the Presbyterian minister in the Musquodoboit Valley. Already a successful lawyer with experience in politics, he was an ardent Dalhousian and an ardent reformer in the field of legal education. One of the first dozen people to graduate from Dalhousie after its revival, he had been for nearly ten years the representative of the Alumni Association on its Board of Governors. Trained as a lawyer in Cornwall, Ontario, office at a time when the Law Society of Upper Canada's law school was struggling unsuccessfully to be born, he had been one of the

promoters of the abortive Halifax Law School. And it was, once again, probably he who was primarily responsible for getting Weldon. He lectured on
Equity until 1887, when he went to Ottawa as Deputy Minister of Justice; in
1893 he was appointed to the Supreme Court of Canada.

Benjamin Russell, who would later be known to many generations of students as 'Benny' and would in twenty years' time become Mr Justice Russell
of the Supreme Court of Nova Scotia, was at this time supplementing what
little he could earn from 'a not very lucrative practice' by journalism and by
acting as editor of the law reports. In the School's opening year he was one of
the unpaid lecturers – the subject assigned to him was Contracts – but in
April 1884 he was appointed Professor of Contracts on a half-time basis at a
salary of a thousand dollars and in the course of the next few years there
came into his hands three other basic subjects, Bills and Notes, Sales, and
Equity. From 1891 on, he was in effect doing a full-time teacher's job at half
a salary. In any event he was from the beginning Weldon's right-hand man.
The two were close friends from their college days on; Russell stayed with
Weldon at the family farm, went to see him when he was teaching at the
country school, and made the long journey to Yale to see him receive his
doctor's degree; and when in the summer of 1883 Weldon was in Dartmouth
looking for somewhere for his family to live he stayed with Russell there and
studied with him the British North America Act cases on which he would be
lecturing in the fall. In their lives at the School they would complement one
another. Russell was only a little bit more than five foot tall, excitable and
disputatious. Weldon was six foot two and a half, with a commanding presence and a strong moral sense. Although Russell did not have, as Weldon
did, any formal training as a legal scholar he would later on write a textbook
which was well known in its day, Russell on *Bills and Notes*. And he had, as
any reader of his *Autobiography* can see, a feeling for literature. He and
Weldon would together be 'the School' for all the students who graduated
from it between its very early days and Weldon's retirement in 1914.[12]

And now for a brief note on each of the remaining members of the original
faculty. Wallace Graham was one of the leading counsel of the day – so leading in fact that in that first session of 1883-84 he could not begin his lectures
until after Christmas because he was tied up all fall in the Supreme Court at
Ottawa; in 1889 he was elevated to the Bench of Nova Scotia but continued
lecturing for two more years; he would end his career as Sir Wallace Graham,
Chief Justice. John Y. Payzant had been – as had also Russell and

Sedgewick – one of the group of lawyers who tried to start the Halifax Law School; in later years best known as a businessman (he became president of the Bank of Nova Scotia), he was in 1883 a successful counsel and had the reputation of 'having remained a student'; for nine years he taught the demanding subject of Torts. About James Thomson, who lectured on Conveyancing for four years, we know nothing except that, according to the *Gazette*, he had in one of those years to miss some lectures because he was on a business trip to Texas. Hon. S.L. Shannon had been a member of Dalhousie's Board of Governors ever since the reorganization and revival of 1863. He was a man with a distinguished legal and political past – the title of 'Honourable' had been conferred on him in recognition of his services in the cause of confederation – and in 1883 he was, at the age of sixty-seven, living in semi-retirement. Widely travelled and widely read – he had in his youth made the grand tour of Europe, studied the classics, learned to speak French, and would have become a professor if his father had let him – he was ideally equipped to lecture, as he did at various times in his nine years of service, on subjects as diverse as Real Property, Criminal Law and Roman Law (which was for a year or two on the early curriculum).[13]

What a distinguished group of men! What diverse backgrounds they had! And what a large proportion of them were men of culture – not mere 'lawyer-barbarians'! All that is obvious. What does need to be emphasized about this original faculty is that all of them except one, the Dean, were what later came to be called the part-timers or the downtown lecturers – judges and leading practitioners who came up to the School to give their classes in the afternoon or evening. Without their aid, freely and readily given, there would have been no Dalhousie Law School. So from the very beginning the School has belonged, emotionally, as much to the profession as it has to Dalhousie. In more earthy terms the part-timers will remain essential to the School's survival until the nineteen-fifties. They will also continue to bring with them their one really serious disadvantage; it must have leapt to the reader's eye as he read through the last few paragraphs. Like Mr Justice Thompson and Robert Sedgewick, some do not last very long or, like Wallace Graham and James Thomson, they sometimes have more pressing business elsewhere and have to cancel classes. Weldon ran very early into an extreme form of this problem; in 1886 the lecturer in Crimes (not the always devoted Shannon) resigned after two years and the subject was not taught in 1886-87; and in 1887 a class in the then very important subject of Shipping, instituted only one year earlier, had to be dropped from the curriculum because the lecturer, a Harvard graduate and soon to be a judge, found the task too onerous.

As one would expect of an able group like the original faculty, they did not just go blindly ahead and 'do their own thing' with a School which was largely an experiment; they sent three emissaries, Mr Justice Thompson, Wallace Graham, and Robert Sedgewick, to visit law schools in Boston and New York City and see how things were done there. We know for a fact that they went to the prestigious, but at this time highly innovative, Harvard Law School and to the wholly orthodox Boston Law School, which had recently been started by some Boston practitioners who objected to the new-fangled ideas and methods that had been introduced into the teaching of law at Harvard by the famous Dean Langdell; they probably also went to the established law school at Columbia in New York. In a letter to his wife, Annie, on Tuesday 17 April 1883 Thompson tells her that they spent Monday at the Harvard Law School and 'got a great deal of insight into matters. We had four Nova Scotians who were there (Tupper, Parkin, Silver and Sawyer), to dinner with us last night and then went to see *Iolanthe* played which was delightful. Today was spent at the Boston Law School.'[14] The three emissaries have left no record, direct or indirect, of the ideas they brought back with them to Halifax.

There is a persistent local tradition to the effect that the School's founders drew their inspiration from the Harvard Law School. That much they certainly did: Weldon in his inaugural address pays a glowing tribute to it and then goes on to hope that his new School will do for the Bar of Nova Scotia what the Harvard Law School had done for the Bar of Massachussetts. But there is no historical evidence behind the assertion, fathered by Horace Read (who was addicted to viewing Dalhousie Law School through a rainbow, and preferably a Harvard rainbow), that the School was 'modelled explicitly on the Harvard Law School.'[15] On the contrary, what evidence there is runs in an entirely opposite direction: the really distinctive characteristic of the new Dalhousie Law School was the attention paid by it to Weldon's 'cultural' or 'public law' subjects of Constitutional History, International Law, and Conflict of Laws, but the Harvard curriculum of the day did not contain any of them and confined itself to subjects which would be of immediate use to the hard-shell practitioner.

The emissaries did, however, learn from their trip, and publicly record, the importance of a good library. At a public meeting held in August to drum up public support for a library for the School, Thompson said, we are told:

It was to some extent an experiment, and it would be well to understand at once that the experiment could not be successful without a library. Three of the faculty had visited several law schools last spring in Massachusetts and New York, and they had found in each of these schools just such an equipment – as far as the lecturing staff was concerned – as the profession in Nova Scotia might be expected to supply, but in each case the most prominent feature of all was the ready access which the students had to a valuable and well stocked library in close proximity to their lecture rooms. It might as well be acknowledged that without some collection of the kind the School, as he had already said, could not be successful in giving the proper instruction and facilities for study to those who should attend its classes.[16]

Getting a library, any kind of a library, did not prove to be as easy as getting a good faculty – hence the appeal to the public. And that first faculty was aiming high, for they already had a first-rate librarian, J.T. Bulmer, who had been appointed at the end of July for one year only at a small stipend. Bulmer was a lawyer without a practice but with a real love of books. He was also a 'character,' with a reputation for collecting, legally or illegally, books for any project with which he was associated. Founder of the Nova Scotia Historical Society, he had been unfairly edged out of his job as librarian at the Legislative Library and now proceeded to give himself enthusiastically to the cause of Dalhousie Law School and its library.[17] In addition to seeking from wherever he could gifts of books and money to the library, he scattered far and wide throughout the Maritimes sheets describing the advantages of the School to law students. It was a great loss to the School when this energetic man – who turned out to be as helpful to the students in the library as he was in collecting books for it – had to be let go at the end of the year because there was not enough money to pay a librarian. There would not be a librarian again until the nineteen-fifties.

Notwithstanding 'the efforts of Mr. Bulmer and the aiding and abetting of these efforts by Nova Scotians at large,' the collection of between one and two thousand books which had been assembled by the opening of term at the end of October was far from adequate. It was to improve to some extent in a year or two – due mainly to generous money gifts from the members of the Faculty – but here is what a student editorial said about it in the Gazette of 7 December 1883:

There seems to be a general suspicion that of these books all are those of which the student has most need, whereas the real fact is that there are a great many such as

Sessional Papers and Parliamentary Debates, besides a somewhat heterogeneous collection of literary curiosities which, although extremely interesting and useful as
books of reference, when one has time to dip into them, are nevertheless of little use
to Law Students. ...what causes the passing pang is the scarcity or rather comparative
scarcity of those that are more earnestly to be desired – text books and reports. ...
[But we do] have the use, owing to the care and foresight for which the faculty is
distinguished, of the barristers' fine selection of books [i.e., the Barristers' Library].

By 1887 the library will have 'a good set of English and Canadian Reports and
will be found to contain almost all the books which an undergraduate will
have occasion to consult.' 'Almost all' – these are the key words. And that is
all, with the exception of a few special collections given from time to time by
generous private donors, it will contain until even later than the end of the
nineteen-fifties.

Two formal ceremonies were held to mark the opening of the School. In the
evening of Tuesday, 30 October, Weldon gave his inaugural address as Professor of Constitutional and International Law at the Convocation of Dalhousie
University in the Legislative Assembly Room of the Province Building. And
two evenings later there took place in the same room a public meeting to mark
the formal inauguration of the School, for the School was more than a Dalhousie project; it was a community project. Sir William Young, Chairman of the
Dalhousie Board, presided; Honourable Adams G. Archibald (who had been
continuously Lieutenant Governor first of Manitoba and then of Nova Scotia
from 1873 to 1883 and would in 1884 succeed Young as Chairman at Dalhousie) gave the principal address; Chief Justice MacDonald of Nova Scotia and a
judge from the Supreme Court of New Brunswick, Mr Justice Palmer, also
spoke. The two judges had one single theme: that the new law school was not
meant to be for Nova Scotia only but for all the Maritime provinces; to which
Sir William Young replied that 'such had been the intention of the founder,'
George Munro.[18]

The addresses given by Weldon and Archibald may still be read in a pamphlet entitled *The Inaugural Addresses, etc. delivered at the opening of the
Law School in connection with Dalhousie University*. In addition to the two
addresses the pamphlet contains an article on 'Advantages of Study at a Law
School,' the tuition fees, terms of admission and degrees, and finally a page
devoted to 'The Faculty of Arts.' It is a substantial piece of work, well worthy
of the event. It was compiled by Bulmer and paid for by Sir William
Young – who was, as appears from a semi-acrid correspondence reproduced

in a history of the School written by George Farquhar ('27) in 1958 but never published, in effect tricked by that irrepressible character into paying for the printing and circulation of it in Canada, England, the United States, and the West Indies when all he had undertaken to do was to pay for the printing and local circulation of a few copies of the addresses themselves.

Both the addresses are 'set pieces' prepared for delivery on a formal occasion before an audience of our forefathers who liked speeches and liked them long and learned. Archibald's proved, as next day's *Morning Chronicle* put it, 'to be an exhaustive treatise on the growth of legal science, particularly English law, and the necessity for a school for its study.' In his hour-long discourse he was obviously trying to justify to the lawyers the establishment of that strange new thing, a law school. The address of Weldon, not yet a 'name,' was not reported in the press. Forgetting the hidden nuggets which later deans have laboriously mined from it for their own 'on parade' pieces, we can see that he was trying to do the same job on the university people as Archibald was trying to do on the lawyers. Expatiating at some length and with much learning on rather distant history in England, long-established practice in Germany, and more recent developments in the United States, he devoted two-thirds of his speech to the message that professional training in law has a place, and a proud place, in a university. Well, then, said he: 'In Canada, I believe, there is not one law school with endowed chairs and adequate libraries. Do we not need them? Can we any longer do without them?' He then dreamed a dream: 'To build up in this city of Halifax a university with faculties of arts, medicine, applied sciences and law ... that shall influence the intellectual life of Canada as Harvard and Yale have influenced the intellectual life of New England.' He concluded 'with a few words as to our course of study.' Although 'by far the greatest part of our time and thought must be given to more useful and practical studies – to the study of the common law of England,' the 'historical and general subjects' of International and Constitutional Law of which he is Professor will, he assured his university audience, give to the lawyers-to-be a truly university slant.

One thing he said in this connection he later made so central to the policy of the School that, although so often quoted as to be almost trite, it has to be set out in full here:

In drawing up our curriculum we have not forgotten the duty which every university owes to the state, the duty which Aristotle saw and emphasized so long ago – of teaching the young men the science of government. In our free government we all have political duties, some higher, some humbler, and these duties will be best performed by those who have given them most thought. We may fairly hope that some of our students will, in their riper years, be called upon to discharge public duties. We aim to help these to act with fidelity and wisdom.

It was by pursuing this policy that, as Premier Angus L. Macdonald said many years later: 'He gave the School personality and he gave it distinction. He made it not merely a Law School but a breeding ground for public service and public men.'[19]

For its first four years the School lived in makeshift quarters and was engaged in making changes in its experimental course of study. During that period it had to move no less than twice but succeeded nevertheless in achieving the following ends: lengthening to three years a course which had in the beginning been for most students no more than two; giving to the curriculum the shape that it would retain for many years; arranging with the Nova Scotia Barristers' Society that the law student apprentices should be allowed to attend the School full-time while it was in session; and getting underway with the Society the concession that these students should, if they were successful in earning the LLB, be exempted from the Society's professional examinations (which second, and vital, gain was in sight in 1887 but was probably not realized until 1891). So in these four short years and by as early as 1887 legal education in Nova Scotia moved from the traditional and unsatisfactory method of unadulterated apprenticeship to the system of three years at university law school plus a shorter period as an apprentice in a law office, the system which is today standard throughout Canada.

The School's first home was in rented rooms in what was then a notoriously disreputable neighbourhood, two 'commodious rooms' on the ground floor of the new High School at the corner of Brunswick and Sackville Streets; because of increased enrolment in Dalhousie College, there was no room for it in the College building on the Grand Parade. The new High School, now old, time-worn, and no longer a high school, is still in existence. So is the Register in which Weldon wrote down the name, and some of the particulars, of each student and the amount of the tuition fee paid over by him – $30 for each year of the degree course.

At this opening session of 1883 there were twenty-five undergraduate students: thirteen of them were classified as second-year students by reason of their previous study of law while articled clerks (incidentally, most of the subjects they would have to take in their next and graduating year seem oddly 'fringe' ones to the modern eye); twelve others were classified as first-year students. Of these twenty-five degree students four were from New Brunswick and in each of the next three years the incoming first-year class would always contain three or four students from New Brunswick and occasionally one from Prince Edward Island; thus from the beginning the School was a Maritime and not merely a Nova Scotian institution, and thereby fulfilled the hopes of the judges who spoke at the formal inauguration. There were also thirty or so 'general' students – many of them practising lawyers, aged from twenty-four to forty-two – who came in to take just one subject, Weldon's Constitutional Law or Mr Justice Thompson's Evidence; one of them, George Ritchie, was a recent Harvard Law School graduate, and became a tower of strength as a downtown lecturer in as many as three subjects from 1892 to 1902. Easily the most popular subject with the practising lawyers was Thompson's Evidence. One of the second-year students took down these lectures in shorthand and transcribed them in long hand; 'it was assumed that [they] would be published but they have never seen the light';[20] the student, W.B. Wallace ('85) who would in later life be a county court judge and another tower of strength as a downtown lecturer, would one day publish a book of his own on a difficult and practical subject, *Mechanics Lien Laws in Canada*, which ran into two editions.

In 1885 the School produced its first graduates, ten of those who made up the second-year class in 1883. (Standing first in the alphabetical list of them was Albert Bennett of Hopewell Cape, New Brunswick; he was still living, a very old retired county court judge, in 1958 when the School reached its seventy-fifth birthday, and was given, as the University's first law graduate, an honorary degree at a Convocation celebrating that birthday.) But by graduation day the faculty and students were homeless, with no new home in sight; in November of 1884 the School Board had given the Law School six-months notice to quit 'the two commodious rooms' in the High School and there was still no room for it in the College buildng.

What now was the School to do? The advice given by two Halifax newspapers in that November was that the faculty and the students should betake themselves and their belongings to the Court House and that there should be a thorough amalgamation of the School and the Barristers' Society – which shows how highly experimental the new university-based Law School was at this time still thought to be.[21] Fortunately for the future of the School, the advice was not taken. At a meeting with the Board of Governors at the end of March 1885, Weldon had put the School's problem before them and told them, among other things, that the friends of the School 'would furnish a subscription list to put up such a building as was required by the Faculty, if the Governors would furnish a site for the same.' But to the Governors the Law School's problem was only part of a much larger problem brought about by the increase in enrolment in the University as a whole: should they enlarge the present College building or sell it and build a new one on another and more suitable site? So all they did at that meeting was appoint a committee to consider that question. Three weeks later, however, they decided to approach the government of Nova Scotia for assistance, at which time two members of the faculty, Mr Justice Thompson and Judge Johnstone (the then lecturer in Crimes), submitted a memorandum setting out their version of the story of the School to date – a memorandum so comprehensive and so interesting that it must be quoted in full:

Its staff of nine, all but two unpaid; the subjects taught; the degree course; fifty-three students from the three provinces attended its first year and sixty-two in its second; before the school opened an average of a dozen students a year went abroad for study and none had left since, except one who went to complete a course; the gross revenue from fees for the two years was $2,100; the Faculty itself had given over $3,000 in money and a large number of books besides; friends of the school, among all classes, denominations and parties, had given $2,000; no part of these monies went for salaries but was used to expand the Library; the Library was useful for public purposes and open to all; Osgoode Hall gave no regular instruction at all yet had an annual revenue of $40,000 and was given aid from government; McGill and Laval, which taught only the Civil Law, were aided by their government, while Laval had less students than Halifax and McGill had only twenty-three; the operating expenses of the school required an additional $2,000 a year, a burden too great for the Faculty, which was already giving time and labour; a new building must be provided immediately since the High School was no longer available; and that no part of any funds granted by the government would be used, directly or indirectly, for the payment of members of the Faculty.[22]

The appeal to the government was unsuccessful, as had been a similar plea made to it for aid to the library at the public meeting in August 1883. The government gave nothing. It would not give the School anything until the end of the nineteen-forties, when Angus L. Macdonald, an old student and old teacher there, was Premier.

Faced with what might be a ruinous interruption in the life of the School, Weldon and Russell took the matter into their own hands. In July they approached the Board with a proposal that they buy at their own risk the old Halliburton House, the Board to pay them $400 a year as long as the building was used by the Faculty of law. Their proposal having been accepted, the two old friends bought the house subject to a mortgage of $4000 and spent the rest of the summer making shelves for the library and seating for a couple of lecture rooms – quite a lark, as Russell describes it in his *Autobiography*. The students were delighted with their new home; the house had historical associations – it had belonged to Sir Brenton Halliburton, the second Chief Justice of Nova Scotia – and was, unlike the High School, in an excellent residential neighbourhood. Here the Law School spent two happy years, a close-knit family, so much so that when it moved into the new University building the students looked back with some nostalgia to 'the coziness, the seclusion and the good fellowship that existed among us in Haliburton [sic] Hall.'[23] After the move Weldon and Russell sold the house and paid off the mortgage, so that everything ended happily for them too. The house still stands, but the portico and stone front which it then had have been torn down, and the building itself has been converted into a duplex, numbers 5184 and 5186 Morris Street, between Barrington and Hollis.

In 1886 a committee consisting of Dean Weldon, Professor Russell, and John Y. Payzant undertook a fundamental revision of the course of study, 'part-timer' Payzant's qualification for the job being that he (and also Russell and Shannon, by the way) had played a leading part in framing the curriculum for the 'private study' LLB degree of the University of Halifax, an examining but not a teaching body which started up in 1887 and collapsed for ever in 1881;[24] their recommendations were confirmed by the Faculty. The revision came fully into effect in the fall of 1887 and, with comparatively minor changes, remained in effect until after the retirement of Weldon in 1914. This is therefore a convenient place to describe in broad outline the course – using that word in its widest sense to include such things as admission requirements, length of course, subjects taught, method of teaching, exams, etc. – as it was in the formative years 1883-87. And do not, please do not, judge it by modern standards; ask, rather, whether the people who are teaching at the Law School in 1976 can even begin to compare with those who were teaching there in 1883.

All that a student needed in order to enter the School in 1883 was less than the equivalent, in modern terms, of a Grade XI certificate; he had to have passed either the preliminary examination set by the Barristers' Society for those seeking to be student apprentices or the matriculation examination set by the School itself, both pretty simple tests of general education. Once in, he would find himself with a load of seven or eight class hours a week, spread over a teaching term of twenty-one weeks. These standards would remain unchanged until shortly before the advent of Dean MacRae in 1914.

A student would also find that although the course nominally took three years there were ways of getting through it in two; three of these ways, purely temporary ones to attract customers in the early days of the experiment, did not survive the revision of 1886; one of them, the 'affiliated student' way, did. The affiliated student privilege, invented in 1885 in order to encourage bright, hard-working people with Arts degrees to enter the Law School and the legal profession, allowed Arts graduates who had taken the three Law School subjects of Constitutional Law, Constitutional History, and Contracts as part of their Arts courses to get through in two years by taking and passing in those two years all the other subjects in the three-year curriculum – a privilege which would continue, with some modifications, until as late as 1923.[25] But apart from this privilege, of which quite a number of Arts graduates availed themselves, the course was from 1886 on a three-year one.

Our student of 1883 would also find himself a prisoner of the office where he was serving his apprenticeship and unable to attend classes until after business hours; in that opening year, therefore, all classes, even Weldon's, were held in the late afternoon or evening. By the next year, however, he must have been allowed to leave the office for some classes because both Weldon's and Russell's classes were now held in the morning. And from 1886 on he was, no doubt by arrangement with the Barristers' Society, allowed to attend the Law School full-time; for in the calendar for 1886-87 there appears for the first time the following significant statement: 'The Faculty urgently recommend that students devote their whole time during Sessions to the work of the School ... The course having been very considerably enlarged, the Faculty apprehend that students who are doing regular office work during Session will find it quite impossible to pass the required examinations'. Henceforth the School will always be a full-time school in the sense that the student does not, as he did in Ontario until around 1950, only come to it from the 'practical' office to attend a daily hour or two of classes but spends his whole time there on 'academic' study.

Were the mere seven or eight hours a week of classes really as demanding as this and subsequent calendars make it out to be? The answer is almost certainly yes. The students, nearly all of them just out of school, were, as we can see from the course descriptions and the examination papers (for the first dozen years or so of the School's existence last year's examination papers are printed in this year's calendar), expected to be able, by their study of an assigned textbook and of the cases discussed in class by the lecturer, to answer questions designed to test their understanding of a range of topics far wider than would be the case today: the pass mark was, then as now, 50 per cent, raised, for what that is worth, from 30 per cent in 1885.

The first of the two really important things about the curriculum itself we have already emphasized *ad nauseam*: it was from the beginning a mix, which would for many years be a distinguishing mark of Dalhousie Law School, of political science, cultural or public law (the labels are interchangeable) subjects, and professional or strictly legal ones. The second is that almost from the beginning a distinctive curriculum was being taught by distinguished teachers. From 1886 on Weldon, the public-law man, and Russell, the superb teacher of 'lawyers' law,' were the students' teachers for as much as nearly half the students' class-time; by 1892 Russell was doing the basic private-law subjects of Contracts, Sales, Negotiable Instruments, and Equity, and the two of them together were taking the students for an even larger proportion of their time than that. Most of the other members of the faculty, busy practitioners taking on without pay a task for which they would not have much time to prepare, were chiefly interested in getting across legal information; their examination papers rarely rise above the level of 'what is the rule where' or 'state the principle in.' But, says Russell in his *Autobiography*: 'As for Weldon and myself I can vouch for it that we were teachers and not merely lecturers. We taught our classes to criticize the authorities they read and we criticized them ourselves and condemned them when they appeared to have been erroneously conceived. Professor Weldon's comments on the decisions of the Privy Council interpreting the British North America Act were of great value.' Russell too had bees in his bonnet about at least two well-known leading cases in his specialty, Contracts; in the Contracts course he gave in 1884 he used the American Langdell's *Select Cases on Contracts* and *Survey of Contracts* as well as the recently published English book by Anson; and he set at the end of that year an examination paper which shows that he must have discussed with his students in a searching way most of the crucial issues in the subject – a practice he seems to have continued in subsequent years and to have extended to the three other subjects he later took on.[26]

Before giving what will be little more than a bare list of what subjects were taught and in what year, both before and after the revision of 1886, we had better state expressly what we have earlier implied: the downtowners' courses were all survey courses, designed for the general practitioner of the day who was expected to know just a little bit about a great many topics in each of the areas into which he was most likely to run. For example, after twenty one-hour lectures on Torts from John Y. Payzant – and what must have been a considerable amount of reading on his own – the first-year student in 1884-85 was expected to be able to answer moderately simple questions on all of the following topics: negligence, defamation, seduction, conversion, nuisance, and trespass.

Here is a list of the subjects comprised in the curriculum as it was during the first three years of the School's life; the figure in brackets after each subject denotes how many class-hours per week were devoted to it; although the mere name of the subject gives no clear idea of the topics covered in it, we cannot, for reasons of space, go more deeply into the matter than this. First Year: Real Property (1); Conveyancing (1); Contracts (2); Torts (1); Crimes (1); Constitutional History (2); Total 8. Second Year: Evidence (2); Negotiable Instruments (1); Sale of Goods (1); Equity (2); Conflict of Laws (1); Constitutional Law (2); Total 9. Third Year was a very odd affair with what seems to be a very light load: International Law (2); Procedure (?) – no course description and no examination appears in the calendars; Marine Insurance (1); and examinations on, but apparently no lectures on, the following books: Hunter's *Introduction to Roman Law* ('Roman Law') and Maine's *Ancient Law* ('Jurisprudence').

Where did this, the original, curriculum come from? It looks as if it were an amalgam of (a) the subjects that the endowed professor, Weldon, was capable of teaching, (b) the professional subjects prescribed by the Nova Scotia Barristers' Society for their Intermediate and Final Examinations which had to be taken and passed by all candidates for admission to the Bar, and (c) the cultural subjects that formed so large a part of the curriculum for the LLB degree of the University of Halifax with which, as we said earlier, Russell, Payzant, and Shannon had had something to do. It was in other words a makeshift, designed to take account of the most pressing local exigencies and get the experiment started. But why bother with speculations like that? For by 1886 the experiment had proved to be a success, and the curriculum which emerged from the revision of that year would, with minor changes backwards and forwards, be *the* curriculum for the whole of the Weldon-Russell period, 1887-1914.

Here is the new 1886 curriculum. First Year: Real Property (1); Crimes (1); Contracts (2); Torts (1); Constitutional History (2); Total 7. Second Year: Equity (2); Evidence (1); Sale of Goods (2); Constitutional Law (2); Total 7. Third Year: Conflict of Laws (1); International Law (1); Marine Insurance (1); Conveyancing (1); [Shipping (1)];[27] Partnership, Agency and Companies (1); Negotiable Instruments (2); Total 7. That was a very substantial revision. The course has been 'very considerably enlarged,' by adding Partnership and by lengthening Sale of Goods and Negotiable Instruments to meet the needs of the day. It has, by the reshaping of the Third year, been made into an instrument that will give equal play to both professional training and university education. And it has been made to make pedagogical sense by giving the student an even load over all his three years instead of the lopsided arrangement that existed previously.

According to the Law Valedictorian of 1887 the new course was officially recognized by the Nova Scotia Barristers' Society as soon as it went into effect, for he refers to a recent Act 'whereby the degree in Laws conferred by this University admits to all the honours and privileges of the bar of Nova Scotia.' Two years before that the Faculty had appointed a committee to take the first steps towards persuading the Society to exempt the School's graduates from its professional examinations and the *Gazette* had published a well-reasoned editorial in support. But the Valedictorian probably read too much into 'the recent Act.' The significant event he was recording probably did not occur until 1891; it was, however, well in sight in 1887.[28]

The three significant events of 1887, one of minimal, and the other two of major, importance, were: the arrival of the first students from outside the Maritimes; the Dean's election to Parliament; and the School's move to its third, and what proved to be its 'real,' home. Two first-year students, Frederick Howay and Richard McBride, came all the way from British Columbia on the recently completed Canadian Pacific Railway. When they graduated three years later a student editorial in the *Gazette* trumpeted: 'Dalhousie Law School is no longer a mere local institution – it is Canadian'[29] – the first sounding of a theme which Deans Vincent MacDonald and Horace Read will, in a flight of fancy quite equal to that of the student of 1890, restate in the fifties as the theme of 'a national law school.' As it so happened, however, one of the two students from British Columbia, Richard McBride, did in his own person attain national prominence; only eight years after he graduated from the School he was elected to the British Columbia Legislature, became Premier of the Province from 1903 to 1915, and was knighted.

Viewed from the hindsight of today's Weldon tradition with public service as one, perhaps the chief one, of its elements, when Weldon accepted the nomination as Conservative candidate for the Dominion House of Commons in Albert County, New Brunswick, the home county of the Weldon family, he was not doing anything startling or controversial; he was only carrying out in his own life the ideal he had urged upon others in the passage from his inaugural address which we quoted earlier. In the actualities of 1887 he was faced with a real problem. Suppose he were to be elected, could he, the administrative head of and the only full-time teacher at the infant Law School, justify to himself, his Faculty, and the Board of Governors an attempt to serve two masters – his students in Halifax and his constituents in distant Albert County? And how, as a practical matter, could he attend the three-or-four-month-long sessions of Parliament in Ottawa, which in those days usually began at the end of February, in March, or early in April, when he would have to be in Halifax until the end of the first week in April giving his classes and until the end of the last week in April attending to his administrative duties as Dean? For in the University, and so in the Law School, lectures ran from the end of October to the beginning of April and the academic session from the middle of October to the end of April.

In this strait, Russell tells us in his *Autobiography*, Weldon 'frankly put himself in the hands of his friends. The faculty was consulted and it was with the unanimous and cordial consent of the faculty and board of governors that he accepted the nomination and entered upon his parliamentary career'. He was elected. In order to enable the Parliamentarian-Dean to attend Parliament the Law School year was, beginning with the session 1887-88, changed so as to run from the first week in September to the middle of February and so end before Parliament opened. This radical departure from the year of the rest of the University, made to accommodate Weldon, was continued in 1896, when Weldon was defeated but Russell elected (in the Liberal interest and in a Halifax constituency), in order, presumably, to accommodate Russell; it persisted thereafter, through sheer academic inertia, until 1911 – all this time at considerable inconvenience to the students. The students did not, as things turned out, lose anything by what to the modern mind seems an oddly easy-going way of running a law school. Quite the contrary. They already had Weldon the man and Weldon the teacher of public law; they now gained in addition Weldon the man of public affairs.

But when, in pursuance of the new September-February schedule, the School opened on 7 September 1887, it was once again homeless, this time only temporarily. Pressured by an increasing enrolment in the University as a whole and spurred on by their inability to find room for the now established Law School in the old College Building on the Grand Parade, the Governors had in 1886 succeeded in making an arrangement with the City whereby that site would be exchanged for a new site on Carleton Street and $25 000; to this $25 000 Sir William Young had added $20 000 of his own and had in April 1887 laid the cornerstone of the imposing new 'Dalhousie College and University' building, known since 1919 as the Forrest Building. The way was now open for the School to join for the first time the rest of the university community. Rooms on the first and second floors in the north wing of the new building were reserved for it and during the summer it moved out of the Halliburton House. But when the time to begin lectures arrived the building was not quite ready. For the first few weeks lectures were held in the rooms of the Medical College and the Barristers' Society gave, once again, the use of their library, until in the late fall of 1887 the school moved into the quarters that would be its home until 1952.[30]

Now settled in its corner in the Forrest Building, what had begun only four years before as a daring experiment turned out to be an unqualified success. In purely statistical terms, from 1885 on, the year of the first law class to graduate, there would be in every year until as late as 1893 almost as many graduates in Law as in Arts. In 1885 there were ten from Law and twelve from Arts, and in 1893 there were twenty-one from Law and twenty-one from Arts; or, putting the same thing another way, there would be in the ten-year period 1885-94 a hundred and thirty seven LLBs and a hundred and eighty BAs.[31] In terms of quality the following comments of two knowledge-able outsiders are worth quoting. In an article criticizing the state of legal education in Ontario, E.D. Armour, the editor of the *Canadian Law Times*, made an assessment in 1888 that, coming as it did from an Upper Canadian, will gladden the heart of any Nova Scotian: 'The Province of Nova Scotia with its well regulated and well officered Law School is as far ahead of Ontario in the practical education of its lawyers, as the Province of Ontario is ahead of

Nova Scotia in vanity and self-adulation.'[32] And Sir Frederick Pollock, editor of the prestigious *Law Quarterly Review* in England, who had made the first of his approving comments on the School in 1886, gave an appraisal in 1900 which is just as applicable to the School of 1887 as it was to the School of 1900: 'The current calendar of the Law School of Dalhousie University, Halifax, N.S., continues to give evidence of a far higher ideal of legal education than it has yet pleased our Inns of Court to recognize.'[33]

This is the end of the story of the beginning of Dalhousie Law School. It is also, as far as Dalhousie and the Nova Scotia Barristers' Society are concerned, to all intents and purposes the end of the story of the genesis of the 'Dalhousie-Nova Scotia model' of legal education – the system under which a student gains admission to the profession by attending full-time for three years a university law school with a curriculum that is a mix of liberal and technical subjects, obtaining an LLB degree there and serving for a shorter period as an apprentice in an office. For that system was as good as already in effect in Nova Scotia at the time of the move to the Forrest Building. By the end of the nineteen-fifties, but not until then, the Dalhousie-Nova Scotia model would be in effect in every province (except Manitoba) and would have become the Canadian system of legal education.

And now begins the story of 'Dalhousie's Little Law School.' In the late fall of 1887 the School, with its liberal-technical curriculum and Weldon's public-service aims already established, was 'just like a little family.' It had a little faculty consisting of Weldon full-time, Russell half-time, and six distinguished downtown lecturers; there was a little student body of forty-one, all of them working in the School's own quarters in a few rooms on the first and second floors of the Forrest Building. With minor changes in curriculum and in aims, it remained almost exactly the same until shortly after the end of the First World War: a full-time faculty of one, assisted by downtown lecturers; a normal student body of between forty and fifty, all housed in the north wing of the Forrest Building. Even as late as the end of the Second World War, it would still be recognizable as the same, despite an increase in the number of full-time faculty to four in the twenties and an increase in the normal student body to seventy-five in the thirties, all of them still squeezed into the same corner of the Forrest Building. It could indeed be said that it was not until after the School moved to its fifth and present home in the Weldon Building that 'anything really happened,' so that this history might well end here in 1887 and begin again in 1966. So well and truly did the founders of Dalhousie Law School lay its foundations.

PART II

Dalhousie's Little Law School: 1887-1945

With the move to the Forrest Building in the fall of 1887 there came into being what to many graduates still living will always be the 'real' Dalhousie Law School: this small group of students, these two or three small rooms in the north wing of the building, a small but competent faculty, all working with a small but adequate collection of books in a course of study combining both the university and the professional approaches to Law. Not until the swollen enrolments that came with the end of the Second World War and the move in 1952 from its corner in the Forrest Building to its own Law building on the Studley campus – 'something akin, I think, to removing the Vatican to Sydney Mines'[1] – does it begin the slow process of changing into the very different kind of institution depicted in its recent glossy brochure, *The Dalhousie Law School.*

The true flavour of this long period is best caught by reading the Law School items in the student-run *Dalhousie Gazette* from 1887 to 1916 – ranging as they do from critical appraisals of the curriculum and of the teachers down through detailed reports of moot courts and mock parliaments to class histories and little 'in' jokes about fellow-students – and then turning to the January 1976 and December 1977 special issues of *Ansul* for the evocative reminiscences written by some of those who were there during the years 1916 to 1960. It is in those reminiscences that one senses most clearly what the student members of that tightly knit little society 'dedicated to the study and worship of the law' felt about each other and about the School. In the words of a member of the class of 1929: 'There was great esprit de corps among the students. We were all proud of the Law School and we were proud to be members of the Law School.'[2] Exactly the same note had been struck forty years earlier, but in the more strident tones then customary, by two students in the *Gazettes* of 1887 and 1889: 'We have been and are today a class united in fellow-feeling and good-will. In the Moot Court and the Law Club we have fought as law students only can, armed to the teeth with wordy weapons, but we always parted friends'[3]; and 'We are prepared at all times to maintain that the Dalhousie Law School is far and away the best in Canada, and inferior only to one or two in the United States.'[4] Added to these feelings of esprit de corps and pride in the School was a sense of belonging to a tradition: 'All of us studied the pictures around the Law School and saw the names of the graduates who had passed through'[5]; and 'no one who ever sat in the old third-year room in the Forrest Building needed to be reminded of those who had gone before. Each class had for decades inscribed its initials on the old benches which had been there since the building was erected.'[6]

This history will not attempt to reproduce except incidentally the picture of Dalhousie's Little Law School which has built up in the writer's mind as he read the *Gazette* items and the *Ansul* reminiscences. And it will resist the almost irresistible temptation to describe such choice morsels of a now long-vanished student way of life as the 'Christmas tramp' of 1886 ('Mr. Graham [i.e. Wallace Graham QC, one of the original downtown lecturers] was met on the street and they [i.e. the students] would not let him go unless he blessed them'),[7] the Law School dinner of 13 December 1899 with its gourmet menu and its many after-dinner speeches,[8] and 'the familiar Law Yell'[9] which seems to have been considered a fit and proper way to end a meeting addressed by 'an eminent jurist of Ontario' in February 1912.[10] All that it aims to do is to set forth for the information of 'the faithful' the relatively uneventful high spots – uneventful, that is, when compared with the high spots in 'Beginning.'

Because, and only because, a history is supposed to move forward in time, this story of Dalhousie's Little Law School is divided into four periods:
Section One, 1887-1914: Weldon
Section Two, 1914-24: MacRae
Section Three, 1920-33: the Golden Age
Section Four, 1933-45: the Great Depression and the Second World War.

Of these time-periods, the first, which begins with Weldon in Parliament and ends with his retirement from the School in 1914, is by far the most important. It is important because, as we said earlier, it was during these thirty years that Weldon and Russell, men of affairs as well as teachers, put their stamp on more generations of students – and more nationally notable students – than anyone else has since. It is important because, as we have not yet said but should have said, it was this thirty-year-long domination of the School by Weldon and Russell as teachers that gave permanence to what had in 1883 been the novel Dalhousie approach to the teaching of law. It is, for the purpose of this history, even more important because it was during Weldon's time as Dean that there first emerged patterns – such as an outspoken student body, a struggling library, and a faculty that comes and goes – which will persist throughout the whole sixty-year period, and it was Weldon who, with Russell's help, formed the intangible traditions such as public service and the ever-open door policy and fostered the tangible ones, such as the Moot Court and the Mock Parliament, which are still part of the heritage of the School today. There are, however, no events on which to build the chronological record that a history is supposed to be – unless one rates as events such happenings as the rare address given to the students by a distinguished visitor, the holding by the long-forgotten Canadian Bar Association of 1896-98 of its second annual meeting in the Law Library in 1897,[11] or the abortive attempt by a group of students (students, mark you) in 1906 to raise, in anticipation of the twenty-fifth anniversary of the founding of the School, $30 000 for a library fund and an additional professor, 'the need [for both of which] is apparent to all.'[12]

SECTION ONE: 1887-1914

Weldon

Both the Moot Court and the Mock Parliament were in full swing by the time of the move to the Forrest Building in 1887. Weldon and Russell for many years ran the Moot Court as an integral part of the curriculum, providing the fact situations to be argued and presiding as judges – exacting judges too – at the hearings. And although the Mock Parliament was started by the students and has always been run by the students, it was no doubt the presence among them of Weldon and Russell – real live members of the House of Commons for seventeen continuous years, Weldon from 1887 to 1896 and Russell from 1896 to 1904 – that inspired them to make of it something more than a place where embryo lawyers could learn to think on their feet; it was a place where aspiring young politicians could learn how to debate the public issues of the day in accordance with the rules of the House and could acquire practical experience in the art of combining with one another to form and defeat governments. Both the Moot Court and the Mock Parliament were held for many years in the so-called Moot Court room in the Forrest Building, so that on the occasion of the School's fiftieth anniversary in 1933 the *Gazette* was able to say: 'The shrine of the traditions of the School is the Moot Court room. Men now prominent in public life first tried their wings in forensic combat and in Parliamentary debate in the Moot Court room.'

From the very beginning of the School every candidate for a degree was required to take part in arguing points of law in moot courts. For, as the Inaugural Addresses booklet put it in 1884, 'it is the aim of the School to make practical as well as theoretical lawyers.' It was this requirement which drew from Sir Frederick Pollock in 1886 the first of his approving comments: 'truly Nova Scotia is in advance of the mother country in this matter.'[13] – and it has remained in effect to this day.

In the early days the moot courts were regarded as so basic an educational tool that all students, and not merely the contestants, were for a short time required to attend each and every one of them and the presiding judges were always members of the faculty or practising lawyers; as can be seen from the *Gazette*'s detailed reports of many cases, the students took them very seriously. Some time shortly after 1915 control of the Moot Court system passed to the Moot Court Committee of the Students Law Society, with the judges coming from third-year and counsel from second-year students. Since then, as is liable to happen in any student activity, there has occasionally, but only occasionally, been a little too much fun and games. In the last fifteen years the Faculty has from time to time considered ways and means of reasserting to some extent its control of what it has never ceased to regard as a serious academic enterprise, but fifty years of student control has created a tradition of student control and in an institution so tradition-minded as Dalhousie Law School the argument of tradition is hard to overcome. In any event the standard of the Moot Court has usually been reasonably high and the very high level of achievement reached year after year by the four contestants in the annual Moot Court Competition for the Smith Shield – a trophy given by Sidney Smith (of whom more hereafter) and first competed for in 1927 – before a bench consisting of members of the Bench and Bar of Nova Scotia seems to show that there is nothing fundamentally wrong with things as they are.[14]

The Mock Parliament, said to be the oldest in Canada and still an honoured tradition at the School, grew out of a debating club which the students formed in December 1884 for 'the improvement and development of the oratorical gifts of the member'; the subject discussed at the first meeting was 'Resolved that the House of Lords in England has outlived its usefulness.' At the beginning of the 1886-87 session they decided to change the debating club into a mock parliament – a change which should occasion no surprise, for the students have throughout the School's history always shown as much interest in politics as in law; in 1951 indeed 'two classmates, Earl Urquhart and Al Baccardax, took several weeks off to run against each other in a by-election in Richmond County.'[15] The 'prime minister' at this first session of 1886 was Hector McInnes, in later years one of the stalwarts among Weldon's part-time lecturers and in the nineteen-thirties Chairman of the Board of Governors of the University, but his government was short-lived and another student was called upon to form a new government, which government soon fell too. This was to be a familiar pattern, for in the parliaments down through the years many governments were to meet this same fate – the idea being to give as many students as possible a chance to sit in the seats of the mighty.

From the extensive reports of the proceedings which the *Gazette* carried until 1914, it can be seen that the Mock Parliament was from the beginning, and was meant to be, what it still is, 25 per cent fun and 75 per cent serious discussion of contemporary political issues, carried on in accordance with the rules of the House of Commons. Typical of the fun is the mock pomp and pageantry with which the session has opened since some time in the early nineteen hundreds – complete, to quote from a description of the opening in 1947, with 'Professor Hancock, dashingly garbed in white tie and tails ... as Gentleman Usher of the Black Rod and Scotty McLeod of the maintenance staff [as] Sergeant-at-Arms with a new wooden mace turned out by the Halifax Shipyards.'[16] Typical of the serious side is the occasional course of lectures on parliamentary procedure, given at the request of the students: for example, one by Weldon in 1905 and one by Professor Lorne Clarke in 1959. The Mock Parliament has had its ups and downs: 'after the stormy session of last year, and the revolutionary measures taken to restore Mock Parliament to what it ought to be ... may it always be as successful as it was this year' (*Gazette*, 22 January 1896); and as recently as 1976 it was successfully revived after having died for a year, and was given the new and non-traditional name of '*model* parliament' 'in order to prevent it being a circus' (according to a member of the class of 1977).

The only official record of its proceedings that has ever been kept is the minutes for the session 1898-99; they are at the back of a sturdy notebook containing the minutes of the Students Law Society from 1898 to 1908, a volume which still exists. This record shows the same mixture of serious political discussion and fun that has always characterized this venerable institution. One of the many resolutions debated during that session was 'that Nova Scotia withdraw from Confederation and form with New Brunswick and Prince Edward Island a new confederacy to be known as the Maritime Provinces of America'; and on a motion disapproving of the present conduct of the Parliamentary Hansard, 'Mr. O'Connor spoke to resolution, said jokes were ancient and produced affidavit to prove antiquity.'[17]

It appears from the minutes of the Students Law Society, to which we have just referred, that the Society did not acquire a constitution or by-laws until 1905, but long before that there had been 'general meetings of the law students' and the Society was clearly in *de facto* operation by 1898. It also appears from those minutes that the Society was in these early days directing its activities along three main channels: 1, scholastic, such as sponsoring debating teams and organizing the mock parliaments; 2, athletic, arranging for hockey and football games; and 3, social functions. It continued to function along these humble lines until after the emergence of 'the big School' in the late nineteen-sixties. Not until then did it become the important organization that it is today, giving an official helping hand to the members of the entering first-year class and acting as an official organ of communication between a student body of four hundred and fifty and a full-time faculty of thirty-six. It is with a sense of yearning for an uncomplicated and unsophisticated past that the writer records that the only item of business to engender any discussion in each of the years 1899 to 1905 was what form the annual social function should take and here sets down for posterity what the decisions were: in 1899 a dinner; in 1900 an At Home; in 1901 a smoker; in 1902 another At Home, this time with a band; in 1903 a dance in the Law Library; in 1904 a complimentary dinner to Benny Russell on the occasion of his elevation to the Bench; and in 1905 no function of any kind.[18]

Inaugurating a pattern which will persist throughout the period of Dalhousie's Little Law School, and indeed throughout the School's whole history, the students were from the beginning quick to say what they liked and what they disliked about the School. So much so that it is from the columns of their *Gazette* that we derive almost all we know about the Weldon period. About Weldon and Russell they were always, and about what the School was trying to do – 'giving us broader and more humane ideas of the law as a science' – they were nearly always, enthusiastic. About the struggling library, the in some ways deficient curriculum, and the sometimes unsatisfactory downtown lecturers, they were understanding but critical. The general tone of their comments was 'this is a good School, but ....' From these comments we can see what problems Weldon – and to a lesser extent his successors – had to cope with in order to keep the School going.

Quite apart from the malaises which will be found in any law school library (even the well-ordered Sir James Dunn Law Library on the top two floors of the Weldon Building today), malaises such as stolen books, marked books, and noise – 'A few students drop in there whenever they have nothing to do and spend the time with someone who is not very particular about working' (1895)[19] – we can see that the struggling library of the Weldon period was recognizably the same then as at the end of the Second World War. It was located in the same large, airy, and well-windowed room on the second floor, though less crowded no doubt with ecclesiastical-looking stacks than it became later. There was no full-time librarian, except in one year, 1892-93. For that one year A.H.R. Fraser ('92) served, to the delight of the students, as Law Librarian and Tutor, but, like Bulmer before him, he had to be let go at the end of the year because there was no money to pay him; the very next year he became librarian of the Cornell University College of Law and by the time of his early death in 1911 he had succeeded in making Cornell's Law Library second only to Harvard's in excellence. The small collection of books was watched over and order was preserved – or was supposed to be preserved – by a series of students annually appointed by the Dean at a tiny salary on the basis of financial need and scholastic performance; among them were two who would later be the School's greatest benefactors, R.B. Bennett ('93), destined to become rich and Prime Minister, and James Dunn ('98), destined to become a prince in the world of finance and one of the last of the multi-millionaires. In the hungry twenties and thirties the Dean was still making these appointments 'with a care and solicitude that would raise the eyebrows of a modern welfare officer' and was appointing men who are still living and have made their mark in the world.

The collection of books itself was both in Weldon's time and in 1945 an adequate student working library – no more than that – but it was not until some time in the early 1900s that the library acquired what it did not have before then, a university appropriation for its support. From an article in the *Gazette* in 1905 complaining that the library is 'sadly in need of replenishment' we learn that as late as that 'there is no fund at the back of this library, and whatever reports or text books there are, are entirely due to the liberality of the Faculty who contribute generously to its sustenance.' No wonder that in earlier *Gazettes* we find items begging the Dean to procure 'a few at least of the leading law magazines, such as *Canadian Law Times*, *Harvard Law Review*, *Law Quarterly Review*, as they come out' (1891) or to raise some money for later editions of textbooks (1894) – material which, we hasten to say, had long before 1945 become part of the standard equipment of the library. As for books outside the normal pabulum of the practising lawyer, there were practically none in Weldon's time, unless we count such doubtful items as 'some ... very costly and rare books in the science of Jurisprudence' that were left to the School by Sir William Young in 1887; even in 1945 what few there were had come from infrequent casual gifts by private donors, such as the Bennett collection of books on the history of English law which was established by a series of almost annual contributions from R.B. Bennett that began in 1922. In a word the library was, like the libraries at all the other Canadian law schools, always pathetically starved for money until the 1950s; the dramatic illustrations just given from Weldon's time are no more than extreme examples of a condition that continued for many years.

Far more pressing for Weldon than the problems of the library were the problems of getting and keeping satisfactory downtown lecturers and so, in a School which depended on them for teaching most of the bread-and-butter subjects of a lawyer's life, of preventing the quite adequate revised curriculum of 1887 from developing serious gaps. By 1892 the last of the original downtowners had gone; who, when the initial driving enthusiasm of starting the new project was spent, would be willing, and competent, to carry on what they had begun? Part of the slack had, to the lasting benefit of the School, already been taken up by Russell; by 1892 he was for a pittance of a thousand dollars a year teaching the basic subjects of Contracts, Sale of Goods, Negotiable Instruments, and Equity. Some of the rest of it Weldon had perforce to take up himself, and this at a time when, also to the lasting benefit of the School, he was as a member of Parliament spending two months or so of every year in Ottawa and continuously looking after the interests of his constituents in distant Albert County, New Brunswick.

Weldon stood, and had to stand, ready to move into any breach that developed. In 1891 he had to take on Crimes, a subject which had already been shuttled back and forth between two downtowners and in one year had not been given at all; he continued to teach it until 1902. In 1893 he had, in response to repeated student comments, such as 'in a law school ... which depends so largely on seaport towns for its students, we note, and we blush to note it, ... no lectures on shipping are delivered,'[20] to take on Shipping too; this subject had been added to the curriculum at the time of the 1887 revision, had been taught by a highly qualified practitioner for a year – just one year – and then left in abeyance for four. So adept did Weldon become at it that a few years later he became counsel to the best shipping firm in Halifax and was still teaching it in 1914 when he retired. And all this in addition to his own public-law subjects of Constitutional History, Constitutional Law, Public International Law, and Conflict of Laws. In 1905, at the age of fifty-six, he had to turn his hand to yet another new subject, Torts, and for the same reason as he had earlier taken up Crimes and Shipping: after a long series of unsatisfactory downtowners, there were two successive years in which he couldn't find anyone at all and so he had to do it himself. Here, please note, is the beginning of another pattern which will not disappear until the emergence in the late 1960s of the young 'specialist' just out of graduate school – the full-time teacher at Dalhousie Law School who has to be, and is, ready and willing to turn his hand to anything.

Weldon did, of course, have some indispensable stalwarts among the downtowners. In the early days there was Sidney Harrington who took over Evidence from Mr Justice Thompson when he left for Ottawa in 1885, took on Agency and Partnership when it was added to the curriculum in 1887, and taught both of these courses until 1904; there was George Ritchie, a graduate of the Harvard Law School, who took over Real Property from that devoted old man Shannon in 1892, filled a glaring gap in the curriculum with Conveyancing in 1894, added Wills in 1897, and taught all three courses until 1902; and there was Hector McInnes ('88), the first in a long line of old students to come back as a downtown lecturer, who filled another glaring gap in 1894 by giving the first course in Procedure ever given at the School and was still teaching it when Weldon retired. (Of these two glaring gaps more in a moment.) In later years there were Judge W.B. Wallace ('85), a member of the first graduating class, who relieved Weldon of Crimes in 1902 and continued teaching it until 1922, and Judge George Patterson ('89) who from 1907 to 1922 came every two weeks from New Glasgow to lecture on Evidence.

The students were loud in their praises of these stalwarts, but they were very outspoken about the deficiencies in some of the downtowners, deficiencies that will also evoke comment from their successors of later days, the authors of the reminiscences in *Ansul*: irregularity of attendance and lack of preparation. Two examples, chosen for their explicit outspokenness from a host of similar criticisms in the *Gazette*s of the Weldon period, are the following. 'By means of a "short" course delivered intermittently, they [the members of the first-year class in 1910] thoroughly imbibed the abstruseness of Real Property from Controller ... who contrary to his prefix could not control his attendance and was therefore conspicuous by his absence.'[21] And 'We sympathise with the man who rushes away from his work to attend to the duty of lecturing to a class; not having time enough to completely familiarise himself with the lecture about to be given, and the cases upon which it bears, he is compelled to read closely, make a few comments here and there, and, when time is up, he rushes away leaving a list of cited cases, varying somewhat between fifteen and twenty, which the student has to read' (1895). Again and again during this period the students extolled their two 'paid professors,' Weldon and Russell ('their lectures are ideal ones'), and sounded the theme 'the Law School's greatest need is an extra professor.'[22] There would be no 'extra professor' until 1920.

And now for the two glaring gaps in the curriculum which were filled by George Ritchie and Hector McInnes in 1894, but only after persistent pressure from the students. From 1889 to 1892 there are a number of sympathetic but quite strongly worded items in the *Gazette* drawing the attention of the Faculty to 'certain known defects in our curriculum.' These known defects were: the course of study is not practical enough; there are too few lectures; and admission standards are too low.

The course of study not practical enough? A recommendation that International Law ('like geology ... though interesting ... not of any great utility') be struck out of the course and that Constitutional History ('it is not practical') be cut down to one hour a week and the law of (say) domestic relations, construction of statutes, agency, or bailments be substituted therefor was, naturally and properly, ignored by the Faculty: it struck at the heart of the public-law-minded curriculum that was distinctive of Dalhousie Law School. But 'the long felt need of practical lectures on Conveyancing ... which would deal with matters of every day work and would constitute fully one half of the work in the average law office' the Faculty could not, and did not, ignore: this basic subject had formed part of the original curriculum and had only ceased to be given when the original lecturer, James Thomson, resigned in 1887 and (presumably) Weldon had been unable to find anyone to take his place.

The students' request for a course on Procedure ('the most important of all subjects to the young lawyer and the one which will give him the most trouble') was in a rather different category. 'It is generally admitted that it can only be acquired by office work and practical experience'; and, what is far more important, the Nova Scotia Barristers' Society had, when in 1891 they accepted the Dalhousie LLB degree as satisfying all the academic requirements for admission to the Bar, specifically excluded Procedure from that arrangement and continued to require the Law School graduates to pass its own examination in the subject. Because, however, 'a series of lectures to students of two or three years office work is vastly beneficial to students of this all important branch' the Faculty also added Procedure to the curriculum. George Ritchie's lectures on Conveyancing and Hector McInnes' lectures on Procedure were a great success, and in 1899 the Barristers' Society completed its acceptance of the Dalhousie degree by exempting the graduates from its Procedure examination. By 1894, then, the serious practical gaps which had developed in the reasonably adequate curriculum established by the revision of 1887 had all been removed. Thereafter the curriculum remained substantially unchanged until after Weldon's retirement and the arrival of the new broom, MacRae, in 1914.[23]

To meet the other two criticisms voiced by the students in the early nineties – that there were too few lectures and that admission standards were too low – the Faculty did nothing, and continued to do nothing for twenty years. 'We believe that more lectures should be given a week. Summing up the whole course, we find that it only amounts to nineteen hours per week [i.e., about six hours a week in each of the three years of the course]. This is a smaller quantity than is prescribed in most other law schools. In Osgoode Hall the number in the whole three years amounts to twenty-six hours a week' (*Gazette*, 13 March 1890). Although the number of lectures scheduled had, as a result of the addition of the classes in Shipping, Conveyancing, and Procedure, risen to twenty-two by 1894, there were still no more than that in 1907. And, coming down to hard actualities, the number of lectures actually delivered must, because of hours missed by downtowners, have always been less than that; from 1911 to 1914 it was, as clearly appears from the attendance records kept by the downtowners, a good deal less.[24]

The complaints that admission standards are too low begin as early as 1887 and ten years later we are told that 'one half of Dalhousie Law Graduates have never had any preliminary training or educational experience beyond a common school education' and that 'a change is necessary' – and this at a time when half of those attending Osgoode Hall Law School had university degrees, 'many of whom have been trained in the political science subjects before entering the School.' The 'necessary change,' and then only to a prerequisite of one year of college work in certain prescribed classes, did not come until 1915, and then only because it had been in effect forced on the Law School by the Barristers' Society.[25]

In terms of mere educational statistics, then, the School of the Weldon period was not particularly impressive. Why then did it make such an impression on so many of those who were there in those years: 'it is the crowning glory of this law school that it has kindled in many a heart an inextinguishable fire' (*Gazette*, 28 February 1906)? Because of the two men who were running it, Russell the half-time lieutenant and Weldon the Dean.

John Read's appraisal of the team of Weldon and Russell is so compelling that it is here reproduced in full:

Both men were great teachers, but it would be difficult to find two individuals who were more unlike. They differed in method and intellectual approach to problems, political views and in stature. Indeed, almost the only things they had in common were a common love of their common work, a zeal for the public service of their country and an intense interest in the law. There can be no doubt that Weldon and Russell, as a team, accomplished a work that can only be adequately compared with that of Langdell and Ames at Harvard or of Dicey and Geldart at Oxford.[26]

Russell was, as the reader already knows, with Weldon from the very beginning of the School and was still teaching there when Weldon retired; he did not resign until 1921, by which time he had put in nearly forty continuous years, a record which has not been, and is not likely to be, surpassed. He was that godsend to young law students, a man of affairs: from 1896 until 1904 a member of Parliament and from then on a judge of the Supreme Court of Nova Scotia. 'A wee bitty man and quite lively' as late as the middle of the First World War,[27] Benny treated the students as friends, giving them the occasional party at his house (duly reported in the *Gazette!*) and always turning up at Law Dinners. As can be seen from his *Autobiography* and from his occasional learned addresses (for example, the one he gave as long ago as 1886 on 'Legal Education and Law Reform,'[28] as alive today as it was then), he wrote like an angel; even his outdated textbook on Bills and Notes – he was a scholar too – is readable. But it was as a teacher, a great teacher – 'worthy to rank with Langdell and Ames, his own heroes,' one of his old students, Dean Vincent MacDonald, has said[29] – that his students knew him best and best remembered him. He did not lecture them, as other teachers did; he discussed the cases with them. So his classes on the down-to-earth, bread-and-butter subjects that he taught were memorable experiences: 'when his book on Bills and Notes was in the press ... he used the proof in his classes, every paragraph going under dissection in the classroom'; 'balanced on a chair, which in its turn was balanced on one leg, Russell was trying to get into our heads some very subtle point in the law of contracts'; and (said of a student by one of his fellows) 'He's fond of giving Benny points, and gives them free at that.'[30]

But it was Weldon – 'far above the ordinary man in every way'[31] – who made the truly enduring impression on his students and on the School. 'He was not merely the Dean of the Law School; he was the Law School.'[32] And, as we have already indicated by the quotations from John Barnett ('07) in the Introduction, it was Weldon who by his idealistic approach to public affairs, both in and out of Parliament, created the Weldon tradition of public service and it was 'dear kindly Weldon' who by his easy-going ways with the little group of students started the tradition of the ever-open door policy.

The nine years that Weldon sat in Parliament – to have as their Dean a member of Parliament must in itself have been an inspiration to the students – were not just an interlude in a life devoted to teaching. Long before he came to Dalhousie in 1883 and was elected as Conservative member for Albert County in 1887 he had been taking an active part in the political life of the county. While in Parliament he took a distinguished part in the work of the House: in the first of his two sessions there he was chosen to move the address in reply to the Speech from the Throne; he was successful in promoting an important private bill, known for many years thereafter as the Weldon Act, to amend the Extradition Act; he was twice offered a seat in the cabinet; and, Russell tells us, 'there was a time when it seemed as if he might become the Prime Minister of Canada.' After his defeat in the general election of 1896 – deserted by his party because he had, characteristically, listened to his own sense of what was right and had spoken against them on the Manitoba school question, a matter involving great issues of constitutional law and minority rights – he did not give up politics. In the next general election, in 1900, he stood once more in Albert County but lost by a small majority. And in 1906 he stood yet again in what must have been a particularly nasty by-election in Shelburne-Queens, Nova Scotia: the main issue was corruption and he was asked to stand because of his 'high character, attainments and reputation'; in this, his last election, he suffered an overwhelming defeat at the hands of Hon. W.S. Fielding, the Minister of Finance in the Laurier government.[33]

Did the School suffer in any way from Weldon's long involvement in practical politics? In some minor ways the answer may be yes. In the *Gazette* for 11 February, 1896, a time when Weldon was still in Parliament and Russell was about to face an election, there is a letter from 'Alumnus' complaining that 'the professors [i.e. Weldon, the Professor of Constitutional and International Law, and Russell, the Professor of Contracts] have private interests

widely apart from their professorial duties, interests which frequently conflict with those duties to the great prejudice of the School.' Early in the twentieth century, he was failing in health – the reports of Law Dinners show him
'absent due to illness,' brought on perhaps by the strain of living two lives
and having to take on extra downtown subjects in addition to his own – and
for the last two or three years before he retired the School 'was allowed to fall
into a loose state,' to use the words of the new President, A. Stanley
MacKenzie.[34] And it may also be that it was these strains which prevented
him from publishing anything out of his great store of knowledge of international and constitutional law. But in all that really matters the answer is a
resounding no. By his example, in his lectures, and in his conversations with
individuals he inspired his students with the ideal of unselfish, upright, public service.

His political experience illuminated his lectures on International and Constitutional Law; 'with the happiest faculty of making these lectures interesting in the light of our own times and the conditions of our own country, he
inspires his students to go through life with their eyes open.'[35] So also with his
conversations with individual students on the current topics of the time; 'frequently they were lit up by personal reminiscences but most frequently by
tales drawn from his own experiences as a Member of Parliament.'[36] Unlike
Russell, who in teaching his nitty-gritty 'lawyer's law' subjects 'delighted in
chasing a point down to the ultimate,'[37] he taught his own great public law
subjects in the grand manner. From the notes taken by a student in his
Constitutional Law class in 1891-92, which are preserved at the Law School,[38]
and from the examination paper for that year we can see that, while he spent
half his time on the cases dealing with the division of powers in Sections 91
and 92 of the BNA Act, he put his subject in very broad perspective. He dealt,
for example, with the federal constitutions of Switzerland and the United
States and with the legal position of the Executive, the Senate, and the House
of Commons, referring to Sessional Papers and the practice of the House of
Commons where relevant. His Constitutional History class was, John Read
('08-'09) has told us, 'traditional' – i.e., a glorification of British institutions
such as Magna Carta – 'and you get something from the traditional that you
don't get when you strip it off and get to the bare bones.'[39] 'The Dean's
eloquent lectures' said Humphrey Mellish ('90), 'always brought the "ma-
jesty" of the law before his hearers in the great subjects which he taught such
as International Law, Conflict of Laws and Constitutional History. The very

"greatness" of his teaching particularly in dealing with such a subject as the growth and expansion of the British Constitution excited a pride and enthusiasm in which, for the time at least, Subtlety and Art were forgotten.'[40]

Often expressed in his lectures was the idealism which was the bedrock of his character: 'I well remember the closing words of the last lecture of his I attended. Dean Weldon said "Gentlemen, I ask you as you go your several ways in life, to be proud men – very proud men – too proud, gentlemen, to do anything mean." '[41] 'He possessed such superior qualities as a teacher that I am certain every man who was privileged to be a member of his class had a finer conception of life and a firmer resolve to maintain the best traditions of the noble profession for which we were being trained.'[42] And what drove that idealism home to Weldon's students was their feeling for him as a man. Predominant among the items about him in the *Gazette* and in 'appreciations' delivered on more formal occasions are such sentiments as: 'and of course we love him as a man no less than we appreciate him as a lecturer'; 'dear, kindly Weldon'; 'Dean Weldon, whose great stature and rugged and kindly face reflected not only his strength of character but also his great intellectual powers.'

Each in his own very different way a teacher of distinction, Weldon and Russell made, when put together, a remarkable team. George Patterson ('89), an old student and later a part-time colleague of theirs, has said why:

Russell had the faculty of teaching us how to learn law, a faculty that very few professors have ... Let me not be misunderstood ... Dr. Weldon, was the heart and soul of the University ... his influence with and upon the student body came not from his learning, great though it was, but from his glorious personality ... the subjects he professed were cultural rather than practical .... It was Weldon who made us, if we ever became, good citizens; it was he who equipped us for public life if ever a discerning electorate sought our services; but it was Russell who taught us the law and enabled us intelligently to advise clients and properly and convincingly represent their cases. In a word, we were the better men because we had known Weldon, the better lawyers because we had learned of Russell.[43]

When Weldon retired in 1914 the experiment he had helped to start and had fostered for more than thirty years was an established reality. Dalhousie's Little Law School had graduated more than four hundred students and, as it so happened, the enrolment in that year was nearly the largest it had ever been, sixty-two. A few years earlier he had said of it to John Barnett: 'It hasn't done all I hoped it would, but it is my child, I love it.' But others thought well, very well, of it. So many of his old students had made their names in one of the great chapters in Canadian history, the settlement of the West, that for years the majority of people in the four western provinces thought of Dalhousie only in terms of the Law School. And, leaving entirely aside what Weldon himself would have cared about most, the honest day-to-day job done by those of them who stayed in Nova Scotia and the Maritimes and were 'just lawyers,' it was his old students who made on the national scene an impact unequalled by their successors. The overwhelming majority of the students in Weldon's time came from Nova Scotia, and from the country in Nova Scotia. Poor boys that they were, they lived on a scale comparable to that announced in the Inaugural Addresses booklet of 1884: the estimated annual cost of attending the School is there given as $150 (books, $20; tuition fees, $30; and board for 25 weeks, $100) and there is added thereto the comment that 'students have taken the course and paid all expenses for one hundred dollars, but it is advisable to come prepared with the larger amount.' When they graduated they found work hard to get, so that in the 1890s and in the first two decades of the twentieth century about one in four of them went to the raw Canadian West where there was a demand for lawyers; 'we couldn't,' as one emigré from Nova Scotia has forthrightly put it, 'compete with those that remained.'[44]

The earliest of these emigrés went mainly to Vancouver, Victoria, and the Lower Mainland of British Columbia; the later ones went mainly to the three Prairie provinces, many of them to small towns with names unfamiliar to a Maritimer; their greatest concentration was in Alberta. Some of them did very well and very quickly. By 1904, for example, Aulay Morrison ('88), a bright boy from Baddeck, 'Dalhousie's first and only artist' and a great football player, had become a judge of the Supreme Court of British Columbia – the same year in which his old teacher, Benny Russell, was appointed to the Bench in Nova Scotia. By then too Richard McBride ('90), who, it will be remembered, came all the way east to the School in 1887, was Premier of British Columbia. In the Territories (in Calgary, in what was soon to be Alberta) 'Dick' Bennett ('93), who would one day become Prime Minister of Canada, was regarded as 'the most brilliant orator among the younger politicians. He has kept true to the faith of the Dean.'[45] As to the lesser lights in the West, most of them, says John Barnett, brought from the north corner of the

Forrest Building so desirable a combination of qualities – including 'a college and clan spirit which was not to be found in any other large group among the members of the legal profession with which they were associated' – that they 'gave to the Dalhousie Law School ... a high country-wide repute.'

Coming back again to 'names,' there would be in 1932 one of Weldon's old students on every Supreme Court in the country except Ontario, Quebec, and Prince Edward Island.[46] In the political field also his old students did him proud: in addition to McBride and Bennett, there came from among them two premiers of Nova Scotia, a premier of New Brunswick, and a prime minister of Newfoundland.[47] The best known of these political leaders, R.B. Bennett, was, as Bennett himself was never tired of acknowledging, deeply indebted to Weldon: in a practical way because Weldon gave the poor boy from Hopewell, New Brunswick, a helping hand at two crucial stages in his career, appointing him student librarian to supplement his meagre resources when he was at the Law School, and later, when he had graduated and was practising in Chatham, recommending him to Senator Lougheed of Calgary who was looking for a bright young man as partner; and in a far deeper way because in his oratorical style of public speaking and in his devotion to 'the British connection' he was Weldon all over again.[48] And in the world of international finance there was James Dunn, once a poor boy from Bathurst, New Brunswick; he too received help from Weldon in the form of an appointment as student librarian and a letter of recommendation which he treasured and kept for the rest of his life; shortly before he died he told a classmate that he attributed much of his success in life 'to the wholesome influence and guidance of Dr. Weldon.'[49]

Weldon's Law School may not have done all he hoped it would. But Weldon's old students have, by what they did with their lives and what they said about him, made the name and fame of Weldon himself secure. For the students and teachers who work in the Weldon Building today this brief and inadequate account of what Weldon did to start the School and shape it in its early days should serve as a reminder that the word 'Weldon' is something more than a prefix which has somehow attached itself to a tradition and a building.

SECTION TWO: 1914-1924

MacRae

With the end of the Weldon era in the summer of 1914 we come to what are almost modern times in the history of Dalhousie's Little Law School. For the first time there is information, sometimes too much information, about what is going on; for we have now arrived at the beginning of the age of paper and, what is even better, at a period which is within the memory of those still living. With the departure of those revered sons of the age of oral communication, 'Lord John' Forrest, the long-time President (1885-1911), and Weldon, the long-time Dean (1883-1914), and the arrival of their more businesslike successors, President A. Stanley MacKenzie and Dean Donald Alexander MacRae, Faculty minutes and files of correspondence are thereafter regularly and carefully kept. And beginning with Emelyn MacKenzie and Vincent Pottier, both of whom entered the School in the fall of 1916, we have from then until the end of the fifties a series of enchanting descriptions by old students of what it felt like to be there.[1] There are in addition such sources as reports of the President, Dalhousie University *Bulletins*, and the *Alumni News*. No longer do we have to rely almost exclusively on items painfully dredged out of the *Gazette*.

Compared with the Weldon period and with the two later periods of the Golden Age and the Great Depression and the Second World War, the MacRae period, 1914-24, is full of events – as far as there can be said to be any events in the history of a School which, as we said earlier, had by 1887 already achieved the fundamental shape that it has ever since retained. Events of a non-academic kind include: the removal of the main body of the University, i.e., the Arts and Science Faculty, from the Forrest Building to the new campus at Studley; the arrival of the first women students; an abortive first attempt to start a kind of student law review, if that is what it was; two first attempts, both abortive, to create a law alumni association; the coming, in the shape of the veterans of the First World War, of what is one of the most distinguished groups of students that the School has ever had; and the realization for the first time of the dream that the students of the Weldon period had so often dreamed – the appointment of first one, and a year later of yet another, full-time teacher in addition to the Dean. These two men were, as it happened, themselves veterans and were destined to become as distinguished as any of the veterans that they taught.

As to events of an academic nature, one of those two men had the courage to abandon the traditional 'lecture method' of teaching and use for the first time in Canada what has since become the now almost equally traditional case method; the first in a long line of later students to do so went on to the Harvard Law School for graduate work; and the first in a long line of later faculty members to do so wrote and published articles in the newly established *Canadian Bar Review*. But the last two of these three academic events happened right at the end of the period and were no more than a by-product of what is by far the most important event, academic or non-academic – the persistent and successful drive by MacRae and others, nameless others, to raise the academic standards of the School.

When MacRae came in 1914 the standard of admission to the School, and to the profession in the common-law provinces right across Canada, was still no higher than that upon which the *Gazette* had time and again poured scorn in the nineties; when he left in 1924 the standard at Dalhousie Law School had become two years of college work, a standard which stood until as recently as 1957. Until shortly before MacRae came the students were on a leisurely schedule of eight or nine class hours a week – if they were all given – for twenty-one weeks a year; when he left they were scurrying for twenty-seven weeks a year on a treadmill that called for fourteen class hours a week in the first year, nineteen in the second, and twenty in the third – a load far in excess of the twelve or so that the leading American law schools of the day imposed and considerably in excess of the much more reasonable load of fifteen that is the rule at Dalhousie in 1976. And it was during this period that MacRae (and, once again, nameless others), building on the curriculum that he found when he came, fashioned the 'cover-everything' and 'professionally-oriented' curriculum that was in effect copied by the Legal Education Committee of the Canadian Bar Association and was promulgated in 1920 by the Association as its 'standard curriculum' for suggested adoption in all common-law provinces. This curriculum, familiarly known to all Canadian law teachers of the writer's generation as the MacRae curriculum of the twenties, remained, with comparatively minor modifications, the curriculum in effect at all common-law schools in Canada, including Dalhousie Law School, for nearly fifty years.

It is therefore only fitting that MacRae should have his name attached to the period covered by this section. If Weldon earned that honour in respect of the period covered by Section One – as earn it he did, by being the creator and for many years the personification of the School – so also did MacRae earn it by the new start he gave to the School and by the enduring influence that his measures of reform had upon the School and, indeed, upon the whole spectrum of Canadian legal education. He will be the last dean to be so honoured, for none of the deans that followed him made any truly significant impact on the School. The first truly decisive change since MacRae in what the School was doing or trying to do did not occur until the late sixties or early seventies and by that time it was, as we shall see, no longer the Dean but the Faculty that was in the driver's seat. As to our insistence, twice repeated, that it was not the Dean, MacRae, alone but also the nameless others with him who gave the School its new start, our aim is to warn the reader against thinking that even in the one-man School the Dean was the sole source of 'all things bright and beautiful.' Even the great Weldon had, as we have said, his Sedgewick, his Russell, and others to help him. MacRae too had, of course, others to help and to inspire him – among them the reformer-president A. Stanley MacKenzie, the reform-minded Council of the Barristers' Society, and perhaps also the forward-looking Dean R.W. Lee of McGill, the chairman of the Legal Education Committee of the Canadian Bar Association, with whom, as a member of that committee, MacRae became associated in 1918; we have called these and other helpers 'nameless' because we do not know, as we do know in the case of Weldon, precisely what help they gave.

Now to Donald Alexander MacRae himself and how he came, as the *Canadian Law Times* put it, to be 'called to preside over an institution with [such a "high reputation"] and to follow in the footsteps of his distinguished and revered predecessor, Dr. R.C. Weldon.'[2] When this tall handsome man of forty-two was appointed only two weeks or so before classes were due to begin in the fall of 1914 – and he did not arrive in Halifax until just one week before classes – he must have seemed to Halifax lawyers an odd man to have been chosen to follow in those footsteps: he was only a year out of Osgoode and was the most junior man in a firm of lawyers in Toronto. But, like his predecessor, he was, as it so happened, the right kind of man to head up the university school of law that Dalhousie Law School was. Born in a village in Prince Edward Island, he came late, and by his own choice, to the world of learning. For seven years after leaving school he worked in a clothing store but, like so many Maritimers of his time, he thirsted for higher education. Against heavy odds and despite some discouragement from 'Lord John,' the Principal, he won at the late age of twenty-two an entrance scholarship to Dalhousie. From then on all was plain sailing. He graduated with high honours in classics and with the University Medal, spent six years at Cornell as instructor in Greek and in getting his PHD and then four years at Princeton as assistant professor and preceptor in Greek. When, then, he decided at the age of thirty-seven to turn to the study of law – 'partly with the intention of becoming a law teacher if the occasion ever presented itself' – he had behind him a record of solid achievement in teaching at the university level a subject no less demanding than law.[3]

But why the long delay between the retirement of Weldon and the last-minute appointment of MacRae? Because the Board had, on the insistence of Benny Russell (and no doubt others), decided in the first instance to let the School coast along without a new dean until they could find someone worthy to stand in Weldon's shoes, but then later, and at the last minute, it came around to the position taken by the President: 'I feel most decidedly that what the Law School needs more than anything now in the loose state into which it has been allowed to fall, is a man whose whole time and attention is given to it and to its problems and to putting a life and energy and snap and go into it which it does not now possess.' Of the Law School's loose state and problems at the end of the Weldon period, more in a moment.

And how did the Board come to appoint as Dean of Dalhousie Law School a man who 'was at the tail end of Mr. Bicknell's firm'? Because he was all they could get for the price they were prepared to pay, i.e., $3000 a year – which is all that Weldon was getting after thirty-one years of service. What the President had to say in this regard is worth quoting in full for the light it throws on the difficulty of getting good men for the job of full-time law teacher, particularly in 1914 when there was as yet no such thing as a law teaching profession in Canada:

there is no doubt in my mind that if he were a man very high up in Mr. Bicknell's firm, or even a very much smaller firm, he would not leave any such position for a place that could only offer him $3,000 a year. That is the point that we have to take into consideration all the time in trying to find professional men to take poorly paid academic teaching positions: namely that if they have already got well set in lucrative practice they certainly [would] not be drawn away by anything we have to offer them. We can only expect to get a man who has a taste for teaching, and that MacRae has.[4]

In the two or three years prior to MacRae's arrival the School was at one of those low points that every academic institution goes through from time to time. Weldon was obviously failing: he had 'lost some of the influence he should have had with [the students],' and Russell, not Weldon, seems to have been more or less in charge of the School. At least two of the downtown lecturers were 'far from satisfactory' and one or two or others were missing more than the customarily acceptable number of lectures. To the outsider the School probably seemed to be just as good as it always was. Two Supreme Court judges, in addition to Benny Russell, had recently joined the part-time staff to give newly instituted courses in subjects that had lately acquired great practical importance, Corporations and Insurance. Enrolment, 62 in 1913-14 and 68 at the beginning of 1914-15, the first of the war years, was the largest it had ever been. And the *Gazette* items of the time give an impression of more than usually light-hearted normalcy (e.g., 'the great, white-haired Dean Weldon, loved and respected by all who know him'), though some of their jocose references to the downtowners do have a biting edge.[5] The insiders, President MacKenzie and the Council of the Barristers' Society, were of a very different opinion, and, acting together, had removed, even before MacRae's arrival, three serious deficiencies in the School's course of study.

The first and most long standing of these deficiencies – a glaring example of sheer academic inertia – was the School's teaching period. It was, to begin with, too short, much shorter than Osgoode's – only twenty-one teaching weeks – and it ran for a period which meant that the law student in his graduating year had to hang around for two months after he was through, and knew he was through, before he could receive at Convocation the degree he needed for his admission to the Bar. As the reader may remember, this odd arrangement was originally, and perhaps pardonably, instituted to accommodate Weldon's, and later Russell's, Parliamentary ambitions. But by

1904 those two Parliamentary careers were over and yet in 1911, despite frequent student objections, the arrangement was still in effect. In the very first session after the new broom, A. Stanley MacKenzie, moved into the President's office this anomaly was swept away. From then on the Law School year was timed to end at the same time as the University year and, what is even more important, three teaching weeks, and in 1914 three more teaching weeks, were added to it – making the twenty-seven or so that has been, with upward variations, standard ever since.

The second deficiency – of equally long standing and even more frequently criticized by the students in the *Gazette* of the nineties – was the low standard set for admission to the School. The minimum prerequisite should, those students thought, be like the Harvard Law School's since the early nineties – an Arts degree or, if that were asking too much, at least enough exposure to a university atmosphere to ensure that the would-be lawyer could read and write, using those words in the university sense. But it was not until shortly before Weldon's retirement that anything was done to remedy this deficiency and when it was done the initiative did not come, as one would have expected, from the Law School but from the Council of the Barristers' Society. In 1912 the Council raised to a Grade XII certificate from High School (or maybe even to one year of college) the standard of admission for those who were proceeding to the Bar via the old apprenticeship system (which was then still in existence, and still exists, at least nominally, today); it was the first of the common-law law societies in Canada to take this significant step. In the spring of 1914 the Council made it quite clear to the Law School that it would have to fall in line if the Council was to continue to recognize the results of its examinations. At the last faculty meeting attended by Weldon the Law School not only fell into line but went a little better: it resolved that 'the requirements for entrance upon study for the degree from the Law School should after the session of 1914-15 be that the student shall have *spent one year in an Arts College* and taken at least five classes and passed in them, four of which shall be Latin, English, Mathematics, and French or German' – should have had, in other words, at least an exposure at the university level to the basic elements of a literary education.[6]

The third, and by far the most serious, deficiency in the School's course of study at the end of the Weldon period was – or so the Council of the Barristers' Society seems to have thought – the inadequacy of the legal instruction given by it. We do not, alas, know any of the details; all we can do is read between the lines of what hard evidence we have. In 1908 the Society withdrew, for some reason or other, the subject of Procedure from its blanket acceptance of the School's degree as satisfying all academic requirements for admission to the Bar, and in 1912 may even – to judge from a mysterious entry in the calendars for 1912-13 and 1913-14 – have considered withdrawing other subjects as well. In any event a delegation from the University met with the Council several times in the spring of 1914 to 'discuss ... the subject of Students' Examinations,' and at one stage in the discussions it was tentatively suggested that 'the Council should have a voice in the curriculum of the School.' What was it that was bothering the Council? Was the then curriculum in their view an inadequate preparation for the practice of law; or were the existing subjects, or some of them, in their view being inadequately taught; or were the examinations in their view being made too easy? We do not know. In any event there emerged from the discussions the 'conjoint examination' system – an admirable *modus vivendi* between a university law school's right to say what shall be taught and how it shall be taught and a law society's right, and duty, to see that inadequately trained lawyers are not let loose on the public.[7]

In the calendar for 1914-15, therefore, there appeared for the first time an announcement which, with minor variations and in recent years in less formal language, has appeared in all the calendars ever since:

An arrangement has been made between the University and the Nova Scotia Barristers' Society whereby the University appoints two co-examiners for each subject of examination, one of whom is nominated by the Barristers' Society. The Barristers' Society in return will exempt from its Intermediate and Final Examinations the holder of the degree of Bachelor of Laws from Dalhousie University but expressly stipulates that the examinations passed by the student must have included one on Procedure and Practice.

The following two comments by a knowledgeable outsider in 1924 – by which time the School had acquired three full-time teachers – on the way the system operates in practice have remained so lastingly true that they must be quoted in full:

in Nova Scotia the system of 'conjoint examinations' is somewhat of a misnomer in so far as it suggests that the Barristers' Society exercises any great degree of control over the Law Faculty of Dalhousie University. It serves however a valuable purpose. Better than any device known to the writer, it stimulates a fruitful interchange between practitioners who are too busy to teach and teachers who are withdrawn from practice.[8]

It was, then, into an atmosphere already charged with reform that MacRae, 'the man at the tail end of Mr. Bicknell's firm,' came a few weeks after the beginning of the First World War. By the end of his first year at the School the curriculum had undergone its first general revision since 1886 and, purged of at least two of its 'sleepers' and now including in its ranks no less than four Supreme Court judges and several other Supreme Court judges to be, the part-time faculty was stronger than it had ever been since that opening year of 1883. And all this at a time when the students were melting away to the war: by 1915 there were only thirty-nine of them and by 1918 only twenty. The few that remained were on the receiving end of the new and rigorous academic standards imposed by the revised curriculum ('The thing that stands out most vividly in my mind was working in the library at night reading cases. We worked like blazes'[9]), carried out though they were under conditions that were, understandably, less formal than in normal times ('on occasions we would go to their [the voluntary lecturers] homes in the evenings. This created no difficulty, as classes were small in number'[10]). What undoubtedly contributed to the students' acceptance of their increased workload was MacRae's out-going and vigorous personality and his own devotion to hard work.

At the very first annual dinner of the Students' Law Society after he became Dean he was, the *Gazette* tells us, 'greeted with prolonged cheering which in some measure indicated his great popularity among the students.'[11] This erstwhile Greek scholar turned out to be a great mixer at all levels. For example: he corresponded regularly with R.B. Bennett, giving him news of the School; he wrote to judges of the Supreme Court of Canada about their opinions; when he made, as a part of 'the Million Dollar Campaign,' a two-months trip to the West in 1920 to visit the Law School graduates there he also took in the Rotary Convention at Atlantic City; a year later he was a delegate to the Rotary Convention in Edinburgh and when he came back he gave a talk to the Commercial Club in Halifax about his impressions of 'the Old Country'; he was, as a key member of its Legal Education Committee, a familiar figure at the annual meetings of the infant Canadian Bar Association from 1918 on; and, coming closer to home, it was probably he who inspired the two first, but abortive, attempts to create a Law Alumni Association.[12] He was also a great worker. Although in his first year he only took on three classes, Weldon's subjects of Constitutional Law, Constitutional History, and Conflict of Laws, in 1915 he took over and expanded Mr Justice Drysdale's course in Corporations, started a wholly new course of his own on History of English Law (for ever after a great favourite of his), acted as 'preceptor' in one of the three tutorial groups which in that year were added to Benny Russell's first-year Contracts class, and wrote an article for the *Canadian Law Times*.[13]

The coming into force of the revised curriculum – the curriculum which, as it turned out, would govern the School and, indeed, all the common-law schools in Canada for nearly fifty years – was not the only event to take place in these war years when Dalhousie's Little Law School was the littlest it had ever been. The following events call for no more than a mere mention. The Mock Parliament was suspended, but only temporarily; when the war was over it was revived with even more than its customary mock pomp and true political vigour. The Students' Law Society took into their own hands – in this case for keeps – the Moot Court which had ever since the opening of the School been run by the Faculty. In 1918 there was established, at last, a University Medal in Law with terms of award that are the same today as they were then: it 'may be awarded on graduation to the student standing highest among those taking the full regular third-year curriculum, provided he reaches a very high standard of excellence, and obtains First Class distinction in at least all but three of the subjects of examination.' And two years after the end of the war the Carswell Company, the law publishers of Toronto, gave, and have given ever since, a prize in books available in each of the three years and awarded to the student who leads the class in his year. The Carswell Prizes are a 'first' and a very important 'first.' In the very early days of the School there were one or two prizes but they soon disappeared, so that the Carswell Prizes have the distinction of being the oldest in the long list of prizes to be found in the calendar today. But there are two events which positively demand a paragraph each to themselves: the departure in the fall of 1915 of the main body of students, the Arts and Science students, from the Forrest Building to the new campus at Studley; and the arrival, also in 1915, of the first woman student ever to enter the Law School.

The moving out of the Arts and Science students and the moving in in their place of the 'Medicals,' the traditional enemies of 'Law,' seems to have made the tightly knit little group of law students in the north wing more conscious than ever of their separate identity. There was a move to dissociate themselves from the Students Council – and its fees – and manage their own affairs; after two acrimonious debates, reported at length in the *Gazette*, the move came to nothing. Then there appeared, but for one issue only, what may have been an embryo *Gazette* for law students only, or maybe a kind of student law review, called *Dalhousie Law Monthly*; nothing survives of it except the titles, and very odd titles too, of three articles in it – for example, 'Why I am a De Cujus.'[14] And then, inspired perhaps by the same feeling of separateness, there came into being in downtown Halifax first the Weldon Law Club and then a few years later, in 1922, the Dalhousie Law Association – both seemingly first attempts, but abortive attempts, by old students of the School to create a Law Alumni Association separate and distinct from the Dalhousie Alumni Association.

All we know about the Weldon Law Club is derived from two brief handwritten entries in its Minute Book, which is still preserved at the Law School; it had two lunch meetings in the late winter of 1916. The Dalhousie Law Association had a slightly longer and certainly more effective life. Formed to 'promote the interests of the Law School in various ways' and 'to keep in touch with all the graduates by the issue of quarterly "Bulletins" containing matters of interest to those who have passed through the Law School,' it held several lunch meetings, issued four *Bulletins* (which still exist), and had achieved a membership of forty and a bank balance of $300 before it became inactive. Ten years later it came, in a sense, briefly to life when Judge R.H. Murray ('96), its founder and president, acted by virtue of his office as chairman of the dinner held to celebrate the School's fiftieth anniversary, and its bank balance was, or so the story goes, spent on giving the members of the third-year class free tickets to the dinner. Not until the establishment in 1976 at the Law School of the Office of Alumni Affairs with its news bulletin, *Hearsay*, would there be anything even remotely resembling the Dalhousie Law Association.

In 1915 and 1916 'the first women ever' came to the Law School: Frances Fish, Emelyn MacKenzie, and Caroline McInnes. It had been settled as early as 1881 that 'ladies can be admitted to Dalhousie'[15]; what had not been settled was whether they could be admitted to the Bar. After Emelyn MacKenzie, the first of the three to apply to have her articles registered, had appeared before one of its committees, the Nova Scotia legislature settled that issue too in favour of women. Miss MacKenzie came from a small farm in Victoria County, Cape Breton; she put herself through Law School by doing part-time teaching at the Halifax Ladies College; when she was through, 'there were not enough places for the law students in the Halifax law firms and so most of them had to travel. I went to New York'; and for the next forty years she engaged in legal work there.[16] Frances Fish was the first of the three to enter the School. She came in the fall of 1915 – the other two did not come until a year later – and so became in 1918 the first woman graduate of Dalhousie Law School and the first woman to be admitted to the Bar of Nova Scotia: 'She won,' she has said, 'the trust of her [male] classmates by not tattling about such things as the poker games that went on in the Dalhousie library.' Miss Fish came of a political family in Newcastle, New Brunswick, and 'from the time I was very young I always wanted to be a lawyer.' It was not however until several years after she had graduated and had been admitted to the Nova Scotia Bar that she was able to realize her ambition to practise law in either Montreal or Newcastle; neither in Quebec nor in New Brunswick were women then 'persons' so as to be admissible to the Bar. After that obstacle had been removed in New Brunswick she went for the rest of her working life into practice there on her own, specializing in criminal law – 'I've dealt with a lot of tough characters ... but I'm not afraid of them' – and in the thirties stood, unsuccessfully, as a candidate in both a federal and a provincial election.[17] Caroline McInnes was the daughter of Hector McInnes ('88) of Halifax, a part-time lecturer at the School in Procedure since 1894; when she was through she went into her father's distinguished firm and in the twenty years she spent there became known as a first-rate general practitioner.

That paragraph about the first women has run away with itself. As originally conceived, it would have recorded the following facts about Dalhousie Law School: it was in 1915 that the first woman came; from then on there would usually be one or two, and sometimes more, of them there; but not until the early seventies would there be a 'woman explosion' so great that it is now normal for one in every four of the students to be a woman. The paragraph turned into capsule career histories of Misses MacKenzie, Fish, and McInnes. That does not matter: these three lives are in their diversity of background and of later life work typical of all the students of sixty years ago, male as well as female, and they stand as a reminder to the 'women's libbers' of today that even sixty years ago women of no more than normal character and determination could lead legal lives as normal as any man's.

We have deferred until now any extended reference to what we have several times called the most important and most far-reaching event in the whole MacRae period, the framing and coming into force of the revised curriculum – our reason being that the transformation of what was in origin a purely Dalhousie project into the standard curriculum suggested by the Canadian Bar Association for all common-law provinces in Canada transcends the year-by-year framework that we have adopted for telling the story of this eventful period. It was in the fall of 1915, just one year after MacRae arrived and at a time when the School would, it was clear, have only a handful of students until the war was won, that the new curriculum went into force. It was in 1920 that MacRae presented the Report of the Sub-Committee on Standard Curriculum to the meeting of the Canadian Bar Association which adopted that Report and its recommendations, with consequences for the future of legal education in all common-law Canada that we have already sufficiently indicated.

One of the main reasons why the Canadian Bar Association, which had ever since it was founded in 1914 shown great interest in legal education, was minded to promulgate a standard curriculum was 'that a curriculum of respectable standard uniformly adopted in all the Provinces would tend to establish on a creditable level the standards of the Canadian Bar as a whole.'[18] In January 1920 MacRae went, at the invitation of Dean R.W. Lee of the McGill Law School, the then chairman of the Committee on Legal Education, to a meeting of the sub-committee which had been instructed to prepare and present to the Association a standard curriculum for the common-law provinces. The four men who were at the meeting had before them comparative tables, province by province, of various matters connected with legal education, including curriculum, that Lee had prepared a year or so earlier; among the curriculums in those tables was Dalhousie Law School's curriculum of 1918-19.[19] Only a week or so after the meeting MacRae wrote to R.B. Bennett as follows:[20]

One thing I think the meeting showed was the striking superiority of our own curriculum over anything else in Canada. In the number of subjects taught, in the order in which they are taught, and in the extent of the instruction given in each subject, our own curriculum stood out above them all ... the report of the Sub-Committee as at present drafted recommends a curriculum which is practically a duplicate of the Dalhousie Curriculum.

It was Lee who wrote the Report, adding his own notes to it, but it was Macrae who in the temporary absence of Lee from Canada presented, and successfully defended, it in a long debate at the plenary session of the Association which adopted, with a few minor amendments, the standard curriculum recommended in it.[21]

That is how Dalhousie Law School's revised curriculum of 1915 came to be the model for the curriculums of all the common-law schools in Canada and the standard curriculum itself to become familiarly known as 'the MacRae curriculum of the twenties.' Reporting as by then the chairman of the Legal Education Committee, MacRae uttered three years later these prophetic words: 'unless the whole curriculum is reconstructed on some radically different theory, no very extensive changes will be demanded for some time.'[22] The standard curriculum continued, with minor changes – such as the addition, to accommodate the profession, of Administrative Law, Taxation, and Labour Law in the thirties and forties – to dominate all the common-law schools, including Dalhousie, until the late sixties. So it will not be until he reaches the final pages of this history – 'In the Weldon Building' – that the reader will again be subjected to anything more than incidental reference to the content of the curriculum: methods of teaching yes, but content of the curriculum no.

The revised Dalhousie curriculum of 1915 would have gladdened the hearts of those students who in the early nineties complained that there were not enough practical courses. For it was designed to be as far as possible a 'cover everything' and 'professionally-oriented' one, a product no doubt of the pressure currently being exerted by the Nova Scotia Barristers' Society. Its framers, about whose intentions we know nothing more specific than that 'our effort has been to include as many subjects as seem from consideration of their intrinsic importance ... to deserve a place in our curriculum,'[23] almost certainly thought of themselves as doing nothing more dramatic than filling what to them were obvious gaps, but the end result was something strikingly different from what the School had started with. Gone was the balance then established between the cultural and the professional subjects and between public law and private law; the slant of the revised curriculum was clearly in favour of the general practitioner of private law. What, fortunately, had not gone was the tradition, emphasized in their 'on parade pieces' by all later deans who had to administer this curriculum, that 'the founders of the School ... realised that a law school as part of a university should be more than a technical training school for artisans'; as Dean Vincent MacDonald said in 1938, the School's aim continued to be 'to give an adequate training in theory and technical learning for successful practice but also to give to its students the vision of law as a great instrument for social ends and to stress the duty of studying law in all its human implications.'[24]

A few details must be added as a kind of illuminatory footnote to the very general description of the revised curriculum that has just been given. The time devoted to the existing professional subjects was much increased; in the first year, for example, Real Property was given two hours a week instead of one and a few years later was enlarged into what it still is in 1976, an introductory course called Property I covering the elements of both real and personal property and given three hours a week. What had in earlier years been just parts of professional subjects now became subjects on their own. Procedure, for example, ceased to be part of Procedure and Statutes and very shortly became a course in its own right taking up two hours a week in each of the second and third years; the same kind of thing happened with Agency and Master and Servant, which budded off from Contracts and Torts, and with Mortgages and Trusts, which were both split off from Equity. In an effort to meet the changes that were taking place in the world of the practitioner wholly new professional courses, such as Dominion Statutes and Provincial Statutes, were added. As to Weldon's old liberal or public-law courses, they were not only overshadowed by what had become a striking preponderance of professional ones; one of them, Constitutional History, had by the end of MacRae's time at the School actually disappeared forever from the curriculum; and another of them, International Law, was more or less in abeyance from 1915 until revived under Sidney Smith at the end of the twenties. But, and once again let it be said, this overloaded and over-professional curriculum did not, as it might have done, numb the teaching of law at Dalhousie. The spirit in which the full-time teachers – to whose arrival we now come – taught it made sure that that did not happen. A good example of that spirit is the injunction that Dean Sidney Smith gave the writer when he came to the School in 1933 to take up his first law-teaching job: 'Sink a shaft and sink it deep; don't bother overmuch about coverage.'

In 1920 occurred something for which the students of the Weldon period had asked again and again, the appointment of another full-time teacher in addition to the Dean; in 1921 yet another one was appointed, making a full-time faculty of three. By the end of the decade the normal complement would be established at four – three 'men' and a 'boy', the men having what in these learned days we should call tenure and the boy being expected to stay for three years only and then give place to another boy. And there it would remain, with interruptions brought about by the Second World War, until after the end of that war and of Dalhousie's Little Law School itself in 1945. Dalhousie was, incidentally, the first common-law school in Canada to have a full-time faculty of three (McGill, a civil-law school, also reached that level in 1921). That was quite an achievement in a country where, as one observer caustically put it in that same year, 'the prevailing idea has been that the business of teaching law is one which can be sufficiently well done by a busy practitioner and judge in his spare time ...' and university governors 'observe with satisfaction that the law faculty is the cheapest department of the University, and see no reason why it should not remain so.'[25] One of the students who came to the Law School a few years later gives in a nutshell the reason why the establishment of this core of full-time teachers was so significant an advance: 'one thing we learned very, very quickly was that there is nothing like a professional teacher. And few of the downtown lawyers were professional teachers. No matter how well they knew their stuff, it was quite a different thing from knowing how to teach it.'[26]

The School was fortunate in the two men it secured to start off the new full-time faculty. They were John Read and Sidney Smith, both Nova Scotians and both destined for later public careers of great distinction. Had they been born in a more economically favoured region, say Boston or Toronto, they would probably have gone from the beginning into a more glamorous line of endeavour than teaching for a pittance at Dalhousie Law School. As it was, however, the School got them both, if only for a short time.

John Erskine Read, a graduate in Arts from Dalhousie, spent the year 1909-10 at the Columbia Law School and the next three years at Oxford as Rhodes Scholar for Nova Scotia; at Oxford he obtained a double-first – then a rare achievement for a 'colonial' – in Law. On his return to Nova Scotia he was admitted to the Bar, started into practice with a well-known law firm in Halifax, and had just begun a stint as a downtown lecturer in Real Property when the war broke out. He enlisted immediately, served overseas, was badly wounded, and, when the war was over, rejoined the firm in Halifax; in 1920 he became the first full-time Professor (in addition to the Dean) in the Law School. He would in later years become nationally and internationally known as an expert in the 'great' subjects of Constitutional and International Law, but the subjects he started off with were the detailed and tiresome ones of Property and Procedure. His classes in Procedure did, however, achieve an enduring reputation at the School and were remembered long after he left it. He originated, and carried out as long as he was there, the idea of dividing the class into firms; 'he would have one firm institute an action, another put in the defence, and then the reply, and so on ... he would sit as a chambers judge ... It was a great education just to argue a case before him in chambers and it was great fun.'[27] This imaginative, but time-consuming, 'do it yourself' method of teaching Procedure would not be regularly used again at the School until the seventies.

Sidney Earle Smith, an MA from King's College at Windsor, was, like John Read and so many of those they both taught, a veteran who had seen service overseas. On his return he graduated from the Law School in the class of 1920 with exceptionally high marks and second only to Vincent MacDonald. From there he went to the Harvard Law School for a year's post-graduate work, the first Dalhousie product ever to do so. Because Harvard did not recognize an LLB from Dalhousie as qualifying the holder to enter its only, rather rarefied, graduate course of the day (one leading to a doctorate), he – fortunately for the future of teaching at Dalhousie Law School – took several of the basic undergraduate courses, including Contracts from Williston and Trusts from Scott, both masters without peer of case method.[28] Two of the subjects assigned to him in his first year of teaching at the School were Contracts and Trusts and in them he too used case method. This was the first time that case method had been used at Dalhousie and, unlike John Read's 'first' in Procedure, Sidney Smith's 'first' was destined to last.

Langdell's case method was already more than ten years old at Harvard when Thompson, Sedgewick, and Graham, three of Dalhousie Law School's founding fathers, visited there in the spring of 1883 and by 1920 it had become the normal method of instruction in all the principal American law schools. In Canada it was in the air,[29] but no teacher in any of its law schools had as yet made use of it; the prevailing method of instruction was still, to use the words of a young Turk of the day, 'the out-of-date and unscientific' lecture method.[30] At Dalhousie Benny Russell had, as we have seen, always been more than a mere lecturer; he went further than stating principles and using the facts of decided cases as illustrations; he would often insist that the students discuss with him the cases themselves. But the case method is something more – and more rigorous and more demanding both of teacher and of student – than that. In particular it makes such exacting demands on the teacher that only a full-time one can find the time and the energy necessary to prepare himself to conduct a class with it; that is one of the reasons why its arrival at Dalhousie was delayed until the establishment of at least a corporal's guard of full-time teachers. Its great strength is that the law student is forced to participate actively in the teaching process and, as a by-product, learns how to do what he will be doing for the rest of his working life, think and reason like a lawyer.

What, then, is case method? In 1923 Dean Harlan Stone of the Columbia Law School gave the following authoritative description of it to the Ontario Bar Association. The only thing wrong with his description is that it gives no hint of the perplexity, frustration, and anger that many students experience in their early encounters with it.

The steps in the application of the case method are three. The student, before attending a lecture, is required to read and digest a group of judicial opinions, especially selected for the purpose of developing some phase of legal doctrine. In class students are called upon to 'state' the cases which they have read, that is, to state the essential facts of the case, the actual decision of the court and the reasoning of the court in support of its decision. The students are then expected to participate in an active discussion of the cases previously stated, guided and stimulated by the instructor by the Socratic method of question and answer. In the course of the discussion the legal doctrine of each case is subjected to criticism and comparison, and finally the student is expected after class to systematize his classroom notes, to read cases cited in the lecture room discussion and to organize in systematic fashion the knowledge which he has acquired by the combination of extra-class-room reading and classroom discussion.[31]

Smith had a fairly easy ride, all things considered, when he, only a year out of Law School and junior in age and in military rank to many of his students, subjected them to that 'strange new thing,' case method – a result due in part of his own good sense in using with them the casebooks with which he himself was already familiar, Williston's *Cases on Contracts* and Scott's *Cases on*

Trusts. With his first-year class in Contracts he had no difficulty at all; they were not ex-fellow-students, only half of them were veterans, and, like all first-year students, they had a fresh interest in law. Horace Read was a member of that class and he reports that: 'As the year progressed the students became progressively more convinced that Contracts was the most valuable subject in the curriculum. Despite the heavy work load of case study it became their favourite course.' His third-year class in Trusts was much more of a problem. Most of the students in the class were veterans, many of them senior to him in age and military rank, and after two years in law school they objected to the new and unusual burden of case study. And then there was a silly little *contretemps* at the beginning of the very first hour he met them. He was calling the roll (yes, they took attendance in those days!) and, being shy and merely an ex-gunner himself, he made the mistake of calling one of these students of his who was an ex-colonel 'Colonel' – whereupon the rest of the class set up, after the hour was over, a kind of campus confrontation with him. To add to all this, they were, as sometimes happens even today, reluctant to take part in the classroom discussion which is the very heart of the case method. After several weeks of deliberate student non-participation Smith seriously considered resigning. But all came right in the end. When the students heard what they were doing to Smith – most students are very kind people – they reversed their stand and from then on gave him their full support.[32] So that he got better treatment from those Dalhousie students than Christopher Columbus Langdell did from his Harvard students of fifty years earlier; 'Attendance at Langdell's class dwindled to a faithful handful called "Kit's Freshmen" by their sceptical classmates.'[33]

The third-year class on which Smith sprang case method, the class of 1922, rates a paragraph to itself. It was the first of the post-war classes and therefore the first one of any size under the new regime, that is, since the coming into force of the new expanded curriculum. It was also the largest but one that had ever graduated from the School; there were twenty-six of them. Of these twenty-six eight were from outside Nova Scotia, viz. one from Newfoundland, two from New Brunswick, one from Prince Edward Island, two from Alberta, and two from British Columbia. Nearly all of them had seen some kind of war service and about half of them had held commissions.[34] Notwithstanding their claims on 'patriotism and all that' these veterans did not, as the returned men of the Second World War would, receive any financial aid from the government. Nor were they given any time off their law school course. In 1885 a member of that first class ever to graduate who went off to fight in the Northwest Rebellion just before examinations was given his degree without taking them; and in Ontario every law student who served at the front in the First World War was let off a whole year of law school. But the new regime at Dalhousie Law School took legal education seriously. And so did the veterans there: 'the war vintage,' says John Read who taught them, 'was simply terrific. It set a pace for students that was almost impossible for the non-military ones.'[35]

Before passing to the last of the fundamental and lasting academic reforms over which MacRae presided, a further tightening up of admission requirements, we must briefly record three events that took place in 1921. Mr Justice Russell – Benny Russell to many generations of delighted students – resigned after nearly forty years of continuous teaching and thereby severed the now almost modern School's last remaining link with the almost forgotten School of 1883. He was paid the inadequate tribute of being made (in effect) Professor Emeritus and also Doctor of Laws Honoris Causa, but his real reward came ten years later when he received a rousing reception from his old students at the fiftieth anniversary dinner in 1933; the writer was at that dinner and so can boast that he 'once saw Russell plain,' a living reminder of the School's past. The second event involved two of the School's old students: James Dunn ('98), by this time a financier in England, became a baronet, and Richard Squires ('02), by this time Premier of Newfoundland, became a knight. A few years earlier another old student, Richard McBride ('90), longtime Premier of British Columbia, had, as they used to say in those days, 'received the honour of knighthood from his Sovereign.' These three men were up to that time the only Dalhousians to have been so honoured – all three of them, be it noted, Law School men. Men from Dalhousie's Little Law School in a corner of the Forrest Building in Halifax, Nova Scotia, were making their mark in England, Newfoundland, and British Columbia. The third event involved the Law School itself and was a great disappointment. In April 1921 the cornerstone was laid on the Studley Campus for a building intended to house the Faculty of Law; first 'two commodious rooms' in the High School, then the makeshift, made-over Halliburton House, then a corner in the Forrest Building, and now, at last, a building of its own! But the first post-war depression intervened. By the time the handsome new building was finished, there was no money left for the projected and absolutely necessary Arts Building. So the Law Building was loaned temporarily to the Faculty of

Arts, which would, as things turned out, occupy it temporarily for thirty years. The School stayed in the Forrest Building until 1952.

In 1921 the Faculty decided to tighten still further the standards for admission to the School, a decision that had two prongs, both to become effective at the beginning of the 1924-25 session; the decision was announced in the 1922-23 calendar. The first prong raised to the equivalent of two years in Arts the minimum preliminary education requirement that had, the reader may recall, been raised to one year in Arts just before MacRae arrived at the School in 1914. The second prong abolished the affiliated student system under which a student with an Arts degree from one of the Maritime colleges (including, of course, Dalhousie itself) could cut a year off the three years he would normally have to spend at the Law School by taking certain law subjects as part of his Arts course. The two-years-of-Arts admission requirement would remain unchanged until 1957. And with the abolition of the affiliated student system the School became for the first time, and has ever since remained, a simon-pure three-year law school.

The raising of the admission requirement from one year of Arts to two was the work of MacRae. He was a great proselytizer for the idea that all law students should come to law school with a good general education: 'The question of a proper standard of preliminary education for law students is fundamental to all other questions of legal education. The foundation must be well and truly laid before the superstructure can be well builded.' He was, indeed, as chairman of the Legal Education Committee of the Canadian Bar Association at the time, the man mainly responsible for the Association's recommendation, made in 1922, that that be in future the standard in all the common-law provinces[36] – a recommendation that was put into effect at Dalhousie Law School in 1924 but ignored at Ontario's Osgoode for many years.

Two comments must, however, be made before we leave this important but not very interesting topic. The first is that this raising of the minimum requirement does not tell us anything about what we really want to know: what was the educational level of the general run of students who came to the School in the years that followed? Our impression, and it is not much more than an impression, is that about half of them came in with more than the minimum: they came in with Arts degrees. Which means that the general educational level of the student body was then much lower than it is in 1976; ninety per cent of them now come in with college degrees. The second comment is that at Dalhousie the required two years of college work was no mere rag-bag of 'free choice' courses. It had to be done in certain prescribed subjects, subjects that were regarded as providing either the basic general knowledge or the mental discipline that every would-be lawyer should have. One of these prescribed subjects, by the way, was Latin. In later years the increasingly irrelevant subject of Latin became such a stumbling block for many of the students, even good students, that during Dean Vincent MacDonald's regime strenuous efforts were made by the youngish full-time teachers to get rid of it, which efforts were successfully opposed by the older and more conservative downtowners. Latin did not cease to be required until 1949.[37]

The affiliated student system had become a problem long before MacRae arrived. When it was started, within two or three years after the beginning of the School in 1883, the idea behind it was: in part to lure good students to the School, students with Arts degrees, by holding in front of them the bait of getting through the law course in two years instead of three; and in part to draw the other Maritime colleges into the orbit of the would-be-one-and-only university in the Maritimes, Dalhousie, by rendering them affiliates of Dalhousie for the purpose of instruction in law. Without going into the details of the arrangement, which varied from college to college and from time to time, a student at, say, Acadia would take as part of his Arts degree program at Acadia four of the subjects required for the LLB degree at Dalhousie – say, Constitutional History, International Law, Contracts, and Torts. Armed with this Acadia Arts degree he would go straight into the Second Year at the Law School and would take the first-year subjects he had not already taken, i.e., Crimes, Property, and History of English Law in addition to his ordinary second- and third-year work, thereby graduating in two years instead of three. Even in the old days of the limited curriculum and of limited educational objectives the arrangement was not really defensible. What kind of a training in the fundamental subjects of Contracts and Torts would our Acadia student get from a practitioner in rural Wolfville and without a law library? From that aspect alone the arrangement was, as Benny Russell remarked in 1913, 'a farce.'[38] The reader will be spared the dramatic illustrations that might be given to show why the Faculty decided, at last, to abolish this long-standing short-cut. MacRae himself has, in his usual measured tones, said why:

The plan may have worked well enough with the limited law curriculum of the old days, but it does not work well today. It is utterly too heavy a task for any student to attempt to finish all but four of the subjects of the present curriculum in two years. Moreover the instruction which affiliated students get in law at other colleges such as Acadia, St. F.X., U.N.B. *et al.* is I fear under par. Then, again, as law is training rather information ... time is of the essence in training. The process of acquiring information may be accelerated by the wet towel route etc. but ... it is otherwise with the processes of reasoning. It is therefore of considerable importance that the student should have at least three years to devote wholly to the study of legal subjects.[39]

With its much expanded curriculum, its full-time staff of three, its two-years-of-Arts admission requirement, and a course that was for all students without exception a three-year one, the School had substantially raised its standards from where they were when, only two years before, the Harvard Law School had refused to recognize Sidney Smith's Dalhousie LLB as qualifying him to become a candidate for the doctorate there. Harvard had meanwhile started a new graduate course, one leading to a Master of Laws degree. As a tribute to the memory of Horace Read, a life-long devotee of Harvard, we here quote from his first draft of this history: 'June 30, 1922 became a day of historic importance for Dalhousie when the Secretary of the Harvard Faculty replied [in answer to an inquiry made by Dean MacRae]: "We shall be prepared to admit as candidates for our graduate degree any graduates of your School who have completed satisfactorily your three year course ... It would also be necessary of course for the applicants to ... have completed the three years of law work with high rank." ' In the fall of the very next year the first in a long line of Dalhousie Law School men to do so thereafter went on to get their LLM at Harvard. By no means all of that long line were after what would for many years be 'the union card' for entry into the law teaching profession in Canada, but, as it so happened, the first three of them to secure it all went into academic life. They were: J. Forrester Davison ('23), who collaborated with Felix Frankfurter in producing one of the earliest case books in the then infant subject of Administrative Law and became a professor at the George Washington Law School in Washington, DC; 'Larry' (N.A.M.) MacKenzie ('23), who began his working life by teaching the then very 'in' subject of International Law at the University of Toronto and ended up as a university president, first at the University of New Brunswick and later at the University of British Columbia; and Horace E. Read ('24) himself, who, after a few years as 'just a law teacher' at Dalhousie Law School, became a pioneer teacher and scholar in the then just-born subject of Legislation – all three, be it noted, 'public law men' in the tradition of Weldon from whose School they had come.

In 1923 there was yet another 'first,' this time a first for the Faculty and a highly visible one too – the first in what would thereafter be a long stream, and for the next fifteen years or so quite a full and continuous stream, of articles in legal periodicals emanating from the School. With the honourable exception of that redoubtable scholar John D. Falconbridge, by now dean of Osgoode Hall Law School, no Canadian common-law academic had up to this time made any contribution to legal scholarship; even the scholarly Weldon had never published anything. Now, with a full-time faculty of three, the School was about to break that unhappy aspect of the Weldon tradition. This was the year in which the *Canadian Bar Review* began publication; its first editor was Charles Morse ('85). In the very first volume there were two articles by MacRae, one on a strictly legal topic and the other his valuable 'Legal Education in Canada,' which was the report presented by him as chairman of the Committee of the Canadian Bar Association on Legal Education at the Association's annual meeting in 1923; there was an article by Vincent MacDonald, the Gold Medallist in 1920 and now part-time lecturer on Agency, which would prove to be only the first of many later contributions by him; and there were 'Notes on Offer and Acceptance' by Benny Russell, now retired from his long-time teaching of Contracts, which put in print for a wider audience the characteristically light-hearted swings at two received doctrines with which he had been delighting his students for many years: making four contributions in all from the faculty of Dalhousie Law School. In the next three volumes there were articles by other members of the full-time faculty, articles by Horace Read, Sidney Smith, and John Read. Overloaded though they were with teaching – in 1924-25 one of them was teaching twelve and a half hours a week, the other ten, and the Dean eight in addition to his administrative duties – the full-time men were beginning to write. When the writer came to the School as a young teacher in 1933 he found that he and his colleagues were *expected* to write.

In 1924 MacRae resigned and went to Osgoode Hall Law School at the invitation of John D. Falconbridge, who had recently been appointed dean and was hoping to wake it up after its long sleep of thirty years under 'Daddy' Hoyles. Why did MacRae give up being Dean at Dalhousie Law School, 'which in these years had an enviable reputation' to become just 'one of the boys' at a school which, as one of its part-time lecturers said at about this time, 'people are not proud of attending or graduating from'?[40] Probably because he was discouraged by his inability to obtain from the University the money that he felt was needed to run the School properly: money to keep John Read and Sidney Smith from looking around for something better elsewhere; money to add to and otherwise improve the barely adequate library; money to enable him, chairman as he was of the Canadian Bar Association's Legal Education Committee, to go to an annual meeting of the Association in Vancouver; and also, perhaps, money to increase his own salary. Because we have in this section concentrated on the enduring academic reforms carried out while he was Dean – which were all successes – we have forgotten to mention the equally enduring problems which he, like Weldon and his own successors, had to face: a changing and sometimes not very satisfactory corps of downtown lecturers; a mass of administrative chores to be done (in those days the Dean did everything, with only a share in a stenographer and a share in the one telephone in the Forrest Building); and that perpetual struggle for money. In any event to Osgoode he went, at a starting salary of $5 500 a year, a substantial increase from the $4 500 he was getting at Dalhousie, and had only been getting since 1922.

In the twenty years he spent at Osgoode, MacRae was a kindred spirit to Falconbridge in their moves, not very successful ones, to reform legal education there. And he is remembered 'by former students as being a remarkable man, a lecturer of fluency, force and unusual vividness'[41] and by the profession as being the author of what was for Canada and especially for Ontario a trail-breaking text on the law of Evidence.[42] But his best work was done while he was at Dalhousie. Not only did he put into the School the 'life and energy and snap and go' for which the President had hoped in 1914; with nameless others to help him, he set it on the course that it would follow for many years to come. Rather than summarize all over again the advances that were made during the ten years that he was there, we will here set down what his old student, one-time colleague, and life-long friend, the effervescent President Sidney Smith, felt about him: 'I regard him as the most worthy of the "worthies"'; and 'I have spoken to Larry MacKenzie and some others and they do feel that a portrait of the Dean [MacRae] should be placed opposite Weldon's in the "Promised Land" [the Law School, by then in the Law Building at Studley].'[43]

Now that Dalhousie's Little Law School has in a sense been re-born and is about to go into what the writer thinks is its golden age, this is an appropriate moment to look back and compare the School's position in 1883 with its position in 1924. In relation to the university of which it was a part, it was no longer as important as it had once been. Once a struggling competitor for students with several denominational colleges, Dalhousie University has become, says a Carnegie Report of 1922, 'the largest, best equipped and most important institution for higher education in the Maritime Provinces.'[44] The School's claim on the university dollar – the university now has *some* dollars – has been correspondingly lessened and for the next thirty or forty years it will, in common with the other university law schools in Canada, be re-echoing the complaint made by Professor H.A. Smith at a meeting of the Canadian Bar Association in 1923: 'All that we want for our teaching is men – and very few men compared with what [medicine and science] need – books and a building to enable us to sit down in, yet we do not get it.'[45]

In relation to the world of Canadian common-law law schools, Dalhousie Law School was no longer the only school in the country. In Ontario there had been since 1889 the Law Society of Upper Canada's part-time Osgoode Hall Law School, always by far the largest of all the schools (in 1925 it had three hundred and fifty students, Dalhousie had fifty) and always firmly dedicated to the proposition that the two hours or so of every day which the student spent there is far less important in his legal education than the rest of the day which he spends in the office where he is serving his apprenticeship. In the three Prairie provinces of Manitoba, Saskatchewan, and Alberta there had grown up within the last ten years three little law schools, each of about the same size as Dalhousie; after a period of hesitation between the Osgoode model of a part-time school run by the profession and the Dalhousie model of a full-time university school, Saskatchewan and Alberta emerged as university law schools and Manitoba as an uneasy compromise between the two models. Of all these schools Dalhousie regards itself, and quite rightly, as the best.[46]

It is, however, only the best of a rather poor lot. A forthright observer with an English background may have gone a bit too far when he said in 1923: 'Legal education in Canada is in a very backward state as compared with almost every other important country.'[47] But an immensely tactful American observer was not much more complimentary when he set down 'with some hesitation certain general impressions for what they may be worth': 'The English-speaking schools, pretty generally, seemed to him to possess the invaluable enthusiasm, combined with the awkward self-consciousness, of youth. ... He was impressed more by their vitality and promise of future development than by their current achievement.'[48] And with respect to Dalhousie Law School itself, MacRae himself concluded a summary of some of the recent advances there – a full-time staff of three, a curriculum which has 'received ... the compliment of being followed almost literally by the curriculum recommended by the Canadian Bar Association,' and a number of hours of class work 'considerably greater than any other Canadian Law School – by pointing out that 'as compared with the Law Schools of the United States, it cannot count itself as having made anything more than a good beginning.'[49]

SECTION THREE: 1920-1933

The Golden Age

No, it is not by reason of a mere mistake in arithmetic that the next period in the life of Dalhousie's Little Law School, 'the Golden Age,' overlaps by four years the previous one, 'MacRae.' For many of the significant events of the years 1920-33 involve MacRae. It was he who taught the veterans, with whose arrival at the School the Golden Age begins, and it was he who inspired the two deans who succeeded him, John Read and Sidney Smith, to try and turn the School into 'a centre of legal thought which is given expression by writing.'

But why call this period the Golden Age? Because, when seen in retrospect, there were in the years 1920 to 1933 more 'names' working in the School than at any other time in its history. Among its students, to mention just three of them, there were a future president of the University of British Columbia (N.A.M. MacKenzie ('23)), a future justice of the Court of Appeal, and later Lieutenant Governor, in Ontario (J. Keiller MacKay ('22)), and a future head of the Newfoundland Commission which negotiated the terms of that ancient colony's entry into Confederation and later Chief Justice there (A.J. Walsh ('28)). And all the members of its staff of full-time teachers were – with the exception of MacRae himself and of two who were just passing through – drawn from a pool consisting of a future judge of the International Court of Justice (John Read), a future president of the University of Toronto (Sidney Smith), a future successor to Joe Howe in the hearts and minds of all Nova Scotians (Angus L. Macdonald), a future judge of the Supreme Court of Nova Scotia (Vincent C. MacDonald), and Horace Read who would become a scholar of international repute and then Dean of the Law School in the period 1950-64 when it was in the process of changing from Dalhousie's Little Law School into the School as we know it today.

This golden age begins with the return from the First World War of the remarkable post-war classes of veterans; as one of them has truly said: 'The Dalhousie Law School has long been famous for the men it has drawn to it as teachers and students. We all like to claim that 'our time' was the best or the most important, but I do think that the period immediately following World War I was one of the high points in the history of that famous institution.'[1] It ends with the dinner held on 30 October 1933 to celebrate the fiftieth anniversary of the opening of the School, a dinner graced by the presence of two old students who were provincial premiers, Premier L.P.D. Tilley of New Brunswick ('93) and Premier Angus L. Macdonald of Nova Scotia ('21), and by the reading of a nostalgic letter from another old student who was Prime Minister of Canada, R.B. Bennett ('93) – a fitting climax to a period filled with teachers and students who would in later years become almost as distinguished as those among their predecessors whose names and achievements were so often called to mind in that anniversary year.

It was that anniversary year which evoked from John Read his perceptive little piece in the *Canadian Bar Review*, 'Fifty Years of Legal Education at Dalhousie'; it has been reproduced in Appendix III to this book and everyone should read it. In that article John Read publicly recognizes the special debt which the School owed to MacRae for the most important of its academic advances during the period: 'largely as a result of the influence of Dean MacRae, a strong impetus has been given to legal scholarship. This is evidenced in the admirable case books that have been published in recent years and in scholarly articles and notes, originating in the School, which have appeared in this and other legal publications.'[2] A few years earlier Sidney Smith had on two separate occasions privately voiced the same thought. Shortly before he was appointed Dean in 1929 he wrote to Horace Read as follows: 'It is not good enough in this country to lay the foundations of the School in such a fashion that only a house fit to serve the N.S. lawyer needs in the years to come [sic]. I do feel keenly about this – for as I have often said I love the place – and I have yet glimpses of the vision which MacRae, Read [i.e., John Read] and I had in 1920.'[3] And he put that vision in more specific terms when, a few weeks later, he told President MacKenzie of the conditions under which he was willing to become Dean: 'While I believe that the primary function of a law school is to teach ... a law school is also judged by its discharge of another function. That is, it must be a centre of legal thought which is given expression by writing ... Dalhousie Law School, to hold its place, must discharge to a greater degree this second function.'[4]

To the mind of some of the insiders of the time, however, the School seemed very far from being in its golden age and to be declining rather than advancing academically. In the minutes of the 1929 meeting of the Board at which Smith was appointed Dean appears the following: 'The fact that the · personnel of the School is changing so rapidly, and on account of the decline in attendance during the last few years, the impression is abroad among our friends that the School is not retaining its prestige among the law schools of Canada.' Changing personnel? At a time when MacRae and John Read had been pressing the Board to enlarge the full-time staff to four, the School could not even keep the three it had. In the spring of 1924 there were MacRae, John Read, and Sidney Smith; by the spring of 1929 all three of them had gone, MacRae and Smith to Osgoode, and John Read to Ottawa and out of academic life for good. Poor pay, a grinding overload of teaching, and greater opportunities elsewhere had driven them all away. The same thing would happen to Smith, Angus L. Macdonald, and Horace Read who were the full-time staff in the fall of 1929; in five years from then they would all be gone. What the Board did not realize was that the School had been lucky to have got such men as these in the first place and to have kept them as long as it did.

Declining attendance? Attendance had indeed declined; it had gradually fallen from what was almost an all-time high of seventy-seven in 1921 to what was the lowest it had ever been, with the exception of the abnormal years of the war, since the School began in 1883, thirty-five. But the Board was undoubtedly wrong in inferring from that, if infer it they did, that there was anything amiss with the quality of the School. In any event, as we shall see later, with declining opportunities for employment in the years of the Great Depression – and nothing whatever to do with the quality of the School as it was or the outside world thought it was – attendance rose again until by the end of the thirties the student body was, ironically enough, the largest it had ever been – ninety.

Now for a more detailed history of the Golden Age, beginning with the veterans. MacRae was very impressed with them; in a letter to R.B. Bennett commenting on the students who were in the School in the fall of 1919 he was moved to remark: 'In the Maritime mind we have still, as in the past, magnificent material for a really great Law School.'[5] But they had much more than 'the Maritime mind' going for them. They were all ready and eager to make up the years lost to civilian life and to get on with the job of acquiring a profession: Sidney Smith ('20), for example, worked from sixteen to eighteen hours a day and knew the names of all the cases by heart, knew what the facts were, and knew, in many instances, the judges or justices that had decided the cases. They had all been toughened by their experiences in the war and some of them had, even before the war, done rough manual labour: Larry (N.A.M.) MacKenzie had gone ranching in the West; and Keiller MacKay, who in his time at the School was known as a 'natty dresser' and would one day be the first Nova Scotian ever to become a judge of the Court of Appeal in Ontario, had worked with a pick and shovel on a railway in order to earn the money to take him through his Arts course at St F.X. And they did not have, as the returned men of the Second World War would, any financial aid from the government, so that some of them had to take part-time jobs at the same time as they were struggling with their work at the Law School; one of them was, for example, a reporter on the *Halifax Herald*, at $2.00 a column. It was no doubt of these very special, highly motivated veterans' classes that John Read – who was himself a veteran and had himself worked for two years as an apprentice engineer on the Halifax and Southwestern Railway – was mainly thinking when he, who had taught them, described the School as 'the teacher's paradise, which is so rarely found in real life. There is never any occasion to prod reluctant students into activity.'[6]

John Read was Dean of the School from 1924 to 1929. Despite the cheerful tone of his 'Fifty Years of Legal Education at Dalhousie,' his time as Dean must have been for him in many ways a frustrating experience. When MacRae resigned in 1924 to go to Osgoode Hall, Read had been a part-time lecturer in Property since the end of the war and from 1920 onwards a full-time teacher, second in rank to MacRae, and, backed as he was by his fine record at Dalhousie, Columbia, and Oxford and by at least two years experience in practice, he might well have expected to have been made dean forthwith. He was not; instead he was asked, and agreed, to carry on the work of the School for a year with the rank of acting dean without in any way prejudicing the selection of a permanent dean. This was not the first time nor would it be the last that this gentle, modest man – 'a darling soul' one of his old students has called him – was underestimated in Halifax. When he was elected a Rhodes Scholar in 1910 there had been 'a good deal of criticism, which unfortunately caused him much anxiety.'[7] And, so the gossip runs, he was in 1927 rejected as not being good enough to be considered as a possible candidate for a County Court judgeship. He was however confirmed as Dean in 1925.

John Read's next blow was that, having taken on a greenhorn in 1924 to fill the gap in the full-time staff left by MacRae's departure – Angus L. Macdonald ('21) of the Attorney-General's Department and a part-time lecturer on Practical Statutes – he had to take on another one in 1925 when Sidney Smith also left for more money and larger opportunities at Osgoode – Horace Read ('24), who had just got his LLM at Harvard after a year spent specializing in such esoteric subjects as Roman Law, Jurisprudence, International Law, and Conflict of Laws. For how was he to know that in these two greenhorns the School had gained two winners? Another blow was that he who had studied International Law under such recognized authorities as John Bassett Moore at Columbia and Sir Erle Richards at Oxford and would in later years become an expert in it himself was denied the opportunity to teach it at the Law School. He spent the summer after his appointment as Dean in preparing his course on it, only to be told on his return that the University had given an undertaking to the then Eric Dennis Memorial Professor of Government and Political Science that he should be the sole lecturer in the subject.[8] The final blow came with the failure, as he considered it, and the subsequent abolition of an honours course that he instituted in 1927 and carried on all by himself in addition to his other teaching and administrative responsibilities.

The abortive Honours Course tells us a goood deal about the vision which John Read had for the future of Dalhousie Law School. He pursued in the main the same objectives as those set by MacRae before him and by Sidney Smith after him: a fourth full-time man, case method, and research. As to case method, he had experienced it at Columbia, was as impressed by it as was Sidney Smith, and had used it in his Conflict of Laws class in 1921, the same year that, as we have seen, Sidney Smith had used it in his Contracts and Trusts; he was, indeed, in 1924 or 1925 the author of the first case book ever compiled in Canada, a mimeographed one on Constitutional Law.[9] As to research, it is sufficient here to note that when in 1928 he was asked to advise what should be done with a $1 000 legacy left by Mr Justice Rogers to the Law Library he recommended that it be devoted to the purchase of books which were of value for research by members of the student body or the teaching staff. But his own slant was less professional and more liberal than MacRae's or Smith's; it was more in line with Weldon's, or to put it another way, it had, as one might have expected, in it more Oxford and less Harvard than theirs had. In a memorandum that he wrote for the President on the urgent needs of the Faculty a few months after he had become Acting Dean he said that Jurisprudence should be a part of the curriculum (it would not get in there until 1950) and that there should be some way of giving the students an elementary conception of the Quebec Civil Law (that would not even be attempted until 1967). Of his interest in the teaching of International Lawn – International Law was Weldon's own special subject and Weldon taught it in the grand manner – we have already spoken. And when in 1924 Judge Leahy ('98) of the Saskatchewan District Court sent him $100 to be used 'for any purpose in relation to the Law School that Read personally is to designate' he used it in bringing to the School from Quebec, Harvard, and Osgoode Hall distinguished men to lecture on the thoroughly non-professional topics of Quebec Laws and Institutions, Extraterritoriality, and Codification.

The idea behind the Honours Course was to expose a small selected group of students to the same kind of experience that he himself had had at Oxford – a training in Roman Law, Jurisprudence, and research methods, together with the benefit of individual instruction given by himself as tutor. To provide these students with the time necessary to take this special course they were to be let off some of the professional subjects. Only one group of students ever took it, five of the members of the class of 1929. In the year they graduated, John Read, with his Oxford ideas, left for Ottawa and Sidney Smith, no friend of Oxford or Oxford ideas, came in as Dean; in the result the Faculty, after hearing both sides, abolished the Honours Course at a special meeting convened in August. Many years later John Read said this of the Honours Course: 'it was probably the worst taught course in the history of Dalhousie Law School because I had my regular courses to teach as well as the Honours Course. On the other hand, I don't think that it did the five students any harm.' Indeed it did not. One of them became an unusually distinguished corporation lawyer in Halifax, another became a member of the Nova Scotia Court of Appeal, another became president of the St Lawrence Seaway, and another attained ambassadorial rank; as to the fifth, who was in the opinion of one of his classmates the brightest man in the class, he died from tuberculosis a few years after graduation. The course they took consisted of a lot of Roman Law, some Jurisprudence, and an extensive research project into what was a burning issue of the day, merchant shipping legislation. To the mind of one of those who took it – but those who took it may have been an unusually devoted group ('We were forgiven, I think, three particular classes. But we still went and took those classes. We just did not want to lose an opportunity to learn') – the course was the very opposite of a failure. 'We spent every Saturday afternoon in [John Read's] office at the School and he taught us Roman

Law. It was a wonderful education and it was a way of getting to understand John Read. He was a remarkable man in many, many ways.'[10]

One of the ways in which he was remarkable was the way he drove himself and drove his colleagues, Angus L. Macdonald and Horace Read, who were, it seems to us today, already driving themselves beyond endurance. Is it too sentimental to suggest that an additional reason for calling this period in the School's history the Golden Age is the devotion of all the full-time teachers to their job?

John Read, Angus L. Macdonald, and Horace Read worked harder than anyone else has since. In the fall of 1925 John Read took on, in addition to his own current specialties, the Procedure and one of the Property courses, two wholly disparate ones that were entirely new to him, Contracts and Constitutional Law, giving him fourteen hours a week of teaching in the first term and nine in the second. Angus L. Macdonald, who had just finished his first year of teaching, had to drop Conflict of Laws and take on Criminal Law instead, for a total load of eleven hours a week. And Horace Read, the beginner just out of Harvard where he had been doing the 'artsy-craftsy' subjects of Jurisprudence, Roman and Comparative Law, Advanced Conflict of Laws, and International Law Problems, was assigned, in addition to Conflict of Laws, the four tough 'lawyer's law' subjects of Property I, Bills and Notes, Equity, and Trusts, so that in his very first year of teaching he had to get up five disparate subjects and teach eleven hours a week. Quite a difference from 1976 where the beginner will usually find himself with three subjects, two of which will normally be related, and with a load of six hours a week! As if this burden was not heavy enough, these three self-sacrificing full-timers decided to have lectures on Saturday morning – which meant they would be teaching six days a week – in order to prevent students who lived not far from Halifax from going home for the weekend and, in many cases, missing Monday morning. A year later Horace Read took on, for just one year, two International Law classes in the Faculty of Arts at Studley in addition to his already overloaded Law School schedule. And in the early spring of 1927 the Dean announced that henceforth every full-time teacher had to take on one new course each year to keep him alive, because 'he wanted to avoid at all costs anyone doing the same old story year after year ad infinitum.' Which was done – but how on earth, how on earth, did they do it?

What was needed, of course, was another full-time teacher to help cut down the load. It had become, as MacRae had realized, quite impossible to rely on the downtowners, self-sacrificing and willing as they were, to operate the vastly expanded curriculum; for one thing they came and went, and for another thing some of them were by no means satisfactory. It was of vital importance, John Read reported to the President at the end of his year as Acting Dean, to have a fourth full-time instructor, but all he succeeded in getting was permission to take on Vincent MacDonald, the winner of the University Medal in 1920, as a half-time lecturer to teach three full-time courses amounting to eight hours a week throughout the year for the miserable salary of $1000. Sweated labour and a penny-pinching Board? Yes indeed, but the Board really had no choice. Despite the comparative success of the Million Dollar campaign in 1920 and a later generous gift from the Carnegie Corporation to wipe out the University's accumulated deficits, they were always hard up; they had not then, as they have now, the governments behind them.

Two little incidents, and a reference to the starvation wages paid the full-time teachers, will show how tight money was during the Golden Age of Dalhousie's Little Law School. After Sidney Smith had been teaching for three years and would soon be receiving an attractive offer from Osgoode, he in effect asked for a raise in pay and some assurances about his future. What he got was no assurances and a raise of a hundred dollars a year, so of course he didn't stay when the Osgoode offer came. And when, a year earlier, MacRae had told the President that he proposed, in order to maintain tighter security in the library, to have four, instead of the customary three, student librarians at a total cost of the enormous sum of two hundred and twenty dollars the President grudgingly replied: 'This makes twenty dollars more than before, and means that there is just that much less for books, binding etc. If you think it is going to add to the efficiency and save us from losing books, perhaps it is as broad as it is long.'[11] As to what the full-time teachers were paid for the devoted service they gave (Angus Macdonald got $2500 a year when he came in 1924 and Horace Read got $2000 when he came a year later) a short comment of John Read's tells us, in these days of inflation, much more than mere figures do: 'In my day the only professor who had a motor car was Sidney Smith and the reason he had a motor car was that he was a bachelor – no married professor could afford a motor car.'[12]

The financial outlook for the University, and so for the Law School, was for a little while – but only for a little while – looking a little bit brighter at the time when, early in the boom year of 1929, John Read resigned to become

Legal Adviser to the Department of External Affairs and was succeeded by Sidney Smith. Even so Sidney Smith had to take, and willingly took, a cut in salary. At Osgoode he was being paid $6 000 a year as a mere professor; all the Board could afford to pay him for being Dean at Dalhousie was $5 000.

Why did the Board ask Smith to come? Leaving entirely aside the wonderful reputation he had made for himself at the School from 1921 to 1925 (when he left for Osgoode, the *Gazette* devoted a whole column to an editorial singing his praises[13]), the Board saw only two real possibilities, both 'old boys.' They were the thirty-year-old ebullient, but sometimes erratic, Smith at Osgoode and the forty-year-old solid, balanced Angus L. Macdonald who was on leave of absence from the Law School doing his SJD at Harvard.[14] Among the half-dozen or so full-time Canadian law teachers that there then were outside Nova Scotia there was no one who would be interested at the price the Board were prepared to pay. But Angus L. had let it be known that he was toying with the idea of going into practice – which left only Smith. As for Smith, he was enjoying himself at Osgoode: relieved from the treadmill of teaching to which he had been subjected at Dalhousie, he was assistant editor of the *Canadian Bar Review*, was preparing for the press what would be the second case book ever to be printed in Canada, one on Trusts, and was writing, in collaboration with his dean, the scholarly John D. Falconbridge, a *Manual of Canadian Business Law* for Commerce students. Why did he come back, and at a cut in pay? Two quotations from letters he wrote at this time to friends give the answer to the question: 'I love that old School and want it to go ahead – I do'; 'The School is plodding along careful lines. Let her plod, says ... but there is no reason why we can't make the whole of Canada look eastward for new thought, etc. That is after teaching, my vision.'[15] Interestingly enough, Sidney Smith's dream for the School was in almost exactly the same words as the one Weldon dreamed in his inaugural address in 1883: 'The light, of course, should come from the east.'

As a condition precedent to his returning to the School Sidney Smith made two demands that were vital to any realization of his (and MacRae's and John Read's) vision of making it 'a centre of legal thought which is given expression by writing' – better pay for the full-time teachers ('It goes without saying that a man will not do his best work if he is continually looking over the fence at other pastures. I do know this condition has prevailed in the School') and another, a fourth, full-time man by 1930-31 to relieve their teaching load and give them time for writing. With these demands the Board agreed and 'were unanimously convinced of the necessity of going into debt for the purpose of putting the Law School on a more modern footing.'[16] The Board would in a year or two be regretting that they had gone as far as that but they were at the time entirely sincere; they thought, as everyone else did in the spring of 1929, that prosperity had come to stay.

In Smith's first year as Dean there were three encouraging 'firsts.' For the very first time in the history of the School the Dean acquired, in the shape of Ethel Macdonald from Cape Breton, a secretary to himself, or as nearly to himself as might be in the imperfect world of Dalhousie's Little Law School. Every Canadian law school with which the writer has been connected has had a 'woman behind the law school' without whom the school could not run at all, and Ethel was the first one ever at Dalhousie. She was there, except for a short interval in the middle of the Second World War, for nearly twenty years: her reminiscences in the January 1976 *Ansul* give an entertaining, and truthful, picture of what the Law School was like during her regime – for regime it was. The second 'woman behind the Law School' was 'Boofy' Keith: 'Boofy was a phenomenon,' one of the post-war students has written, 'supremely efficient and stunningly attractive, she ran the office like a drill sergeant.'[17] Following an interregnum of a few years there appeared in 1959 the third of these indispensable paragons, Mildred MacDonald, who is still with the School. Now enthroned in the recesses of a 'multi-womanned' Dean's office, Mildred is guiding her fourth dean through the incomprehensibilities of such vital mysteries as budgets.

The second 'first' was the beginning of a series of annual exchange lectures between Osgoode Hall, McGill, and Dalhousie Law Schools. Under this triangular arrangement a professor from Dalhousie would in Year 1 give two or three lectures on a legal subject at Osgoode, a professor from Osgoode would do the same at McGill, and a professor from McGill the same at Dalhousie; in Year 2 a Dalhousie professor would go to McGill, a McGill professor to Osgoode, and an Osgoode professor to Dalhousie, and so on. This innovation, an Osgoode idea that Sidney Smith brought back with him, was much more important than it sounds, particularly to Dalhousie Law School and especially to the teachers there. Interesting as some of the papers, most of them inquiries in depth into legal topics outside the ordinary curriculum, may have been, the real gain was the opportunity afforded to the teachers of the three schools to see the other schools in operation: to visit their classes, to observe their teaching methods, and to learn of their problems and the means used to solve them. No one in these days of jets and freely flowing money for travel has any idea how isolated the teacher at Dalhousie was and felt he was – thirty hours at least by train, and with no money to get on the train, from the nearest common-law school, Osgoode – from his colleagues in the rest of Canada. For the five years or so that they lasted until done away with to save money during the depression, these exchange lectures did to some extent alleviate that stultifying isolation, which would, however, continue until the fifties when the Association of Canadian Law Teachers was organized and, with a slowly improving financial situation at the Law School, a little money became available to send some of the teachers to its annual meetings.

The third 'first' was the gift by the Carswell Company of a prize to be known as the Carswell Essay Prize; it consisted of books to the value of $15.00 to be awarded annually to the student of the first-year class who submitted the best essay on a selected topic. In furtherance of the object of the gift – which was to encourage students to do some independent research and to write on legal topics – the Faculty required all first-year students to compete for the prize and to submit a short essay on any one of a number of prescribed subjects, all of them subjects involving disputed points of law that would be coming up in their classes. During the next few years the first-year students produced a number of first-rate articles, some of which were published in the *Canadian Bar Review*, to the greater glory of the student author and of Dalhousie Law School. But the really important outcome of the prize was something quite other than that. For the first time in the School's history the students were being required to put pen to paper and 'do it yourself.' In the early twenties they had moved from the mere absorption of knowledge permitted by the traditional lecture method to the active participation in class discussion required by the case method; they were now being made, to some extent and in a very mild way, to take a step in the direction of the 'do it yourself' method. But not until the early fifties and the advent of Arthur Meagher's course in Procedure and Horace Read's course in Legislation would the 'do it yourself' method, and not until the late fifties and the institution by George Nicholls of his course in Legal Writing would the putting of pen to paper, become the ingrained features of the course of instruction at Dalhousie Law School that they are today.

In the fall of 1930 the School had for the first time four full-time teachers. They were Sidney Smith, Horace Read, Vincent MacDonald ('20), and John MacQuarrie ('29). John MacQuarrie was the extra man, the fourth full-timer who had been promised by the Board; just a year out of law school where he had led his class in all three years, he had been working for a trust company in Montreal; as things turned out, he would only stay for three years and so calls for no special comment. Vincent MacDonald was the replacement for Angus L. Macdonald, who had decided, in his own words, to enter upon a career of 'practice, politics and poverty.' Here once again is the usual mess that plagued the School in its golden age – a full-time faculty that comes and goes (we have spared the reader the many comings and goings of the down-towners). But the going of Angus L was, as the reader already knows, not entirely unexpected; Sidney Smith, and the Board, knew as long ago as the spring of 1929 that he was thinking of it. Angus L had taught at the School for five years and did not, when he left, entirely sever his connection with it; he continued to help out for a year or two as a downtown lecturer and will, as we shall see, be instrumental, as head of the government of Nova Scotia, in giving it a much-needed financial boost at the end of the forties. But that apart, he now passes out of the history of Dalhousie Law School into the wider history of the Province of Nova Scotia and of Canada. As everyone knows, this unknown law professor became Premier of the province in 1933, re-mained, except for a few years in the Second World War that he spent in Ottawa as the Navy Minister, Premier until his death in 1954, and is now a legendary figure in the mythology of Nova Scotia, second only to Joe Howe. To replace him Sidney Smith turned – where else in those days could he turn – to four stars among the School's recent graduates, all of whom were, characteristically or those days, making their careers outside Nova Scotia, two of them in the United States and two in Toronto.

The only one of these old boys who showed any interest – and he came – was Vincent MacDonald. This clever, quick-witted, and articulate man who, despite chronic eye trouble, had beaten, but only just beaten, his able, hard-working, and supremely healthy classmate, Sidney Smith, in their competi-tion for the University Medal in 1920 had, as so many young men in those days were forced to, been 'doing what he could' in practice, first in Halifax and more recently in Toronto. In the ten years he had been out in the world he had had a very varied experience, so that, although not everyone thought so at the time, he was just the man needed to complement his two senior colleagues. To their knowledge of law in books he added his knowledge of law in action. In the intervals of, and as side-line to, practising law he had been, among other things, research assistant to a royal commission and secretary for one session of Parliament to Prime Minister Mackenzie King. And he did not come as a stranger to the academic world. In addition to publishing articles in the *Canadian Bar Review* he had directed the publication of *Dominion Law Annotations*, a collection of commentaries covering almost the entire field of Canadian law. As to teaching, he had been for a year and a half a half-time lecturer at the Law School (the 'sweated labour' of a few paragraphs ago) and in the year before he came back to Dalhousie he was lecturing part-time, and in three widely disparate subjects, at Osgoode.

We have now brought on to the stage all the full-time teachers who were teaching at the School during the Golden Age: MacRae, John Read, Sidney Smith, Angus L. Macdonald, Horace Read, and Vincent MacDonald. We will spare the reader a very minor change in curriculum: a slight curbing of case method in the second and third years in order to cut down the student work-load to what it has remained ever since, fifteen hours a week. We will also spare him Sidney Smith's struggles with the administration to keep his fourth man in a time of deepening financial gloom (he obviously enjoyed them!). Intead we will here briefly record what each of these 'names-to-be' looked like to those who were their students or contemporaries in the days before they became 'names.' The following impressions are drawn from the reminis-cences in the special issues of *Ansul*, January 1976 and December 1977.

They were, as a group, 'discussional' teachers, were admired by their students, and were very close to them. At the beginning of the period they were nearly all, as one would expect with small classes, discussional teachers; by the end of it they were, with one exception, all using a fairly rigorous form of case method, but they were all vastly different in personality and in their methods of instruction. As to their being admired by their students: when Sidney Smith left for Osgoode in 1925, and again when he left in 1934 to become president of the University of Manitoba, the *Gazette* came out with a rhapsodically laudatory editorial about him; and, writes an old student, 'I don't think any of us in later years were surprised when Angus Macdonald became Premier of Nova Scotia or when John Read became a judge of the world court or when Horace Read achieved the great record he did in Canada and the United States as a teacher of law.' As to their being close to their students, we hear for example of: John Read and his five Honours students; of the young Sidney Smith dropping into the library late one night and taking two students back to his bachelor apartment for a midnight snack; of Angus L. Macdonald's 'door being always open to students and of the open and frank way in which he talked to them about their problems, both scholastic and personal'; and of Horace Read being 'the pre-eminent bailer-out and fixer-up whenever a student got into trouble with some section of the establishment.'

Because he was so much older than his students, MacRae is a much more shadowy figure than the others. He is remembered as being kind ('he told me to go home and get well and not to worry'), as 'a wise father to his boys,' and, odd as it seems, he has been gratefully remembered by one student because in his classes in the History of English Law 'he obliged all law students to learn by heart the Latin writs.'

That John Read was 'altogether a darling soul' and that he gave an innovative Honours course and an imaginative procedure course we already know. To complete the picture of this non-conventional man we should add that 'with all his wisdom he always looked remarkably young' (which gave rise to odd incidents) and that 'he took great delight in getting you to go over a case and then disagreeing with you until he got you to agree with him; and then he would immediately start to try and change your mind back again.'

Angus L. Macdonald drew out students too: 'the more the students disagreed [with one another in class] the more Angus encouraged it.' 'On the surface, at least,' this balanced man 'was relaxed and deliberate ... [he] sat at his desk on the rostrum, talking in a slow deliberate way while gazing intently at some spot on the ceiling,' but, reports one old student, 'I thought a pretty good day was the day Angus L. Macdonald lost his temper and cursed.' And another one remembers with gratitude that the man who would become renowned for the lovely English he used in his public speeches gave us 'cases with magnificent judgements. He did this partly to discourage the reading of headnotes; but he also did it in order to dwell on the use of the English language in these judgements. It was a wonderful education.'

'While all the professors at Dalhousie were [by 1929] exponents of the case method, Horace Read was perhaps the one who used it to the fullest extent. He would sit on the edge of his desk and carry on a discussion with the class, from time to time introducing one of his favourite stories.' Like the others, he had his own mannerisms. When, for example, he completed one of his jokes 'he invariably laughed, whether it was good or not. All of us in the class attempted at least to smile. Horace would wipe the smile off his face so abruptly that we would be left sitting there and smiling and he would take advantage of that fact to tell us to get down to work.' And again like the others, he was very accessible: 'he took a great interest in all his students and he was never too busy to discuss a problem with a student.'

Vincent MacDonald's teaching and human qualities were quite different from those of the other distinguished men in this gallery, so that in this, as well having had actual experience in practice, he was an admirable complement to them. Although 'he had a fascinating way with words and an intriguing vocabulary' he dictated notes at great length, to the dismay of some of his bright students but to the delight of those who were more confused than enlightened by the case method that his colleagues pursued. ('They felt that they could understand what he was talking about much better than some of the other fellows.') And, counterbalancing the overindulgence of his colleagues to the weaknesses of the students, he earned the gratitude of some of them by his plain speaking: 'He was a great hand at cutting a fellow down to size, a service which he performed with great skill and effectiveness.'

Sidney Smith has been left to the last because it was he who presided – and was of all men the man best fitted to preside – over Dalhousie's Little Law School at the time when, at the peak of its golden age, it was preparing to celebrate its fiftieth anniversary and to trumpet to the world what wonders Weldon, his helpers, and their successors had wrought. A genial, large, strongly built man with a big head and enormous vitality, he radiated confidence. In everyday life he was always colourful – kicking, in preference to pushing, doors open and given to using expressions peculiar to himself such as 'Bless your little heart.' He had absolutely no side: he treated his students and his young colleagues (the writer was one of them for just one year) as equals. As a teacher he was 'bubbly' and 'amusing' with a stock of striking and useful phrases, such as 'See where its got its mudhooks' – used to indicate the importance of understanding the underlying principle in any given case. And he insisted on his students doing their homework: 'I cannot remember ever going to his class without first having read all the assignments. If I had not done my work, I went to the library instead of to the class and did there the work I should have done previously.' As Dean, 'he was a model of what a dean ought to be. He expected a great deal of his teachers but no more than he expected of – and performed – himself. Immensely hardworking, and with a wide range of outside interests, he was always prepared for his classes: a real inspiration, and a lesson, to a beginner like me.'

We come now to what is the last, and the most exciting event in the Golden Age, the School's fiftieth birthday. To introduce it we will quote, once again, what Laskin said a few years ago. 'For more than half a century [since it was founded in 1883],' said he, Dalhousie Law School 'provided intellectual leadership in the critical study of the common law of Canada.'[18] In the anniversary year of 1933 that intellectual leadership was more vigorous and more visible than it has ever been since. The *Canadian Bar Review* for that year (Volume 11) was practically a Dalhousie Law School production. Its editor was Charles Morse ('85); its assistant editor was Sidney Smith, the School's Dean. Every member of the little full-time staff of four, even young John MacQuarrie, had written something for it. There was Vincent MacDonald's long (two-part!) article on his then specialty, 'Canada's Power to Perform Treaty Obligations'; there was Horace Read's long (three-part!) 'Equity and Public Wrongs' (two years earlier he and Sidney Smith had collaborated in publishing *Cases on Equity*, the third printed case book ever in Canada); and from Sidney Smith's pen there was not only an article, 'The Stage of Equity,' but also a number of case comments covering such diverse topics as *inter alia*, the common-law offence of public mischief in criminal law, the doctrine of frustration in the law of contracts, and the binding effect of Privy Council judgments. Old students of the School were represented by Ray Gushue ('25) and Donald McInnes ('26), with a case comment each. There was even an article by a student still in the School, R.D.C. Stewart ('33), a product of the Carswell Essay Prize Competition. The faculty contributions were, it should be added, only the latest in, and one species of, their scholarly productions in the last few years: Smith, Angus L. Macdonald, Horace Read, and Vincent MacDonald had all become regular contributors to the *Bar Review*; Read and Vincent MacDonald had each compiled a mimeographed case book which was being used in other schools as well as at Dalhousie; and Vincent MacDonald was editor of the *Dominion Law Reports*. To conclude this perhaps tedious recital of what made this volume of the *Bar Review* a Dalhousie Law School production, we should add that, as one would expect from a publication edited by two devoted old boys, it also contains a full-dress article and three editorial notes celebrating the School itself and its founder, Weldon.[19]

Less visible to outsiders but highly visible to, and most often celebrated by, insiders was the evidence of the School's success provided by its roster of distinguished graduates. We have already sounded this theme at the beginning of the Introduction, and sounded it through the mouth of an outsider, Chief Justice Duff speaking at a Dalhousie convocation in 1936, and we are reluctant to sound it again. But we cannot wholly avoid it, for it was at the end of the Golden Age that there were more of them, and of a higher grade of distinction, than there have been at any time since.

In the field of law there was a Dalhousie Law School graduate on every Supreme Court in the country except in Ontario, Quebec, and Prince Edward Island. There was no graduate of the Law School on the Supreme Court of Canada – Mr Justice Newcombe of that Court was 'connected with' the School, but only as a part-time lecturer in Insurance for two years in the early nineties – but the president of the Exchequer Court was a graduate, A.K. Maclean ('92). Most of these judges were, of course, in the West, to which so many young lawyers had fled from the hungry Maritimes and had done well there in the days when it was opening up – in Alberta, for example, eight out of the thirteen Benchers of the Law Society were from the School. And it is worth noting, as a matter of interest merely, that when in 1931 J.A. Chisholm ('86) succeeded R.E. Harris as Chief Justice, the Nova Scotia Supreme Court became for the first what it has, with the occasional exception, remained ever since, an 'all-Law-School' Court.

In the field of politics the prime exhibit was, of course, the then Prime Minister of Canada, R.B. Bennett ('93). But the School could also boast of three then provincial (or their equivalent) premiers, L.P.D. Tilley ('93) New Brunswick, Angus L. Macdonald ('21) of Nova Scotia – nd dare we mention him, because in his second term of office he had just led his Dominion into bankruptcy? – R.A. Squires ('02) of Newfoundland. Not until the seventies with 'the four premiers' – of Nova Scotia, New Brunswick, Prince Edward Island, and Saskatchewan – to which galaxy we referred in the Introduction, will the School be able to 'point with pride' to such an array.

With lists like these of living distinguished graduates there was no need – though in the understandable enthusiasm of these years of celebration it was occasionally done – to invoke the names of the dead, e.g., Sir Richard McBride ('90), long-time Premier of British Columbia, and even of the dead who had only been connected with the School, e.g., Prime Minister Sir John Thompson and Robert Sedgewick of the Supreme Court of Canada who had both played so prominent a part in getting the School on its feet in 1883 and had lectured there as members of the original faculty. We ourselves have not even attempted to make a list of the many graduates who were in 1933 cabinet ministers or members of a legislature at the federal and provincial levels across the country. We cannot however resist the temptation – it is the temptation of geography – to record that the School had at least one distinguished graduate in England, Sir James Dunn ('98) the financier, in the United States G.W. Schurman ('92), a practising lawyer who was sufficiently distinguished to be given an honorary degree by Dalhousie in 1929, and in Hawaii Harry Irwin ('02) who was, or had been, Attorney General there.[20]

Quite as interesting as the visible evidence of the School's achievements provided by the 1933 volume of the *Bar Review* and by the roster of living distinguished graduates are the appraisals made around that time of what the School stood for and what it was trying to do. 'Its instruction and atmosphere have been liberalizing rather than strictly technical'; 'it has sought always ... to give to its students the vision of law as a great instrument for social ends and to stress the duty of studying law in all its human implications'; and 'the walls of [the Moot Court Room] hung with pictures of the succeeding classes daily bring to the students' mind the opportunity for public service which the law affords.'[21] A bit highflown for a little school of between fifty and seventy-five students, all of them tucked into a corner of the Forrest Building? Perhaps – but any institution worth its salt is entitled on ceremonial occasions to contemplate its own navel and to find what it thinks it sees there to be good.

The most interesting of the appraisals is one where the Dean, Sidney Smith, assesses the School in the light of the hopes expressed for it by its founders in the inaugural addresses given at the end of October 1883. On getting the student to think for himself, Smith first quotes from the inaugural address of the Honourable Adams G. Archibald: 'As regards all education, it may be said in the language of Gibbon, that "every man who rises above the common level receives two educations, the first from his instructors, the second the most personal and important, from himself."' He then proceeds as follows: 'This key-note, struck on the opening of the School, has resounded throughout its history. The Honourable Benjamin Russell was the first teacher in Canada to adopt the Langdellian method and through that instrumentality he, his associates and successors have striven to get the student to think for himself. ... The instructor has to talk with and not at the students.' On training men for the public service, Smith reminds his readers of what the first dean, Dean Weldon, said in his inaugural address (we have quoted that oft-quoted passage before but cannot avoid reproducing it once more here) and then adds his own comment:

'In drawing up our curriculum we have not forgotten the duty which every university owes to the state ... of teaching the young men the science of government. In our free government we all have political duties some higher, some humbler, and these duties will be best performed by those who have given them most thought. We may fairly hope that some of our students will, in their riper years, be called upon to discharge public duties.' The story of Dalhousie Law School is above all the story of the fulfilment of the modest hope of Dr. Weldon. The history of the Maritimes and Newfoundland, of Western Canada, and of Canada itself reflects also in considerable measure the realization of the ambition which young Weldon had for his new School. He and his colleague, the Hon. Benjamin Russell, in their own lives subsequently realized for the School that ambition and, by example and precept, gave expression to the policy of training men for public service.[22]

The culminating event of the Golden Age was the dinner held on 30 October 1933 to celebrate the fiftieth anniversary of the opening of the School on 30 October 1883. Among those present were: Benny Russell, the only surviving member of the original faculty; J.A. Sedgewick ('85) of Middle Musquodoboit, one of the three surviving members of the first class ever to graduate (the other two were Charles Morse, then editor of the *Canadian Bar Review*, and Judge Bennett of Sackville, New Brunswick, who would still be living and would be given an honorary degree at the seventy-fifth anniversary celebrations in 1958); and two of the three surviving members of the next class, the class of 1886, Judge Walter Crowe of Sydney and Judge of the Juvenile Court W.W. Walsh (the third one was J.A. Chisholm, Chief Justice of Nova Scotia). The best record for longevity, by the way, was rung up by the class of 1893. After forty years they were all still living; two years earlier they had, also by the way, sent a testimonial signed by all except one of them (who, rumour has it, was in jail) to their classmate, Prime Minister R.B. Bennett, in recognition of the distinction which he had brought upon the class. There were also, of course, telegrams of congratulations from graduates right across the country, including one from J.W. Weldon ('03) of Montreal, a son of Dean Weldon; he would assist at the official opening in 1967 of the Weldon Building, the Law School's present home.[23]

It was an evening filled with eulogy of Weldon and with nostalgic reminiscences, all enlivened by the spontaneous wit of the chairman, Judge R.H.

Murray ('96); he was there in his capacity of president of the Dalhousie Law Association, which defunct organization had been revived for that evening only. Seated to his right, in the place of honour, was Benny Russell, the co-founder with Weldon of the School. He was greeted, of course, by a thunderous ovation from his old students of so many classes. Although he had retired from active teaching in 1921 after nearly forty years of active service, he had not entirely severed his connection with the School. In 1930 the Students Law Society gave him a party in the Forrest Building to celebrate his eighty-first birthday; in tune with the spirit of Dalhousie's Little Law School, 'there was a birthday cake suitably inscribed and lighted with candles' and 'Dean Smith and Professor Horace Read rendered a most successful duet.'[24] And two years later he gave in that building where he had lectured so long his inaugural address from the Russell Chair of Law that had been founded in his honour. It was a characteristically irreverent one, propounding as it did, *inter alia*, that the judges of today were just as good as the judges of old but were paid too much.[25] The brief address he gave at the dinner was also wholly in character. It was a humorous description of happenings at the Guysborough Assizes when, in the days before he joined Weldon and became successively a member of Parliament and a judge, he was a struggling young lawyer and was acting as court reporter there.

The next speaker was Judge Walter Crowe. He 'reminisced about the early days when the School was housed in a room of the County Academy.' He also 'recalled the efforts made by the late John T. Bulmer who was instrumental in founding the law library, a name that was fresh in the memories of the older members of the Bar present.'

The principal speaker of the evening was Premier Angus L. Macdonald. He was at his most eloquent. At the end of a eulogy of the School he sounded the theme 'Dalhousie Law School, even in its infancy, was more than a law school' and went on to a eulogy of Weldon:

He was present at its birth and he saw it grow through its impressionable years to vigorous manhood ... by virtue of his outstanding ability and the nobility of his own character, by the circumstances surrounding his relationship to the School, Weldon really marked out the pathway which Dalhousie Law School has since followed successfully. He gave it personality and he gave it distinction. He made it not merely a law school but a breeding ground for public service and public men.

But the highlight of the evening was a letter from Prime Minister R.B. Bennett. As they listened to Angus L.'s tribute to Weldon and as they prepared themselves to hear what Bennett would say about him, everyone in the room would recall that Bennett was the man mainly responsible for the recent establishment of a chair in his memory, the Dean Weldon Professorship of Law. In 1928, three years after Weldon's death and at a time when everyone believed that perpetual prosperity had at last arrived, he had been the prime mover in a campaign to raise the necessary funds from the graduates of the Law School. The campaign – the first attempt, by the way, to raise funds for the School since the abortive Law School Endowment Fund started by the students in 1906 – was an ambitious one. The objectives were: $100 000 for the endowment of the Weldon chair to enable the Faculty to carry the load of the expanded curriculum; $80 000 for the endowment of the library, together with its administration; and $20 000 for the establishment of scholarships to aid and stimulate work among the better students. 'With these resources,' said the beautifully written, attractively illustrated, and tastefully produced Weldon Memorial Number of the Dalhousie University *Bulletin* that was issued in pursuance of the drive, 'the Dalhousie Law School would be able to give to the students of the Dominion the best possible legal training and to form a centre for research in the fields of law, politics and the social sciences that would make a real contribution to the commonwealth' – would be able to become, that is, the Law School that Weldon himself had dreamed of. Bennett, the Leader of the Opposition in Ottawa, got things off to a good start by giving $25 000 himself and by coming down to Halifax, his first visit since he had graduated more than thirty years earlier. He was met at the train by a bevy of law students, was the principal speaker at the Munro Day celebrations at Dalhousie – Munro Day, the annual holiday to commemorate the University's first great benefactor, had in that year been revived after having been in abeyance for twenty years – and was the guest of honour at the Annual Dinner of the Nova Scotia Barristers' Society.

Despite the efforts of Bennett himself and of a committee of the Society, the campaign was a hopeless failure: for the financial boom of 1928 was succeeded by the financial bust of 1929. The total proceeds, including Bennett's $25 000, came to less than $40 000 – a capital sum that was, of course, wholly inadequate to provide even the annual salary for the professor who was to hold the Weldon memorial chair, which chair was no more than the minimum objective of the campaign. The Board did nevertheless do what it could to perpetuate the memory of Weldon by establishing the chair and in 1932 decreeing that thereafter the Dean of the Faculty of Law was to be designated as the Dean Weldon Professor of Law, a designation that still appears beside the name of the Dean in the School's annual calendars.

Bennett's letter was such a happy combination of nostalgic reminiscence and filial gratitude that it forms a fitting conclusion to the story of the Golden Age and to the fiftieth anniversary dinner which was its culminating event. So here is the main body of the letter:

It is difficult to realise that the Law School was only seven years old when you [Bennett's class-mate, Premier L.P.D. Tilley, to whom the letter, a letter regretting his inability to attend the dinner, was addressed] and I entered our freshman year. Every member of that class must carry forever with him the memory of Dean Weldon, whose great stature and rugged face reflected not only his strength of character but also his great intellectual powers and who, by precept as well as example, inspired us with ambition, courage and determination to live lives of usefulness. He possessed such superior qualities as a teacher that I am certain every man who was privileged to be a member of his class had a finer conception of life and a firmer resolve to maintain the best traditions of the profession for which we were being trained. I frankly admit that I owe him a debt of gratitude beyond words to express. 'Benny' Russell, whose acute analysis of the law of contracts and of sale and whom we admired so much, is still with us after having rendered great service to his country both in Parliament and on the Bench.

I am sure, as your mind goes back to our early days, you will also recall the face of dear old Judge Shannon and his lectures on Real Property. Probably one, if not two, of the sons of the late John Y. Payzant will be present and thus remind you of the pleasure we derived from listening to his lectures on Torts. Nor will you forget the distinguished lecturer on Insurance, who later became the Honourable Mr. Justice Newcombe of the Supreme Court of Canada. After I became Prime Minister he brought to me the original attendance sheet of our class at his lectures. The presence of the Hon. Gordon Harrington will recall his father's luminous exposition of the Law of Evidence, to which we listened with such advantage. Without our training at Dalhousie it would have been most difficult for us to have achieved any success in the practice of our profession; and the celebration on Monday next will, I am sure, be noteworthy for the grateful tribute that will be paid by those present to the teachers who, at great inconvenience, at times amounting almost to sacrifice, made their contribution to the success of the Law School and enabled it to attain the high position which it now enjoys among the Law Schools of the continent.

The influence of Dalhousie Law School is reflected in practically every Province of the Dominion. Certainly the graduates of Dalhousie are well represented on the Bench of Western Canada. I sincerely hope that when the hundredth anniversary of the establishment of the Law School is celebrated there will be even greater cause to rejoice in the achievements of its sons and of the part they have been permitted to play in the growth and development of the institutions of our country.

SECTION FOUR: 1933-1945

The Great Depression and the Second World War

This last period in the life of Dalhousie's Little Law School, the period of the Great Depression and the Second World War, is in some ways an anti-climax to the golden age which preceded it. The list of full-time teachers is no longer a galaxy of 'names;' among the students there are few who in later life will achieve national distinction; and in the place of academic advance there is academic quiescence. But there are two things to be said on the other side. First, the School is for the first time in many years running along on a moderately satisfactory plateau; it has a fairly stable faculty and a growing enrolment, and it is putting into humdrum everyday practice some of the measures, such as case method in teaching and contribution to legal periodicals, that were in the time of MacRae, John Read, and even Sidney Smith not much more than goals to be dreamed about. There are hardly any events, but no events are better than the kind of events that were at this time taking place at Osgoode Hall Law School – events subordinating it still further to the nuts-and-bolts practitioner ideals of its governing body, the Benchers of the Law Society: for example, case method 'which is somewhat on the wane' was being 're-examined by the Legal Education Committee [of the Benchers!!] with the assistance and cooperation of the Dean and his staff with a view to a possible modification of the system.'[1] The second thing to be said is by way of excuse for the anti-climax. The period of the Great Depression and the Second World War was an extraordinary one. Due to the extreme financial stringency which affected every person and every institution everywhere, the question that Dalhousie Law School was asking itself during the Golden Age, 'how can I better myself?,' was of necessity replaced by the question 'how can I survive?'

The depression was, on the whole, kind to the School. It brought two full-time teachers, Curtis and Willis, who probably would not have come there in the first place if they had had anywhere else to go, and, what is much more important, kept each of them there for eleven years; result – a fairly stable faculty. And it brought an influx of students who, if times had been better, would probably have gone to work instead of staying in school; enrolment grew from a low point of forty-two in the boom year of 1927-28 to ninety in the depression year of 1938-39, the highest ever in the School's history. It was, however, less than kind to the other three, but less important, components of the School: the curriculum, the library, and 'the plant.' This time of fear for the financial future did not inspire – indeed it made impracticable – any experimentation with curriculum; the appropriations for the library were cut to the bone and in one year were entirely cut off; and as for the inconvenient and fifty-year-old north wing of the Forrest Building, it was just left to grow older and still more inconvenient.

The Second World War brought with it more financial stringency and then actual disruption, with ever-present threats of more disruption. A year after it started the fourth full-time man was dropped as an economy measure to cope with the prospective drop in enrolment; the remaining three took over his courses, giving each of them five courses and eleven class hours a week, so that they were back, but for the duration of the war only, to the old treadmill of the days before 1930. Two years later the Dean was pressed into service by the government to do a war job in Ottawa, which left only two men to hold the fort. By this time there was only a handful of students, less than thirty in all, but the full curriculum still had to be given. The only thing that kept the School open during the remaining three years of the war was the aid generously and whole-heartedly given by members of the Bar from downtown: they took on and did carefully and imaginatively subjects that would normally be done by a full-time man. So the war years were no more than a holding operation.

With the end of the war there began in the fall of 1945 an inrush of returned men anxious to take advantage of DVA, the rehabilitation grants administered by the Department of Veterans Affairs. There were seventy-seven students in the first year alone and the total enrolment was over a hundred; in two years' time it would be over two hundred, all jammed into the Law School's little corner in the Forrest Building and all still taught by a little full-time faculty of four. The fall of 1945 was therefore the beginning of

the end of Dalhousie's Little Law School. In the course of the next few years
the increase in the revenue from student fees and the generosity of three
benefactors, R.B. Bennett, Sir James Dunn, and the government of Nova
Scotia headed by Angus L. Macdonald, enabled the full-time faculty to expand beyond the four which had become the accepted standard in the
thirties, and in 1952 the School moved, at last, into the Law Building which
had been built for it on the Studley campus in 1921-22. But these, together
with other, important developments are changes that will, in the course of
twenty years and by slow degrees, transform the small closely knit society of
the Forrest Building into the large aggregation inhabiting the Weldon Building in 1976. They positively demand a Part to themselves, the next one, called
'Changing.' To all intents and purposes therefore Dalhousie's Little Law
School ends in the fall of 1945.

Despite the note of triumph with which he had celebrated the School's fiftieth
anniversary, Sidney Smith had in 1933 reason to be concerned about its
future. When he came as Dean in the summer of 1929 he was full of ambitious dreams for it and had, the reader will recall, been assured by President
A. Stanley MacKenzie that 'the Board were unanimously convinced of the
necessity of going into debt for the purpose of putting the Law School on a
more modern footing.' In the intervening four years, however, both the
financial outlook and the President had changed. What had in that summer
looked like an assured financial future for the University and the School had
become, with the stock market crash of the very next October, a time for
tightening belts; the Weldon chair campaign had failed dismally and the
School was piling up an operating deficit of what was for those days the large
sum of about eight thousand dollars every year. As for the President, the
School had in 1931 lost A. Stanley MacKenzie and was now 'faced,' or
thought it was 'faced,' by Carleton Stanley.

The great 'Stanley row' – and the gossip which grew up around it ('how
these academics love one another!') – which began almost immediately after
he was appointed and went on in varying degrees of intensity until he was in
effect dismissed by the Board in 1945, is beyond the scope of this history of
the Law School. It is only referred to here to explain why Sidney Smith and
his colleagues thought they were faced with an antagonist and to allow the
writer to say that in his opinion Stanley did not, in the constricting years of
the Great Depression and the Second World War, put in the way of the

School's advancement any greater obstacles than MacKenzie himself would have been forced to.

MacKenzie was a true and active friend of the School. A Dalhousian and a physicist who, first as a student and then as a teacher, had grown up with the School from its infancy, he came in 1911 to the presidency with a pride in its achievements that was common to all Dalhousians of the day. Finding it in the doldrums, he played a major part in revivifying it; he presided over its expansion and development in its golden age; and after he retired he wrote to its faculty, 'I have to admit how keen was my interest in the development of the School.' Stanley was a very different kind of man. An outsider from central Canada who would know only by repute Dalhousie's 'famous Law School,' as he called it in his inaugural address, and a 'great books and great ideas man' who was not by temperament or by training very sympathetic with what he might consider vocational education, he made from the beginning no bones about saying how disturbed he was to find that at Dalhousie 'the professional schools were riding on the financial back of the Arts Faculty which is the heart and soul of the University.'

With a man like Stanley at the head of the University, Sidney Smith and his colleagues might well be afraid that the interests of the Arts Faculty would be preferred to the interests of the Law School. There was not, however, any real danger that this would happen. There were always a number of the School's graduates on the Board of Governors and from the time Stanley came until shortly before he left, the Chairman of the Board himself was always one of them – G. Fred Pearson ('00) from 1928 to 1932, Hector McInnes ('88) from 1932 to 1937, and J. McG. Stewart ('14) from 1937 to late 1943. That it did not in fact happen is shown by the fact that in 1945, and after nearly fifteen years of Stanley, Stewart, a one-time downtown lecturer, a distinguished lawyer, and as well disposed to the School as President MacKenzie had been, described the School as 'a drain on the general funds of the University' and said that 'for the past 10 years the Arts and Science faculties have been bled white to maintain the professional graduate schools and the weakness at Dalhousie today is in her Arts course.'[2] The progress of the School, as envisaged by Smith and MacKenzie in 1929, was indeed curtailed by the financial exigencies of the depression and the war but that was, as Stanley put it in a letter he wrote to Smith in January 1933, because 'the stern necessities of the moment compel us to shorten sail in all faculties.'

When Stanley demanded that Smith 'shorten sail' in the Law School for the academic session 1933-34, he suggested dispensing with the fourth full-time man. But Smith, to whom such a suggestion looked like a breach of the deal MacKenzie had made with him in 1929, was able in the events that happened to make the required reduction in expenditures without taking that extreme step. He gave Horace Read what had been coming to him for some years but had had until then to be deferred – a year's leave of absence to go to Harvard and take his SJD; that saved the whole of Read's salary, for in those strenuous days no work meant no pay; and he could, he was pretty sure, get a temporary substitute for half the price. And then, as it so happened, the fourth man, John MacQuarrie, who had been re-appointed for 1933-34, decided that he didn't like teaching and resigned to go into practice; for him, too, Smith was able to get a replacement at a substantial saving. But the real price to the School and to Smith was the same as that paid three years earlier: of a full-time faculty of four, two were new boys. In 1930 the two new boys were Vincent MacDonald with some slight teaching experience and John MacQuarrie with none. In 1933 the two new boys were John Willis, the temporary substitute for Horace Read, and George Crouse, the replacement for John MacQuarrie; for each of them it was his very first law teaching job. Not a very reassuring array for those who only four years earlier had thought that the School was going to be put on a 'more modern footing.'

But worse was to come. During the academic year 1933-34 Stanley repeated his suggestion that the fourth full-time man should be dispensed with as a means of reducing the School's operating deficit, and it became clear to Sidney Smith that the School was for the foreseeable future destined to go down rather than up. So that when in the early summer of 1934 he was invited to become President of the University of Manitoba, he accepted – notwithstanding the fact that, as he well knew, he was heading straight into serious difficulties which had been created by a spectacular financial scandal there. He was a magnificent success. Ten years later he became President of the University of Toronto; he was a magnificent success there too. And two years before he died prematurely in 1959 he moved from academic to public life as Secretary of State for External Affairs in the first Diefenbaker government. But he never lost his interest in the School. On his return to Toronto after a brief visit to it in the early fifties he wrote, in his emotional way, to Dean Horace Read as follows: 'You will never know how the cockles of my heart (whatever they are) were warmed on Tuesday last. I had a feeling that I

The following well-known hymn has a special association with Dalhousie University. It was probably written in the Murray Homestead, the home of its author, Reverend Robert Murray (1832-1909). He was a Governor of the University and was made a Doctor of Laws by the Senate in 1902.

From ocean unto ocean
    Our land shall own Thee Lord,
And filled with true devotion,
    Obey Thy sovereign word;
Our prairies and our mountains,
    Forest and fertile field,
Our rivers, lakes, and fountains
    To Thee shall tribute yield.

Where error smites with blindness,
    Enslaves and leads astray,
Do Thou in loving kindness
    Proclaim Thy gospel day,
Till all the tribes and races
    That dwell in this fair land,
Adorned with Christian graces,
    Within Thy courts shall stand.

Our Saviour King defend us,
    And guide where we should go;
Forth with Thy message send us,
    Thy love and light to show,
Till, fired with true devotion
    Enkindled by Thy word,
From ocean unto ocean
    Our land shall own Thee Lord.

Amen.

had never broken my ties with Dalhousie Law School. It is indeed, I realize anew, my true academic home.'[3] In the very same summer of 1934 Horace Read also resigned. During his SJD year he had taken under Roscoe Pound the famous course in Legislation that Landis had pioneered at Harvard and was invited to join the faculty at the University of Minnesota Law School and introduce a similar course there. Realizing, like Sidney Smith, that the immediate prospect for Dalhousie Law School was less than bright, he too accepted an invitation to go elsewhere; he was, by the way, so successful in pioneering the course in Legislation at Minnesota that he compiled, and in 1948 published, the first of the three editions of his well-known case book on the subject.[4] His departure would not, as the reader already knows, end his connection with the School – he would come back as its dean in 1950 – but, to use the words that a contemporary *Gazette* editorial used of Sidney Smith, with Read's departure and Sidney Smith's departure, 'it seemed to many law students that the end must come to the law school.'[5]

The same editorial went on to say however: 'Today the law school is still here, working as it did in former years. Perhaps the average student was too young to realize that an old institution is something more than its leaders and that it will be carried on by its own momentum.' However that may be, the School did carry on and was, despite – perhaps even because of – the Great Depression, at the beginning of a period of comparative stability. When the fall term began in September, the full-time faculty consisted of Dean Vincent MacDonald, John Willis, George Curtis, and George Crouse. MacDonald was, of course, the only possible choice for Dean. But the Board made with him the same mistake that their predecessors had made when they delayed appointing MacRae until a week or two before term opened and made John Read wait a whole year before they confirmed him in the deanship. This time too they failed to realize what a gem they were getting and they made him wait for six weeks after Smith's resignation before appointing him. What manner of men were Willis, Curtis, and Crouse, the raw recruits with whose aid the unfortunate MacDonald was going to have to rebuild the shattered faculty?

Willis was an Englishman, and to use the phrase that MacDonald used to Willis in speaking of Curtis, had been 'on the beach' – as many were in those days of few jobs of any kind, let alone desirable ones – when he had come, a year earlier, to take Horace Read's place for just one year. A 'double first' at Oxford in Classics and Jurisprudence but with no law degree, he had after a year of teaching school won a Commonwealth Fund (Harkness) Fellowship to study for two years at the Harvard Law School; while there he had on the advice of his supervisor, Professor Felix Frankfurter, audited classes given by 'names' like Williston on Contracts, Beale on Conflicts, and Scott on Trusts and had written a book on delegated legislation that was well reviewed.[6] On returning to England at the end of his two years to a promised job in a first-rate department of political science, he was told he would have to wait for it until times got better, and after a year of 'doing what he could' in London he got, and was glad to get, the purely temporary one-year stand at the Law School. When Horace Read, with his eight years' teaching experience, resigned the School took the easy way out and hired Willis, the tyro of just one year, to fill the gap.

George Curtis was in a similar fix when Dalhousie Law School 'picked him up on the beach' in Saskatchewan in the summer of 1934. A graduate of the Law School of the University of Saskatchewan, which was at that time the Dalhousie Law School of the West – and 'a campus wheel' there – he won a Rhodes Scholarship to Oxford in 1928; at Oxford too he did very well, adding to his Saskatchewan LLB two more degrees, a first in BA Jurisprudence and a first in BCL, and the distinction of being runner-up for the prestigious Vinerian Scholarship. The Saskatchewan to which he returned was of all the provinces the one worst hit by the depression; for the next three years he practised, as far as there was any practice, in a firm there and was active in public affairs and in demand as a public speaker. So when he fled Saskatchewan for Dalhousie Law School what the School got was an extrovert with a distinguished academic record and some experience in practice but none in teaching.

These two outsiders, Willis and Curtis – the first non-Maritimers ever to teach at the School – were at the beginning regarded, and justly regarded, as something less than 'finds.' But by the time they left, after what was for Dalhousie Law School an unusually long stay, eleven years each, they would have become – for such is the way of the world – 'good old John' and 'good old George.'

The third member of Vincent MacDonald's staff of beginners, George Crouse, had a more orthodox background. Like MacDonald himself, Sidney Smith, Angus L. Macdonald, Horace Read, and John MacQuarrie before him, he was one of the School's old students, a Nova Scotian from Bridgewater. After graduating from the School in 1932 he went to Harvard on a Langdell

Scholarship to do his LLM. While there he took Glueck's pioneer seminar in Criminology and Landis' pioneer seminar in Legislation and wrote for them jointly a thesis which a year later became the three lectures he gave at the Osgoode Hall Law School under the triangular exchange system to which we referred in the last section. These lectures of Crouse's were published in the *Canadian Bar Review* as an admirable long two-part article, 'A Critique of Canadian Criminal Legislation,'[7] which was itself a pioneer effort in a field which was then totally neglected. He had come to the School in 1933 as the junior or 'fourth man' on the staff and had, when Vincent MacDonald became Dean, just one year's teaching behind him. He was a great loss to academic life when, as 'the boy' on the staff which had been established at 'three men and a boy,' he was in 1936 forced out into the life of practice and business in Bridgewater that has been his ever since. The mention of the 'three men and a boy' policy brings us to the only event worth recording in the years prior to the Second World War, the unfortunate Dean's continuous struggle to preserve in the face of continuing financial stringency the gains that Sidney Smith had made for the School in 1929, one of which was a full-time staff of four.

From 1934 on the School was to outward seeming running along in a normal uneventful way; the place was full, overfull, of students; there was a core faculty with three familiar faces; the standard curriculum of 1920 remained the curriculum; the library was, as it has been for many years, no more than 'an adequate student working library'; the increasingly squalid and cramped accommodation in the Forrest Building was accepted as 'traditional'; and in each year there were the normal highlights such as the Moot Court, the Mock Parliament, and the Law Dance. There were only two 'events,' both of such minor importance that they are hardly worth mentioning. In February 1936, MacDonald, Curtis, and Willis gave a series of radio talks over station CHNS on 'The Administration of Justice in Canada'; the reason for giving them at all was to make the School visible to its local lay constituency, and the theme running through them as given was that law is not a dry-as-dust discipline of interest only to pedants but a subject that deals with problems which touch the life of every citizen. And in August of the same year the Canadian Bar Association held its annual meeting in Halifax, the first time it had ever met there; to mark the occasion Dalhousie University put on a special convocation at which honorary degrees were conferred on four distinguished members of the Bench and Bar of Great Britain and

Canada, including the Chief Justice of Canada, Sir Lyman Duff; it was on this occasion that Sir Lyman paid to Dalhousie Law School the tribute that we quoted in the Introduction to this history. But the over-riding unspoken concern of everyone during this period – of the students ('will I be able to get a job when I get out?'), of the teachers ('will they cut my salary?') and of the Dean ('can I get out of the University enough money to keep this School running more or less adequately?') – was money, shortage of money.

All during the thirties the School was operating at what was for those days a disturbing deficit: for the five-year period 1928-33 the average annual operating deficit was around $7 500 and for the next five-year period it was around $3 500 – despite the fact that student fees had been raised twice and were the highest in Canada. So that 'pare your expenses to the bone' was the order that again and again came down to MacDonald from President Stanley at Studley. MacDonald did not protest overmuch against the cuts the School could live with: from 1936 on, for example, the exchange lectures with Osgoode and McGill were discontinued in order to save the trifling amount it would cost in travelling expenses to send the Dalhousie man to Montreal or Toronto; and from 1937 on one-quarter of the time of Ethel Macdonald, 'the woman behind the Law School' who was the Dean's secretary, the typist, and mimeographer for the other members of the Faculty and general doer of all the minor chores that it takes a dean's office to do today, was, as an economy measure, surrendered to the Biology Department. These possibly tiresome details are, the reader should note, given as much for the light they throw on the scale on which Dalhousie's Little Law School was always run as for the evidence they provide, through the picayuneness of the economies, of the financial straits in which the University was in the thirties. What MacDonald did most strenuously, but quite unsuccessfully, object to was the starvation of the library and the reduction of Sidney Smith's fourth full-time man to a 'boy' or, to put it more elegantly and more precisely, to a temporary assistant, definitely junior in rank and in salary to the others, who was appointed from year to year for a maximum period of three years and for a maximum salary of $2 500.

'The place of a Library in a School is unique in that it is as much a Laboratory as it is a Library. It consists of not merely books about law but also of Law Reports and Statutes which are the law itself. To law teacher and student alike it is the place where he does his research work and spends his working hours. It is as essential to him as are laboratories and materials to the scientist.' This is Vincent MacDonald speaking, in a memorandum on the 'Needs of the Faculty of Law' that he sent to the President in December 1938. For this indispensable part of the Law School the average appropriation during the thirties was no more than $1 200 a year – for statutes, reports, periodicals, new texts, and binding, that is, and disregarding the $200 required to pay three student librarians their annual pittance. These figures give, once again, quite a picture of the scale on which the School was operating, as does the fact that when he became dean MacDonald found that $1 500 had been agreed upon as a reasonably adequate appropriation and the fact that even in his 'daring' memorandum of 1938 he asked for no more than $2 000. To put these figures in the perspective of today, the Law School of the thirties regarded $1 500, or about one-third the then salary of a full professor, as an adequate annual appropriation for the library, in the sense of books and disregarding anything payable for the services of library staff; in 1976 it actually spent on the library, in the same sense, the sum of $150 000 or about five times as much as the 1976 salary of a full professor.

Despite the frequent protests of MacDonald, what the Law School normally got for the library during much of the thirties was only $800, about half of what had been agreed upon as reasonably adequate. In one crisis year the appropriation for the library was actually reduced to absolutely nothing and when MacDonald wrote to Stanley saying that he had to have at least $300 to pay for current subscriptions to the materials without which the School could not operate, Stanley replied: 'You say you *have to have more*. I do not dispute that. I only say, and you must treat this as final, that there is no possibility of my finding the money for it.' Acting upon a suggestion made a year earlier by Stanley of which the following gives the gist – 'A propos of bloodletting: a certain ... has been very noisy about Dalhousie. Why shouldn't $500 be pried away from him?' – MacDonald forced himself to write begging letters to more than thirty distinguished, and reputedly well off, graduates of the School. But all he succeeded in getting from them was $415, of which $200 was given by two ever-open-handed friends and supporters of the School in downtown Halifax, neither of whom was the gentleman who had been 'very noisy about Dalhousie.'[8] That was, however, enough to avert the immediate crisis.

MacDonald's other main concern during this period was the position of the fourth full-time man: the files are full of letters about it. That the 'man' envisaged by Sidney Smith should be reduced to the status of a 'boy' who was poorly paid and taken on for three years at the most presented him with many problems, all of which he kept on pointing out to the administration,[9] but to no avail: the difficulty of getting anyone to come on such terms, the dislocation of teaching schedules when one boy left and another came, and the frustration of seeing the boy leave just as he had gained enough experience in teaching to be useful will do as examples. To his always forceful pleading the reply was always the unanswerable one of 'no, no money.'

MacDonald fought, and fought hard, in 1936 to keep the first-rate Crouse, but he lost. The same thing happened with Crouse's successor, Gordon Cowan. He too was first-rate. When he took Crouse's place in 1936 he had just finished his time at Oxford, with an excellent record, as Rhodes Scholar for Newfoundland; previously to that he had graduated from Dalhousie Law School at the head of his class and with the University Medal. He was so effective a teacher that both MacDonald and Stanley were anxious to keep him but when his three years were up Stanley had, once again, to say 'no, no money, he has to go.' When he left, President Sidney Smith, who had dreams for the Manitoba Law School, persuaded him to go out there, but Smith's dreams did not work out and he soon came back to Halifax and went into practice; he is now Chief Justice of the Trial Division of the Supreme Court of Nova Scotia. Being forced out of the School in 1939 did not, however, cause him to pass it by; in the difficult days of the Second World War, of all the downtown practitioners who helped to keep it alive by taking on courses that would normally be done by a full-time man, it was he who shouldered the heaviest load. A year after the outbreak of the Second World War, MacDonald finally lost the 'fourth man' battle. The successor to Gordon Cowan as the boy – Allan Findlay, who had done one year in law at Dalhousie and had gone to Oxford as Rhodes Scholar for Nova Scotia in 1936 – was taken on for one year only and at the end of that year the Board decided to discontinue the position of fourth full-time man for the duration of the war. Allan Findlay enlisted in the air force and at the end of the war joined a well-known law firm in Toronto, where he still is.

Almost everything that is worth telling about the war years has already been recorded in one short paragraph at the beginning of this section; all that remains to be done is to add a few details. Just as in the First World War, the students melted away, leaving only a handful of men who were unfit for military service and two or three women. But the full curriculum still had to be given, and given by a full-time faculty that was now reduced to three, each of them carrying in addition to his normal teaching load one of the subjects formerly carried by the boy. In 1942, however, Dean MacDonald was summoned to Ottawa to do war work, leaving only two. Four practitioners from downtown Halifax stepped into the breach and took over his courses; their names – for by doing what they did they saved the School and for that they deserve to be remembered – were: Gordon Cowan, John MacQuarrie, Arthur Pattillo ('33), and Leonard Fraser ('25). Ottawa wanted Curtis too, but with only one man left the School would have been forced to close, so Curtis stayed. For the next two years Curtis and Willis together ran the School, with MacDonald always available for consultation by telephone and Willis having the formal title of Acting Dean. The two stay-at-homes did their best to prevent the School from becoming completely moribund, putting on a weekly class in which they and the tiny third-year discussed cases reported in current issues of the law reports, inducing a knowledgeable chartered accountant to give a stripped-down rudimentary course on taxation, and subjecting, in a preliminary way, the curriculum to the first critical review it had had for many years. They tried, in a world preoccupied with war, to continue giving their classes with as much zest as in peacetime. But the war years were not, of course, a good time to be at the Law School, whether as student or as teacher.

With MacDonald away in Ottawa as Assistant Deputy Minister of Labour, this is an appropriate moment to say something about his public service while Dean, which was more considerable than that of any dean since Weldon. In the middle and late thirties he played a prominent part in the current drive to revise the constitution which, as he too saw it, had been warped by the Privy Council into an instrument that denied to the national government the power to deal with the very real economic and social problems which were then afflicting the country as a whole and could not be effectively dealt with on a province-by-province piecemeal basis. In 1935 he wrote a classic article on the subject in the *University of Toronto Law Journal* and two years later he gave a public address to the same effect which provoked a commendatory editorial by J.W. Dafoe in the nationally read *Winnipeg Free Press.*[10] In November 1937 he was engaged by the federal Royal Commission on Dominion-Provincial Relations, the famous Rowell-Sirois Commission – appointed to undertake 'a re-examination of the economic and financial basis of Confederation and of the distribution of legislative powers in the light of the economic and social developments of the last seventy years' – as their adviser on constitutional law. As a by-product of the three years he acted as their part-time adviser, he published in the *Canadian Bar Review* a flow of articles on crucial issues in Canadian constitutional law that did not cease until he left academic life.

MacDonald was, then, no stranger to public affairs and public service when in 1940 he gave up two months of his summer vacation to work, in what he called 'the incredible heat and humidity of Ottawa,' in the office of the Custodian of Enemy Property. A few months later he took on, in addition to his Law School work, two wartime posts, first of Arbitrator between the longshoremen and the shipping interests in Halifax and then of Controller of the Port of Halifax; the purpose of both posts was to speed up shiploading operations and so save time in the turn-around of the ships which were carrying food and munitions overseas. And in 1942 he went at the insistent request of the Minister of Labour – MacDonald did not seek the job, it was the Minister who sought him because 'of the very few qualified for the post Mr. MacDonald stood first by a considerable margin' – to Ottawa as Assistant Deputy Minister of Labour, with leave of absence from the University for the duration of the war.

While away on this leave of absence he also performed another public service, in a sense far wider than the meaning usually given to that expression in the 'on-parade' pieces delivered by deans of Dalhousie Law School. He had the guts – 'Vinnie' always had guts – to stand up before a crowd of hard-shell practitioners assembled at the Canadian Bar Association annual meeting and, obviously directing his remarks mainly at the Benchers of the Law Society of Upper Canada with their Bencher-controlled Osgoode Hall Law School, say that 'the Law Societies must emancipate their students and the law schools from the thraldom of purely vocational education.'[11]

In 1943 the Law School received, for the first time in many years, good financial news: R.B. Bennett, now Viscount Bennett retired from politics and living in England, had given it some money, a lot of money. Without going into the details, the Bennett gift established four chairs in the University at the salary level then prevailing for professors, $5 000 a year, one in the Medical School, one in the Chemistry Department, and two in the Law School; the holders of the two Chairs in the Law School were to be called the Viscount Bennett Professor of Law and the Dean Weldon Professor of Law. Like George Munro before him, Bennett did not give his money for buildings or any other such thing: 'In providing,' he wrote, 'that the money shall be used for the payment of salary to suitable professors I have in mind President

Conant's statement that the value of the university is not in its plant or buildings but in its Faculty.'[12] Unfortunately for the Law School, the method Bennett chose to further its interests did not, as things turned out, advance it more than a trifle. All that it did, generally speaking and cutting a long story short, was to relieve the Board of the necessity of finding from the general funds of the University the money to pay the salaries of two of the full-time teachers. As the most influential member of the Board put it in a letter to the Chairman: 'As regards the Law School, my position is this: we should see that the Law School gets the full benefit of the Bennett gift, but it should thereby cease to be a drain on the general funds of the University [referring here, of course, to the School's long-continued operating deficit, of which the reader already knows]. ... With the Bennett Chairs fully endowed the Law School should be pretty well self-supporting. Certainly it should not draw on Arts and Science funds.'[13]

In 1944 Willis decided that it was time for him to leave Dalhousie and resigned; for the next thirty years he taught at various Canadian law schools, including, once again, Dalhousie from 1972 to 1975, with time out for one year with an international organization and five years practising law in Halifax; he is now retired. MacDonald was recalled from his wartime job in Ottawa and had, unfortunate man, to cope with problems as frustrating as those he had had to deal with before the war. The war was still very much on and there was only a handful of students: 'Two-thirds of the senior class consisted of Newfoundlanders – Kevin Barry, Ted King, Claude Matthews and Bill Proudfoot – with Frances Clancy of Vancouver and Bill Reddin of the Island making up the balance of the six.'[14] With the Bennett gift behind him he did not have to worry about money in finding a man to replace Willis but he could not find one, so he and Curtis carried on alone with the aid of the good-hearted downtowners. His main concern throughout the year was to ready the School against the day, expected to be in the fall of 1945 – and so it turned out to be – when the war would be over and a torrent of returned men would be enrolling in first year; for all he had with which to meet the new challenge was working quarters that were inadequate even for seventy-five students, a curriculum that had long been due for extensive modification, and a teaching staff that had been allowed to decline to half its pre-war strength. To bring the staff up to four once more he was, despite the Bennett gift, only authorized to search for one senior man and one junior and even then he found, as he expected, that there was practically no reservoir in Canada of men who were both competent and available. By the end of June, however, he had secured a man who could just be described as a senior, Moffatt Hancock, and, by about three weeks before term began, he had managed to secure his other man, James Bryce Milner ('39), who was definitely a junior.

Hancock – who would in the four short years that he would spend at Dalhousie find himself and become a dazzling success, a teacher who was never forgotten by any of his students – had in 1945 been teaching, with moderate success, for about eight years in the so-called Honour Law course at the University of Toronto. After graduating from that course himself and later from the Osgoode Hall Law School, in both cases with a distinguished record, he had earned an SJD at the Michigan Law School and had published a book on a difficult and controversial topic, *Torts in the Conflict of Laws*, that was promptly recognized as a standard work in its field.[15] All that 'the junior,' Milner, had was an LLB from Dalhousie where he had led his class in all three years and had graduated in 1939 with the University Medal; his ambition was to be a law teacher, but the war intervened and he had spent the war years in Ottawa doing administrative and enforcement work for the Foreign Exchange Control Board. Not at that time very glamorous on paper and only second choice for the job he got, he was destined to make his mark in legal education in Canada.

With only three weeks to go before school opened, MacDonald thought that he had his little staff complete. But only three days after Milner had been signed up, Curtis was asked to become the founding dean of the new – and belated – Law School at the University of British Columbia of which N.A.M. MacKenzie ('23) was by then president. With his record of active involvement in the life of the community in Halifax, especially in the field of international affairs in which he had gained national recognition, Curtis was the ideal man to take on the difficult job of starting the new university law school in a province which had for so many years clung to the long-outdated apprenticeship system of legal education. He felt bound to accept the offer and MacDonald, for his part, felt bound to let him go. So off to British Columbia Curtis went and made such a success of his new school that a few years later – at a time when the only Ontario school recognized by the Law Society of Upper Canada was still its own Osgoode Hall Law School – Erwin Griswold, the dean of the Harvard Law School, is said to have said, 'There are only two law schools in Canada, one on the Atlantic and one on the Pacific.' Curtis remained its dean for thirty years and in 1976 was still teaching there.

In the result poor MacDonald, who had earlier written to the Chairman of the Board – the Chairman was acting as chief executive officer of the University in the interregnum between the dismissal of President Stanley and the appointment of the next President, the Reverend A.E. Kerr – that 'without a fourth man we could not carry on next year,' was forced to carry on with only three, himself and two new boys, one of them wholly inexperienced. And, to add to his troubles, he had to find replacements for three of the downtowners who had been carrying the fourth man's courses, they having resigned. What a mess! There will be similar messes in the next four or five years, but they will be reserved for the next Part, 'Changing.'

There was only one change of any importance in the course of study during this period and that did not directly concern the Law School. It was a change in the apprenticeship system, a change that took effect in 1934. In the days before the School was founded there was, the reader may recall, only one way of gaining admission to the Nova Scotia Bar: the student had to serve for a minimum of three years as an apprentice in a law office. In 1976 he still has to put in some time as an apprentice, but the time he has to serve is only nine months and he must serve it *after* graduating from his three-year course at the School ('consecutive service').

Very soon after the School started, the simon-pure apprenticeship system was, the reader may recall, modified – and to the enduring credit of the Bar Society modified – by allowing the student apprentice to absent himself from the office and spend all his time at the School during the months that it was in session. This arrangement was, the reader may also recall, in sharp contrast with the one that was then in force, and continued in force until the nineteen fifties, in Ontario – full-time attendance at the office with time off for no more than an hour or two every day to go to lectures at the Osgoode Hall Law School. The Nova Scotia system of 'interpolated' service was clearly superior to the Ontario system of 'concurrent' service: the student was not, as in Ontario, torn between two masters, the School and the office, and tempted to play one off against the other; and, whatever may have been the case in earlier days, very few Dalhousie Law School students attempted to carry concurrent school and office work after the increase in the amount of classroom work under MacRae. It was, however, clearly inferior to the system of consecutive service, with various forms of which the Prairie provinces began experimenting in the nineteen twenties. Under the Nova Scotia interpolated system, what happened in practice was that the student spent his fall, winter, and spring at the School and was only in the office during the summer months, the months when least was going on. From the point of view of the student, all he was getting by way of practical experience was three separate three-or-four month periods of doing little or nothing. And from the point of view of the office there were students – always more or less of a nuisance ever since the typewriter and the stenographer took over the students' traditional job of copying documents – from each of the first, second, and third years taking up space and having to be kept busy. In the result, an American observer reported, 'east of Ontario the office work of law school students seems to be generally regarded ... as a good deal of a farce.'

In 1934 therefore Nova Scotia changed over to the system of consecutive service, which is still in force today (it was not, by the way, and still is not, completely consecutive, for two or three of the required nine months can still be served before graduation, i.e., between the student's second and third years). Under this system the student does not go to the office until he has under his belt enough knowledge of law to enable him to have some understanding of what is going on around him and to be of some slight potential use to his office; he is furthermore there at a time, and for a sufficiently continuous length of time, when there is something going on to learn from. As for the office, it made at least one gain from the change; the number of students there at any one time was cut to something between one-third and one-half of what it was before.[16] Despite the 1934 change, however, the apprenticeship part of the Nova Scotia system of legal education has remained, and still is in 1976, far from satisfactory. It is better than the farce it sometimes was before 1934, and both before and after 1934 the aggressive and conscientious student has always been able to get something out of it but, indispensable as everyone agrees it to be, it inevitably runs into the difficulty that we have referred to above: in many offices the student is, and is regarded as, a nuisance.

There were one or two minor changes in the curriculum itself during the thirties and two or three more were suggested, but only suggested, during the Second World War when there were only two full-time teachers and a mere handful of students. Nearly all of them were concerned with remedying what can be seen in retrospect as the outstanding gap in the curriculum of those years, its neglect of Public Law.

In the thirties, thinking Canadians woke up to the fact that two important changes were taking place in their constitution: an immense growth in the amount and scope of legislation; and an immense growth in government by civil servants, boards, and commissions. Many lawyers reacted to these changes by asking whether they were a 'good thing' or a 'bad thing'; very few took time to consider what effect they would have on the kind of legal knowledge that a lawyer should be arming himself with. Dominated as they were by the thinking of the profession, the Canadian law schools took much the same line. It was accordingly the School of Law at the University of Toronto – a school that did not then purport to prepare students for the practice of law and was therefore out of reach of the profession – which was the first to start a course on the law relating to government by bureaucrats (administrative law). And it was the Dalhousie Law School – on which the hand of the Nova Scotia Barristers' Society had always lain so lightly that it was hardly felt at all – which was a few years later the first to institute, in 1937, a course on Legislation and Administrative Law. The course was no more than a feeble first step towards the ambitious and sophisticated Legislation course that Horace Read had fashioned for the Minnesota Law School and would bring back with him to Dalhousie in 1950, and its Administrative Law was by no means as developed as the separate course that would later be given there. It was, however, one green spot in the public-law semi-desert at Dalhousie – there would, incidentally, be no Administrative Law in the Law Society of Upper Canada's Osgoode Hall until 1944 – a semi-desert which would become even more of a desert when, because of the loss of the fourth full-time man in 1940, International Law was suspended for the duration of the war.

Two other public-law courses, Taxation and Labour Law, were suggested during the thirties and early forties by downtown lawyers because of their growing practical importance. Nothing came of these suggestions, except a rudimentary course of special lectures on 'practical points' in Taxation. Fully occupied as they were with teaching the almost obligatory MacRae or standard curriculum, the little full-time staff had no time to prepare such esoteric courses, as they then were. In further defence of the School's neglect of these two practically important public-law subjects, it should be added that, in the supremely practical Osgoode Hall Law School, Taxation and Labour Law did not arrive until 1944 and 1945 respectively.

Now, a brief statement on a projected change in approach to three public-law courses that was discussed in the spring of 1943. It is only mentioned here because of the light it throws on the aridly professional approach that was then being taken to them. 'Consideration should be given to broadening the courses in Taxation, Legislation and Constitutional Law by adding to the law a study of the economic theory behind Canadian Tax Acts and the public administration theory and system which lies behind and is assumed by Canadian Legislation and Canadian Constitutional Law and practice.' There was no 'nonsense' about such things as, say, comparative federalism in, say, the Constitutional Law classes of this period. That kind of broad approach to public law seems to have died out with Weldon. It would not be seen again until the late sixties and early seventies and even then it would draw from a distinguished older practitioner the comment, 'this curriculum was not drawn up by a lawyer.'

There was nevertheless nothing arid about the way the full-time teachers went about their teaching. They were limited all right – 'the emphasis was on close case analysis of strictly legal concepts, almost entirely in the field of private law' – but they were not arid. Much of the limitation was self-imposed: 'like all other law schools on this continent we were at the end of the Langdellian period and our single over-riding aim in all courses, whatever their name and whatever their content, was how to analyze problems and how to handle legal concepts. What we were teaching, and teaching rather well, was legal method ... we felt our job was to teach our students to 'think like lawyers' and we felt we were wasting their time (much as we enjoyed it ourselves) if we strayed off into discussing 'office problems' or 'policy.' What made it impossible for the teachers to be arid was their backgrounds.

Vincent MacDonald had an inborn flair for scholarly polemics, had had a wide and varied experience in the outside world before he came, and willingly came, into academic life in 1930, and was throughout the thirties a central figure in 'driving out the Privy Council scapegoat' whose mishandling, real or imagined, of the Canadian constitution was then the subject of intense public debate. Willis was a product of the Oxford tutorial system and could not help exuding the ideas he had absorbed in his two-year stay at the Harvard Law School, especially those of Professor Felix Frankfurter, his supervisor there. Curtis was an old student of Dean Cronkite, a kind of Harvard-trained MacRae at the Saskatchewan Law School, and he too had been exposed as a Rhodes Scholar to the tutorial system at Oxford. As for the two boys – the School's old students, George Crouse and Gordon Cowan, each of whom stayed three years and was a great loss to academic life when he left it – they too had had experience of two ways of life, Crouse in his LLM year at Harvard and Cowan in his years at Oxford as a Rhodes Scholar. And stimulating all these men to bring the best out of what their backgrounds had made them – however inadequate that best may sometimes have been – was the School's tradition of 'work hard and write if you can' that had carried over from the Golden Age.

The method of teaching they used was case method, or, to be more accurate, each teacher used whatever sub-species of that highly elastic genus best suited him. By the end of the Golden Age, case method, or some variation of it, had become well established, so well established that when Willis came to the School in the fall of 1933 he found that for three out of the four courses he was assigned to teach there were actually case books, Smith's printed *Cases on Trusts*, Falconbridge's mimeographed *Cases on Conflict of Laws*, and Horace Read's mimeographed *Cases on Personal Chattels*. Not all courses were thus equipped; those that weren't used syllabuses and the students had to read the cases in the reports, *if* they could get hold of the volume they wanted in the library. 'The only thing we teachers had in common was that we all used case – and periodical literature – material and that, one and all, we did not bother overmuch with coverage but sank shafts and sank them deep.' Vincent MacDonald was a straight lecturer with a sophisticated discussion and reconciliation of cases; George Curtis a question-and-answer, true-case-method man; and John Willis 'a case a day (if he was lucky) or a case a week (if he was unlucky) man, the argument being mainly with himself.'[17]

To conclude this brief account of what was going on academically at the School in the Great Depression and the Second World War we will make two general observations and then add a few words about the writing that the full-time teachers were doing. The first observation is one of fact: all courses were, of course, prescribed, there were no seminars and the only writing required of the students was the three-thousand-word essay in the first year to which we referred in the last section. The second observation is one of opinion: the full-time teachers did not work their students as hard as did their predecessors in the Golden Age or as their successors do in 1976. As to the writing done by the full-time teachers, how far did it measure up to Sidney Smith's dream of making the Dalhousie Law School 'a centre of legal thought which is given expression by writing'? Vincent MacDonald, for his part, measured up pretty well. In the course of the seven years immediately before the Second World War there appeared no less than eight articles by him, one of them worthy to be called classic or fundamental,[18] on the Canadian constitution; by them he established his right to be called in his day the prime authority on the subject. He would have written more had he not been bedevilled by family problems, decanal worries about money for the Law School, and working for the government during the war. In the eleven years he was at the School Willis published eight articles, one of them an acknowledged classic; he also initiated and edited a pioneer collection of essays on Canadian administrative law in action.[19] Curtis, whose true métier was oral communication both inside and outside the School, published two. An impartial judge would be torn between two verdicts – 'not bad, all things considered' and 'why not, pray, more?' His reasons for judgment, whichever verdict he gave, would include a sympathetic reference to the demands made upon these teachers by the amount of preparation required by case method and by the 'ever-open door policy' under which students would come in ostensibly to discuss a legal point but actually to pass the time of day; it would also include a critical reference to the inertia which creeps up on those who, like these teachers, live remote from where the action is.

Coming now to a brief sketch of what the School was like in, say, 1938, we had better say that what follows is based on the writer's own remembrance of it, supplemented by insights gained from other sources, including the reminiscences published in the special issues of *Ansul*; when we quote, as we often shall, we shall not give the reference; what we have just said is sufficient acknowledgment. We begin with the full-time teachers, and first of all, of course, with the Dean.

'Dean MacDonald reigned over the Law School like an absolute monarch.' He would out of courtesy 'consult with' the rest of us (all three of us!), more often than not *en passant* in the passage, but the latter-day concept of 'Faculty control' was as yet unheard of. As for Faculty meetings, there were only two a year, one in the spring to pass on exam marks, and one in the fall to deal with 'supps.' In short, like Weldon, MacRae, John Read, and Sidney Smith before him, the Dean was in full command of what was *his* ship. He carried the same teaching load as we did, and did, in addition to the more lofty chores that still go with the office of the Dean, the multifarious little 'joe jobs' that today would fall to the lot of lesser mortals, such as ordering books for the library and keeping track of the parts of the reports, periodicals, and the like as they came in. For doing all this extra work he was paid the magnificent sum of a thousand dollars a year above the five thousand dollars that was his as the maximum salary payable to a professor. He was highly visible to the students; he could not indeed be anything else, for the door of his little office gave directly on to the few feet of corridor that were used – there being nowhere else – by the students as a *de facto* Student Common Room and that door was, in accordance with the 'ever open door policy,' nearly always open.

The rest of us three full-time teachers – full-time teachers in addition to the Dean were then, the reader will recall, a comparatively recent innovation – were also well known to our students: they would, during their career at the School, take four classes from each one of us and couldn't help knowing us inside out. We too knew them well, so well in fact that we knew, for instance, that 'Mr X couldn't afford a decent winter coat, that Mr Y was a bright fellow who would make a good lawyer but had better things to do than get good marks, and that Mr Z was a decent man without many brains who needed (and got!) extra help to enable him to get through.' We worked very hard; we were just beginners and we had to, in order to keep that one jump ahead of the students which is all that can ever be expected of beginners. But keeping that one jump ahead was a little harder for us than it is for beginners in 1976. Each one of us had four courses, courses that did not usually mesh and that we were forced by administrative exigencies to change from time to time; during the eleven years he was at the School, Willis, for example, was called upon to cope with the following rag-bag: Trusts, Conflicts, Property I, Bills and Notes, Crimes, Property II, Legislation and Administrative Law, and History of English Law. In the result we probably did not do as good a job as the young teachers of 1976 do, but that was not for want of trying. We were not paid very much – in 1938 Willis and Curtis were getting about $4 000 and Cowan, 'the boy,' about $2 500; but these were the days of the Great Depression, pleasures (such as swimming in the Arm or walking to Herring Cove on the shore road) were free and we were glad – were we glad! – to have a job at all. As to our working conditions, Curtis and Cowan shared a cluttered office – lucky fellows, they were right next door to the library – but Willis, lucky fellow, had one to himself, 'a little hole just partitioned off from the girls' lounge and so right in the middle of their gossip,' and, again lucky fellow, 'in his own office he had a complete set of Chancery and Probate reports and if he wanted Appeal Cases or King's Bench all he had to do was walk down to the passage to the Dean's Office which had a complete set of them.' What about telephones, duplicating service, and a share in a stenographer? Such luxuries were not for us; we were dependent on the goodwill of Ethel Macdonald, the Dean's secretary, and she, thank heavens, was good to us.

The downtown lecturers were no longer the mainstay that they had been before the establishment of a full-time staff in the twenties, but they were still indispensable. In 1938 they were doing the 'practical' subjects of Bankruptcy, Insurance, Procedure I, Shipping, Procedure II, and Evidence. They were a particularly distinguished group of old-timers and took a real interest in the School, some of them even going so far as to attend Faculty meetings. Following immemorial tradition, they gave their lectures at five o'clock and, following a tradition that had been established sometime in the MacRae period, they were paid two dollars a lecture which they were expected to, and did, turn back. A member of the class of 1934 has given the following description of the downtown lecturers of his day. 'In my judgement these part-time lecturers broke down into four classes: (1) old hands, who for years had lectured from the same old dog-eared syllabus and could not be put off it by any ruse; (2) old hands, who could be induced to throw the book away and to talk about something current in the most interesting fashion; (3) new hands, just bursting to impart to us the lore they had picked up by a couple of years head-start; and (4) the judges, as always a race apart. To me, and I believe to all of us, all the part-time lecturers were likeable on personal grounds. As instructors of the young, class (2) won by a mile.' It is of class (2), of course, that the writer is thinking when he says, as he often does, that the absence from the School in 1976 of the veteran practitioners who used to come up at five o'clock and give their lectures is a very real loss to it. He is not thinking of the occasional 'lemon' in class (1), to one of whom Horace Read was subjected when he was a student in the early twenties. 'He dictated every word, including the punctuation, from tattered notes he carried in a side pocket of his jacket. In 1918 an enterprising student who knew shorthand had reproduced the lectures in typewritten form that could be bought for a dollar, so that less than half of the class was usually in attendance. The lectures, including jokes, were repeated verbatim each year and had not been modified after the typing by the student.'

In describing the students of 1938 and comparing them with their predecessors and with those who will be in the School in 1976, we must begin with a few tiresome statistics. There were around seventy-five of them in all, which was about normal for the thirties; in all the previous years of the School's existence the normal had been around fifty; in 1976 enrolment will be limited to four hundred and fifty, all the Weldon Building can hold; and there will be four hundred and fifty, with many more clamouring to come in.

There were four women; every year since the first woman came to the School in the middle of the First World War there had usually, but not always, been one or two of them: in 1976 one in every four of the students will be a woman. Only ten, or about one-seventh of the students were from outside the Maritimes, and that was more than the normal proportion; in 1976 the Maritime complexion of the School will only be preserved by a deliberate policy decision of the Faculty limiting the proportion of non-Maritimers to one-quarter. The student body in Dalhousie's Little Law School was, then, small, male, and Maritime.

When they were through, they did not, of course, all stay in the Maritimes; ten years earlier Sidney Smith had estimated that the Maritimes and Newfoundland could not absorb more than one-half to three-quarters of the small annual crop of graduates. From the nineties to the end of the First World War most of the surplus had, as the reader already knows, gone into private practice in western Canada. In the twenties some of them turned from the private practice of law to the opportunities that were beginning to be available in business for law graduates and went, into business or into law, to the United States or Ontario. But by 1938 the door to the United States had been closed by the new immigration laws there, leaving only Ontario or – a new field that had just begun opening up with the rise of government activity in the thirties – 'taking a government job' open to them. If it was to Ontario that the graduate of 1938 wanted to go he would be faced with two bar fees: one of $175 to be admitted to the Nova Scotia Bar; and another, a crippling 'restrictive tariff' of $1 500, payable to the Law Society of Upper Canada for the privilege of 'transferring' from the Bar of Nova Scotia to the Bar of Ontario. For, as things then stood, had always stood, and would stand until the fifties, the Law Society of Upper Canada gave no credit for the work done in any law school other than Osgoode Hall; it did not recognize a degree from the Dalhousie Law School – or from the Harvard Law School for that matter – as satisfying the academic requirements for admission to practise in Ontario. In 1976 the Law School graduate would not be faced by any such barriers; his degree would, except of course in the civil-law Province of Quebec, be accepted right across the country.

The life-style of the students in 1938 was not very different from what it had been since the School began. They had no government aid, and no scholarships of any kind were available to lighten the burden of the highest annual fees charged by any law school in the Dominion ($282 in 1938). To put themselves through, most of them worked in the summers and some of them were so hard up that they had to stay out for a year in the middle of the course, teaching school for example, in order to collect enough money to finish it; but in the years of the Great Depression 'jobs of any sort were woefully hard to find. After my first year I was lucky enough to get a summer job as helper on a diamond drill prospecting for coal.' There was no Men's Residence and no Student Union Building, but there had always been boarding houses that catered mainly to students, and 'one could obtain board and lodging for $7.00 to $10.00 per week on an average.' Because money was always short, desperately short in the thirties, pleasures were few and simple, so that, for those who could afford it, the Law Ball (which dates from sometime just after the First World War) was the high spot of the year – a social event that was a bit more sophisticated than the sleigh ride to Bedford, the event in what passed for the social whirl in the two or three years immediately preceding the First World War, and a good deal more sophisticated than the annual Christmas tramp which was *au courant* in the first years of the School's existence.

There not being very much to do in the Halifax of 1883-1945 – as there still is not in the Halifax of 1976 when compared with, say, the Toronto of 1976 – most of the students at Dalhousie Law School have always worked, and still do work, pretty hard, much harder at any rate than their opposite numbers in Toronto. But Willis' students of the vintage 1933-40 – leaving out entirely the students left behind when everyone was away at the war – were not on whole very good students, 'excepting always a few outstandingly able ones whose names I could mention if I was going to name names, which I am not. Too many of them were unable to read or write, using those words in the university sense. And they were surprisingly ill-informed; so that looking back at the things I talked to them about in order to put the "law" I was giving them in perspective, I shudder at the contemptuous reception I should get from Dalhousie law students now if I dared to assume that they did not already know them.' Why this apparent decline in the quality of the students, so many of whom were in earlier days so good? It is going too far to say, as one old student of this period has said, that: 'There was no difficulty getting enrolled in the School. The welcome mat was out and recruitment of students was active'; and 'I cannot remember anyone who was turfed out in my time on mere grounds of insufficiency of scholarship.' The writer prefers his own, more moderate but perhaps not very different, explanation (or should it be 'excuse'?) for the apparent decline: 'the group of students we were getting at this period was, because of the depression, unrepresentative; we had far too many fellows sent there by well-off Dad for the one and only reason that there was no job for the boy and we took people we should have rejected but for the one and only fact that the School needed their fees.'

Granted that there was in the years of the Great Depression and the war some temporary decline in the academic quality of the students, there was no change in the warmth, or easy relationship, that had always existed between the faculty and the students and among the students themselves. Here are two impressions, both recorded forty years later; the first is by a teacher and the second by a student. 'There were so few of us – around seventy students all told and four full-time teachers – that we knew one another, trusted one another and respected one another, with all faults. In the now dishonoured phrase we were 'separate but equal,' the student accepting the teacher for what he was, a link (however unsatisfactory) with the experience of the past and with the ideas current in the larger world outside the Province of Nova Scotia, and the teacher accepting the student for what he was (and will, I hope, always be), a gadfly questioning that experience and those ideas.' 'As a society it was cosy, intimate and superlatively congenial. The faculty maintained their station and dignity without pulling rank. There was constant joshing and barbing and any manifestation of pomposity brought down instant and merciless attack. I met no one in the School whom I disliked, then or thereafter. I am proud to be called friend by any of them or to meet any of them in any company. Jammed together as we were each man got to know everybody else very well indeed. My impression is that we rubbed together happily.' This traditional warmth may have been bought at the expense of competitive intellectual drive – which is what one of the outsiders on the Faculty of 1976 was probably thinking of when he said that he never wanted to hear the word 'warmth' again. If that was so, says this writer, the warmth was worth the price.

The library – about which we have already said enough at the beginning of this Part and in the present section – was in 1938 housed in the same room and serviced in the same way, cafeteria-style with a student 'librarian' standing guard over 'the locked press' which contained the textbooks in common use, as it had been ever since the move to the Forrest Building in 1887. It was an entirely different institution from what it would become by 1976 – a wide-ranging collection of about 100 000 volumes, run by a large staff headed by a librarian trained in both law and library science and having in its ranks a number of professional librarians. According to the 1938-39 calendar it comprised, allegedly, 13 000 volumes; the corresponding figure in 1885 was 4 000 and in 1912 8 000. From an administrative point of view it was in an appalling mess: there was no catalogue and nobody really knew what books we had and what books we did not have; what we did know was that there were in the basement and in the attic a large number of volumes semi-discarded and useless – we had carried some there ourselves. But as a working library for students – yes, and for us undemanding teachers of those days – it was good enough. 'The collection of books in the library was, on the whole, pretty good, and, regarded as a students' library, far better than the Students' Library I found at the Osgoode Hall Law School in 1944. We took all the then *worthwhile* legal periodicals and, though I may be wrong in this, our small collection of books on the borderland of law and other disciplines was, for the date, more extensive than I have since found at any other School in Canada. It was not, of course, a research library and would certainly not meet the mindless "number of books" test that is fashionable now; but for our needs and our students' needs it was good enough. Had any of us teachers been bloody geniuses, the library would, no doubt, have been inadequate for our proper development – but none of us were and so the world lost nothing by its inadequacies.'

In 1938 the seventy-five-odd students and the four full-time teachers were squeezed into seven rooms in the north wing of the Forrest Building. Only two of the rooms were of any size, the large library on the second floor and the moderate-sized Moot Court Room, which was also used as the first-year class-room, on the ground floor. Now that the north wing of the Forrest Building has been handed over to 'lesser breeds without the law' and has been subjected to various semi-permanent changes, there is no point in attempting to describe the other five rooms or pinpoint what they were used for. But for those who are interested in such minutiae, it should be pointed out that the School had not been occupying all seven rooms at all times since 1887. It seems, from casual references in the *Gazette* from 1887 to the mid-twenties, that: on the second floor it always had the library; on the ground floor it always had the use, for Moot Court and Mock Parliament purposes, of the so-called Moot Court Room, a large pillared room flanked by two other rooms; but, depending no doubt on its own size and on the space requirements of the rest of the University, it sometimes had as few as only one and sometimes as many as all three of those ground floor rooms for its own as class-rooms; by the mid-twenties at the latest, however, all three of them were recognized as belonging to it and were its three class-rooms, one for each of the three years.

Much more important than these geographical minutiae is the impression made by the Forrest Building – by which we mean the north wing of the Forrest Building – upon those who lived their working lives in it in its latter days. From the strictly objective viewpoint of the Dean this 'plant' was simply deplorable: 'all class rooms are badly ventilated and most uncomfortable when filled to capacity'; 'the students have no room in which to rest or smoke except a room in the basement which they refuse, justifiably, to use. In the result they congregate in one small corridor between classes and seek their moments of relaxation in the same place.' It was comfortless – indeed it was – but to some minds comfort is not all. Here are a few of the impressions to which we referred a moment ago. A teacher (1938): 'The Forrest Building suited me fine. The classrooms were small, "homey" and had windows. I felt at home and natural there in a way I do not in the sterile, impersonal, win-dowless affairs I am saddled with now in the up-to-date Weldon Building.' Another teacher: 'The Law School of 1945 was very different from the School of today. It consisted of some rather shakey old rooms at the end of the Forrest Building. These rooms reeked with the atmosphere of the 1880's. There were pictures on the wall that were kind of interesting and inspiring, pictures of the graduating classes; great big huge-framed pictures of every-one who had graduated.' A student (1929): 'I think all of us studied the pictures around the Law School and saw the names of the graduates who had passed through. We looked at their records and probably wondered what we ourselves would do.' Another student (1949): 'In concept the Forrest Build-ing seemed hardly more than a step or two removed from the single-room rural school house. It was an antique and it smelled "old."'' And yet another student (1932), one who appreciated both the discomfort and the sense of tradition built into the benches with which the class-rooms were equipped: 'The classroom seats were soft-wood benches with low backs, each of which would accommodate two or three people. The desks and benches were covered with the initials of former students, some of them extremely well-known personages. The benches were not comfortable but they served the purpose. And it was easier to stay awake on a hard bench than it is with the more comfortable chairs and desks of today.'

Now that we have finally come to the end of this immensely long Part on Dalhousie's Little Law School and are about to embark on 'Changing,' we must put the School, as it had come to be, in the perspective of the other Canadian schools as they were in the late forties. In his well-known article in the *Canadian Bar Review* for 1950, 'The Condition of Legal Education in Canada,'[20] Maxwell Cohen made a comprehensive review of their main characteristics, though problems or even defects might be a better word. The following thoughts and quotations are taken from that article.

'The resources of the community ... do not seem to have been allocated in any major way to the education and training of law students.' As to 'plant': 'In not one law school in Canada are to be found modern, permanent buildings ... with anything approaching the type of accommodation that frequently is available in many of the other professional schools and often even in the faculties of arts and science.' As to library: 'there is a modesty about library facilities and budgets that parallels somewhat the inadequate level of buildings and classrooms,' though 'many of the schools have the makings of good, small working libraries.' As to teachers: the low salaries offered, ranging from $4500 to $6500, 'will not attract superior and energetic men to the teaching of law'; the normal staff, three or four full-time men, is so small that 'there cannot be the opportunities for specialisation so necessary for a high level of competence and scholarship'; and the teaching load, usually three or four subjects and seven or eight classroom hours (the Association of American Law Schools had set as a desirable standard two subjects and six hours per week), is so heavy that 'there is often too little leisure left for research and creative writing.' As to students: 'law faculties in Canada are easier to enter than any other professional school,' so that the law schools 'have many first-year students who ... should never have been admitted to study law.' And, finally, as to the course of study: major and belated changes are taking place in its emphasis; into what has hitherto been an almost exclusively private-law curriculum there are beginning to come such public-law subjects as Legislation, Administrative Law, Taxation, and Labour Law.

What Cohen says was, generally speaking, just as applicable to Dalhousie Law School as it was to the other law schools. Its 'facilities,' using that word in its widest possible sense, were, viewed objectively, far from desirable; they will in the course of the next twenty years be substantially improved. But to view the mere facilities of Dalhousie Law School and to view them objectively is – like viewing objectively the School's living quarters in the north wing of the Forrest Building – to grasp at the shadow and miss the substance. In the great days of the School, the early years of Weldon and Russell and the years immediately following the First World War, the teachers were men of unusual distinction and the students sturdy Maritimers who were determined to 'get on.' Even in the days of the Great Depression and the Second World War the teachers were quite good and were trying to do their best, the students were serious and hard-working, and both teachers and students had something else going for them. They had inherited from the School's immediate past an approach to teaching that made the boring subject of law seem almost like fun and they were surrounded by evidence – some of it intangible, like the success stories of long-gone graduates who had made good, and some of it tangible, like the old class pictures on the dirty walls and the initials carved on those execrable benches – that what they were now doing had been found to be worth doing by those who had been subjected to the very same inadequate facilities that they were being subjected to now. The School may, that is, have had inadequate facilities but it had something far more important than facilities: conscientious teachers, serious students, and a tradition – above all a tradition.

PART III

PART II

Changing: 1945-1966

In the years between the fall of 1945, when the first great in-rush of veterans resulted in a first-year class that was larger than the normal total enrolment had been in the years preceding the war, and the fall of 1966, when the School moved to its present home in the Weldon Building, the School underwent a slow and undramatic change. By 1966 it had ceased to be Dalhousie's Little Law School, but in some ways it was still much as it had always been and in other ways it was beginning to acquire characteristics that would in the next decade make it markedly different. For Dalhousie University itself this period was also one of change, a slow and undramatic expansion in both size and scope; but here too 'the real change didn't come until the sixties; that's when we saw the great expansion that changed the little college into something closer to a so-called multiversity.'[1] It was, likewise, a period of change in the condition of legal education in Canada generally – and a change for the better; in his 'Condition of Legal Education in Canada; Fifteen Years Later'[2] Cohen is much happier about it than he was in 1949 when he made the rather gloomy evaluation that we quoted a page or two earlier. In line with social and ideological changes in the world about him, there had somewhat earlier also come changes in what a lawyer does and what he is expected to know, changes which, even in institutions so conservative as Canadian law schools then were, began in this period to be reflected in curriculum. In the wider world beyond the law there were, of course, during this period swift and dramatic changes – in international affairs the Cold War and the détente that followed it, in the United States the upsurge of the blacks, and in Quebec the quiet revolution, for example – but these great events had little effect on Canadian law schools and they are in any event beyond the scope of this history of Dalhousie Law School.

At a symposium on legal education held at the University of British Columbia in 1949 Dean Vincent MacDonald so succinctly summarized the change that had, as a result of the depression and the war, come over a lawyer's life since the establishment of the strictly professional and private-law-oriented standard, or MacRae, curriculum in 1920 that the relevant paragraphs in his address will be quoted in full:

The environment of the lawyer has changed in many ways which have produced concomitant changes in the character of the lawyer's work.

Increasing urbanization, the growth of group and large scale corporate activity, the growing intervention of government in the social and economic spheres, the enlarging extent to which enacted law has encroached on the traditional common law as the source of rules of human conduct, the enormous proliferation of subordinate agencies possessing derivative law-making and right-deciding powers – all these significant developments of our own modern age have profoundly affected the lawyer and his task. New economic movements, a new philosophy of the function of government and new techniques of administration have ... produced ... a situation demanding that the profession shall know much more than formerly about matters of strict law, and also many other aspects of community life such as finance, economics and politics which entered relatively little into the professional life of our predecessors at the Bar.

All these suggest the need ... of better professional education, including more emphasis on legislation, accounting, taxation and public law generally ... and the need of widening the vision of the lawyer as to the ultimate purposes of law as a necessary guide to certainty amid changing trends.[3]

One of the basic questions facing all law schools, including Canadian law schools, during the period covered by this Part therefore was: what is it that the Bar and Bench and other users of legal skills expect from legal education today as compared with an earlier period? This question was more pressing for schools located in the great metropolitan centres of Toronto and Montreal than it was for those which were, like Dalhousie, more remote from 'the action' but, hampered as they were by small, inexperienced, and overworked faculties, none of them were able to give much time to considering it. In 1960, however, Dean Horace Read, as one of those deputed to report on the Canadian situation at a conference of British, Canadian, and American law teachers in New York, was able to report at least some over-all progress: 'Present-day curricula have been expanded to include courses in administrative law, community planning law, comparative law, international law, introduction to law, jurisprudence, land use controls, labour law, legislation and taxation, in addition to the courses which, when taught in the grand manner, were successful vehicles in the past for conveying to students a knowledge and understanding of the scope and nature of their public responsibilities.'4 But the expansion in curriculum needed to bring what was taught in Canadian law schools more nearly into line with the diversity of sophisticated tasks that the average lawyer was now expected to be able to perform would not come about until, at the end of the sixties, the law societies allowed the curriculum to be 'optionalized.'

The changes that took place in the other Canadian law schools – and by 'Canadian law schools' we mean in the next few paragraphs the common-law schools only, for what went on in the civil-law schools of Quebec has never had much relevance to Dalhousie – were a little more dramatic than those at Dalhousie. In terms of mere numbers there were the following impressive changes between 1945-46 and 1961-62: student enrolment almost exactly doubled, from about seven hundred to about fourteen hundred; the number of full-time teachers rose from a handful of about a dozen to what was then regarded as a considerable corps, over a hundred; and five completely new schools came into existence, one in British Columbia and four others, all of them in Ontario. Because of its connection, albeit a slight one, with Dalhousie Law School, the minor revolution in Ontario calls for a short paragraph to itself.

In 1957 the Law Society gave up the monopoly over legal education that it had always reserved for its own Bencher-directed and practitioner-oriented Osgoode Hall Law School, put that school on a three-year, full-time, academic basis, and gave full recognition to university law faculties that were prepared to offer a prescribed, but quite loosely prescribed, program. In that year the University of Toronto Law School achieved the status which it had been claiming since 1949 and three new university law schools were established: at Queen's University, at the University of Western Ontario, and at the University of Ottawa. The governing body of what had always been the largest and richest group of practitioners in common-law Canada fell at last, that is, into line with what the Nova Scotia Barristers' Society had been doing with the Dalhousie Law School ever since 1891. All law schools in Canada (including, in function though not yet in form, the Osgoode Hall Law School) were now university law schools. In bringing about this minor revolution – which was in the end successful only because the Benchers' school could no longer cope with the growing numbers that were seeking places in a law school – Sidney Smith, erstwhile student, teacher, and dean at Dalhousie and from the mid-forties on president of the University of Toronto, played a leading part. It was he who in 1949 persuaded the governors, against the will of most of them, to establish a professional law school at the university and to invite 'Caesar' (Dr C.A.) Wright, the real spearhead of revolution against Bencher control of legal education, to head it up; and it was he who stood behind Wright and the new university law school in the eight long years during which the Benchers were strangling it by refusing to grant to its new LLB anything more than partial recognition. The conflict of principle between Wright on the one hand and the Benchers on the other gave rise to the fiercest debate on legal education that Canada has ever known, but that debate was of little interest to Dalhousie Law School – it had been since 1883 a *university* law school with all that the word 'university' implies. Of so little interest was it indeed that Dean Horace Read refused to take part in the controversy; both Smith and Wright asked him for his support but to give it would have risked alienating the Benchers and so perhaps jeopardizing the position of those of his students who wanted to 'transfer,' as was then the practice, to the Ontario Bar after their graduation and admission to the Bar of Nova Scotia.[5]

In other respects the developments that took place in the other law schools were similar to those that, as we shall see, took place at Dalhousie. Despite oft-reiterated complaints that their universities did not seem prepared to support them on the same scale as they did their medical schools, their science departments, and even their departments of social science, the law schools did for the first time get at least *some* money to spend. With this increase in financial support came improvements in facilities and in library.

The standard of law school facilities at the end of the forties was deplorable. By the beginning of the sixties they were better than they had been but they were still deficient enough to evoke the following unflattering description – one that could have been applied without changing a word to conditions in the Studley Law Building at Dalhousie. 'In some schools library space and classroom space are shared; moot court rooms are not provided; enough office space is frequently lacking and good common-room quarters for students – not some "black hole of Calcutta" in a basement ... but attractive, convenient and roomy quarters, where young lawyers in training can rub minds together and kindle a sense of corporate life and loyalty, which should be our hallmark – are wanting. The catalogue, I fear, could be lengthened.' Better accommodation was, however, in sight. 'Happily, the two newest law schools in this country, Queen's and Western, will be well served in this respect. At both universities, buildings of the finest quality, each costing I would judge, at least $1 000 000, are being erected to house legal studies, and exemplify the standing which law should be given among the disciplines of higher learning.'[6] And some five years later Dalhousie Law School would move into the well-appointed building which is its present home.

There was also substantial improvement in law school libraries – and the library is, as everyone knows, the essential base on which the work of a law school rests. Dalhousie Law School made, as we shall see, a similar step forward. Using merely the 'number of books' test, there were in 1949 only two schools that had more than twenty thousand volumes; by 1964 there were three with over forty thousand each. And, what is more, the books covered a wider range than what had hitherto been traditional (the basic reports and principal textbooks); an increasing amount of the wealth of periodical literature was being made available to the students. Nevertheless, much more remained to be done before any school could be said to have a library capable of meeting the needs of first-rate legal education.[7]

As to the changes which took place in what are the most important components in any law school – the student body and the teaching staff – there is nothing much to report about the students. Not until after the arrival of government aid and student activism in the mid-sixties will they become the powerful force that they are today. Nor, despite the raising in 1957 of admission standards to the point that, as a practical matter, nearly all of them thereafter came in with a BA or its equivalent, did they show much improvement in quality; that will have to wait until at the end of the sixties declining employment opportunities for teachers of history, economics, politics, sociology, and the like turned many of them away from the graduate schools and into the law schools. But it was in the period 1945-66 that the most striking development took place in teaching staff.

Up until 1945 the maximum full-time complement of a law school was thought to be four men – even huge Osgoode Hall had but four; all the schools were still relying heavily on the part-time help given by members of the Bar. In the course of the next twenty years this unsatisfactory and outdated system was gradually replaced by one where most of the teaching was done by those who gave their whole time to it, the downtown lecturers only being called upon to handle those subjects which were felt to be beyond the competence of the full-time academics; to take just two examples, in 1961-62 Osgoode Hall, with some 400 students, had fifteen full-time teachers and Dalhousie, with a hundred students, eight. In the result, there emerged for the first time in Canada what had in the United States been for many years a third branch, and a very distinguished branch, of the profession – the teaching branch.

In 1945 there was as yet no career for the would-be law teacher in Canada, so that, as will be gathered when we return to the history of Dalhousie Law School, deans had a hard time finding teachers to deal with the flood of veterans and the unexpectedly large number of students who continued to come in when the veteran bulge was over. And even as late as 1961 Dean Curtis of the University of British Columbia Law School is reported as saying that 'the recruitment of men who will take up teaching as a career is ... in many ways the most difficult of the current problems of legal education in Canada.'[8] Nevertheless, the new third branch of the profession had by that time become solid enough to be conscious of its own identity. In 1951 some of the then handful of full-time law teachers had formally organized the Association of Canadian Law Teachers and by the beginning of the sixties the ACLT had progressed from discussing at its meetings mere 'deans' stuff' (such as library, course organization, and the like) to deliberating on fundamental problems of the law (along the line that would be the theme of the meeting in 1976, 'Public Law on Trial'), had appointed representatives to give papers at the conference of British, American, and Canadian law teachers in New York which we mentioned above, and had established a custom that the current president of its sister organization in the United States, the Association of American Law Schools, should be 'the distinguished visitor' at its annual meetings. The law teachers in Canada had begun to reach out, ending the isolation from one another – and, of course, from their opposite numbers in the United States – that had for so many years been their lot.[9]

To conclude this brief over-all picture of the changes in Canadian legal education in 1945-66, three further comments should be made – all of them as applicable to Dalhousie Law School as to the other schools. First, the law teachers as a whole had not yet made any notable contribution to legal writing and research nor had they participated much in active law reform; for even the beginnings of that we shall have to wait until the last decade covered by this book, 1966-76. Second, whatever may have been the influence of England in the past (and it was to England that the Benchers of the Law Society of Upper Canada had always looked), legal education in English-speaking Canada was increasingly being patterned after the American model – and especially the Harvard model, the reason for this being that up to 1965 or thereabouts more Canadian law teachers had done their post-graduate work at Harvard Law School than at any other institution. And third, as a result of the changes that have been sketched above, the schools were by 1966 no longer seriously undermanned or seriously weak in terms of material resources, such as library facilities; the picture had become one of more schools, bigger schools, and better schools, one or two of which would during the next ten years of government-funded growth dare to aspire to thinking of becoming almost as good – almost as good – as the great American ones.[10]

We come now a little closer to home, to Dalhousie University and the changes that came over it during this period. Some of these changes had no more than an indirect effect on the Dalhousie Law School. For example, the University grew slowly bigger: in the five years before the Second World War registration averaged around 850 students; by 1962-63 it had risen to around 2 500, but that was only a third of what it would be in 1976. And the money problems that had always afflicted it when it was still a miniscule operation (the annual operating budget in 1945-46 was less than $450 000) were continuing to afflict it in 1962-63 when that budget had swollen to $4 500 000 (or 'about as large as was that of the Government of Nova Scotia in 1930'); but by that time they were beginning to yield to the government aid which had started in a very modest way at the beginning of the fifties and was now in the process of becoming substantial – though a mere shadow of what it would be in 1976, with eighty per cent of operating costs being borne by the two governments, federal and provincial. As the retiring President, the Reverend A.E. Kerr, put it in his convocation address in 1963: 'Dean Read said to me recently, as we talked about the Dalhousie of tomorrow, "You and I were born too soon ... [but] ... like the saints in the Epistle to the Hebrews, we may not have entered into our promised inheritance, but we have seen it and greeted it from afar." '[11]

Some of the changes had a more direct effect on the Law School. One whose effect was beneficial to the School and was plain to the eye was the expansion of the Studley campus. In the early stages of that expansion there was built the overpoweringly large Arts and Administration Building and in

1952 the Arts Faculty was able to leave the nearby charming, Georgian-Colonial, stone Law Building that it had 'temporarily' occupied for thirty years and throw open *de facto* to the Law School what had always *de jure* been its own. By 1962-63 the campus had ceased to be what it still was at the end of the Second World War, a hayfield with a few gaunt stone buildings on it, surrounded by rough stone fences. As a result of the addition of several handsome new buildings in the traditional style, it was beginning to acquire shape and grace – shape and grace that was lost when the university population explosion of 1966-76 spawned on its outskirts a congeries of characterless structures, of which the Weldon Building is not the most graceless example!

Less obvious, but just as real, was – or was felt by some of the School's faculty to be – the dampening effect on the School of the University's expansion in academic affairs. During this period there came into being: a new Faculty of Health Professions, comprising the Medical School, a School of Pharmacy, a School of Nursing, and a School of Physiotherapy; a School of Dental Hygiene, operating under the Faculty of Dentistry; a Faculty of Graduate Studies; an Institute of Oceanography; and a reorganized and expanded Institute of Public Affairs which arranged special courses for leaders of labour, management, and government services. It was all very well for the Chairman of the Board to speak in the mid-fifties – as he is said to have spoken – of the Law School as 'the jewel in Dalhousie's crown'; the School was in the opinion of one of the members of the Law Faculty getting the junk jewellery treatment: 'I see this Faculty standing last in the current arrangements and plans for increasing the resources of the various Dalhousie Faculties by government grants. I do not think the Law Faculty here is being allotted a fair or proper share of the available central resources of Dalhousie University.'[12]

Another dampening factor on the progress of the Law School – and this at a time when, as we shall see, the School was receiving from outside benefactions enough money to pay the salaries of five professors and, as we have already seen, was facing competition for leadership from the new and vigorous schools in Ontario and British Columbia – was the penny-pinching attitude of the man who was from 1945 to 1963 the President of the University, Dr A.E. Kerr. Kerr was a clergyman (hence his nickname in university circles, 'the Little Minister') who for most of his working life had had to accustom himself to conserving the unexpandable resources of impecunious parishes; he was emphatically not the kind of man who should have headed up the University in an era that demanded expansion. An extract from his last convocation address, to which we referred earlier, will give the picture. 'Some said that we should go into debt without hesitation ... for the service rendered by the University was so indispensable that governments or the public would have to come to our rescue. Here let me say that they may have been right; but it was not for nothing that I was brought up to believe one should live within the income that one could reasonably expect.' Vincent MacDonald, who was a fighter, would probably have been able to resist such ukases as 'Trust you will suggest lowest reasonable salary' that appears in a telegram from Kerr to him when he was desperately trying to lure to the School one of the exceedingly scarce prospects for the job of law teacher; Horace Read was not. Read fell into line with Kerr, became obsessed with 'budget,' i.e., penny-pinching in the Law School, and would, according to a colleague, spend so much time on it at Faculty meetings that the downtown lecturers stopped coming to them.

Now that we have given a rough sketch of the changes that took place during this period in a lawyer's life, in the other Canadian law schools, and in the main University, we are ready to return, at last, to Dalhousie Law School. We shall for convenience divide its history in the years 1945-66 into three sub-periods:

Section One, 1945-50: Post-war revival
Section Two, 1950-58: Innovations
Section Three, 1958-66: On a new plateau.

There are two general comments that must be made by way of introduction to the chronological record of events – events that are, as usual, uneventful – during the period. The first comment is that there will be changes in each one of the five components that, taken together, determine the character of any law school. As to facilities, the School will for the first time acquire a building of its own. As to library, the collection of books will for the first time become a little better than just barely adequate, and for the first time since Bulmer had to be let go in 1884 a full-time librarian will be appointed to take charge of it. In the curriculum there will be the first significant change since the introduction of case method in 1921 – the beginning of a legal writing and research program, and of its concomitant, the 'do it yourself' method, which is so marked a feature of Dalhousie Law School today. But the most striking change – the change that will for ever take the long-standing 'Little' out of Dalhousie's Little Law School – will be a change in the size of the student body and in the size of the full-time faculty. Instead of the seventy-five students that had become normal in the thirties there will normally be a hundred and fifty of them. Instead of a 'recognized' full-time faculty of four there will be a 'recognized' full-time faculty of eight. And in the two or three years before the move to the Weldon Building in 1966 there will be signs of a population explosion to come in both students and full-time faculty.

The second comment is that because of this increase in mere size the period 1945-66 is the last one in which our story can even attempt to be individual and personal; from 1966 on it will of necessity be general and impersonal. The rough draft which Horace Read made of the history of this period, and the mass of material that he had collected to flesh it out, show that despite the increase in size of the School he was still able to think, and was still thinking, of both students and faculty as individuals. Even in the three formal reports to the President that he made during his time as Dean, he recounts at length the exploits of each individual full-time teacher and actually gives the names and destinations of those students who had brought honour to the School by winning post-graduate scholarships. But if he had in his draft written anything on the years following his retirement as Dean in 1964 – which he did not – he would, the writer is sure, have had to confine himself to the general and the impersonal.

SECTION ONE: 1945-1950

Post-war Revival

When term began in the fall of 1945, Vincent MacDonald, who had just himself and two 'new boys' left to cope with the largest first-year class in the School's history, was in a gloomy frame of mind and sounded a note that will be heard again and again during the period covered by this Part: 'we are in danger of falling behind other schools.' 'As I have pointed out previously,' he wrote to the Chairman of the Board, 'the departure in two successive years of Mr. Willis and Mr. Curtis – and the absence of a fourth man – have definitely impaired our teaching efficiency and our prestige in the public mind; and unfortunately at a time when Law Schools throughout Canada are improving and augmenting their staffs.'[13] He need not have worried so much. Nearly fifteen years later President Kerr would be able to counter a similar prophecy of doom by the following anecdote. 'When people speak to me in terms of discouragement because of the obstacles that be in our way, I invariably recall the fact that my first meeting on becoming President of Dalhousie [in 1945] was with the Dean of Law [MacDonald] who informed me that he was the only full-time member of the staff left (his second-in-command having just accepted the Deanship at the University of British Columbia), that we were facing both the enormous demands of the post-war period, the unprecedented challenge of other law schools and an appalling dearth of qualified law teachers in Canada. Actually we were on the threshold of one of the most significant and progressive periods of development in our Law School's history.'[14]

As it happened, the School was in that fall of 1945 actually right inside the door of what we can now discern as a second but smaller golden age – the four brief years from 1945 to 1949. In those four years seventy-five per cent of the two-hundred-odd student body were veterans just back from the war and there was a little four-man faculty, consisting of MacDonald, Moffatt Hancock, Jim Milner, and, beginning in 1946, Tom (T.G.) Feeney. (Young Feeney who graduated with the University Medal in May was persuaded by MacDonald to give up for the time being his plans to practise with his father and to try his hand in September at teaching returned men who were far older in years and experience than he was – an assignment he carried out with courage and aplomb.)

The reminiscences in the *Ansul* special issue of January 1976 give a vivid picture of what it was like to be at the School during 'the veteran bulge.' All we have space to do here is to give some of the prosaic facts, enliven them with a few quotations from *Ansul*, and urge the reader to read the reminiscences himself. But before we do that we must first insert one brief prosaic comment. The dramatic swelling of enrolment produced by the veteran bulge did not, as happened after the First World War, go down after the veterans were through to the same level that had theretofore been normal. This time the change in size proved to be permanent. The normal size of the School in the thirties was seventy-five; in the fifties it would be a hundred and fifty; and by 1966 it would, after a brief drop at the beginning of the sixties, be on a steeply rising curve that was about to break through the two hundred line. It is because of this change in size which began in 1945 and proved to be permanent – the most enduring, and endearing, element in Dalhousie's Little Law School was its size, how small it was! – that, out of a number of years we might have chosen, we chose 1945 as the year with which to begin the present Part, 'Changing.'

The veterans of the Second World War had the same drive and sense of purpose that their predecessors had in the years following the First World War; 'they wanted to be trained and well-trained and trained quickly. They wanted to catch up with the years they had lost while they were in the services.' They had one advantage that their predecessors did not – the government was subsidizing their education; that is why there were so many of them. But in some other respects they had a harder row to hoe.

Their working conditions were deplorable. No amount of rough and ready attempts to 'improve' the antiquated north wing of the Forrest Building – such as expanding the seating capacity of the library by constructing a mezzanine floor or 'poop deck' in it and taking over as an extra classroom what had in 1887 been the main assembly room for the whole young University (the Munro Room) – could alter the fact that there were two hundred students crammed into quarters that were in the early thirties pronounced by Sidney Smith to be adequate for the seventy-five to which he was at that time hoping to be able to expand. And what was in many cases the cruel kindness of DVA (the educational grants administered by the Department of Veterans Affairs) had tempted into the School many who had little chance of ever getting through. The 'wastage' was terrific; of those who entered the School in these post-war years only a few more than half made it to graduation. For, apart from a slightly reduced admission standard and a slightly shortened articling period, no special concessions were made to men, who, because of their age (many of them were in their late twenties) and the time they had spent away from book learning, were far less able to cope with the rigours of law school than the usual members of a first-year class.

On the contrary: the course the veterans took was tighter and more onerous than it had ever been before; beginning in 1945 any student whose general average in any year was less than 55 per cent was required to repeat that year; and during the next few years the curriculum was expanded to include Accounting, Labour Law, and Income Tax. They were, furthermore, not spared in their first few days at the School the warning that it had by then become customary to give to all first-year classes. 'The practice then was to let in all comers and slash for quality at the end of the first year. The Dean explained the situation in a matter-of-fact way: it was the best school in the country; we all had a responsibility to maintain its traditions; he wasn't going to preside over its decline. Tom Feeney came on belligerently with the news that half of us would not make it to second year – he was just about right – and the great Moffatt Hancock struck an imperial pose and bellowed that heads would roll.' Nor was there accorded to these hard-pressed veterans in classroom discussion 'the respect for his human dignity' which every student will in 1976 be claiming as his right; the treatment they got was the same as that which was from the twenties on customarily given to any student who came to class without having read the cases. 'The fate of the unprepared was not pleasant to behold. Some of us did not favour the rather searching cross-examination which our fellows encountered from time to time.' But it should be added, 'though demanding, the professors were eager to help; they maintained an ever-open door policy which made it easy to discuss whatever questions we chose.'

The general run of the veterans in all universities and in all courses everywhere were a delight to know and a delight to teach. The writer will always remember what fun he had wrangling about basic problems in the then new and mysterious subject of Income Tax with a third-year class of Osgoode Hall students that ran the whole gamut from ex-buck privates to ex-captains of corvettes; compared with the veterans, his later students have always seemed like children, sometimes spoiled children. It was like that at Dalhousie Law School too. 'They were very eager and determined students and that made the Law School an exciting place to be ... they were older men and they were not timid in speaking up, or very few were; and some of them came to class, you might almost say, spoiling for a fight. They loved to argue and debate in the traditional law school manner.' That was Professor Moffatt Hancock speaking. And here is what a member of the class of 1947 has to say about his ex-servicemen classmates: 'at least half of the class would have been outstanding in any year and, I think, the same could have been said of the three succeeding years.' But the energy and drive of these people was not confined to things academic. They brought once more into active operation three traditional Law School institutions which had by the last days of the war ceased to function – the Moot Court, the Mock Parliament, and the Law Ball. In the wider world of the main University they made their mark in the Students' Council, in inter-faculty sports, and in the Glee Club. In the still wider world outside Dalhousie University, they were, as will appear from Appendix V, 'How the Dalhousie LLB degree became "portable,"' the spearhead in an attempt (which was unsuccessful) to break down the tariff barriers which some of the provinces, notably Ontario, had erected against outside lawyers.

On the other side of the desk to this array of challenging veterans was what Moffatt Hancock modestly calls 'a small but competent faculty' – Vincent MacDonald, Moff Hancock, Jim Milner, and Tom Feeney. MacDonald was, of course, a long-term pro., but what, these veterans must have asked, were the rest of them? It was at that time all in the future that Hancock would end up as Marion Rice Kirkwood Professor of Law at prestigious Stanford and an internationally recognized authority on the Conflict of Laws; that Milner would, before he died prematurely in 1969, become at the University of Toronto the quiet, searching kind of law teacher that all really bright students instantly recognize as the best of the lot and make himself well known in Canada as an expert in Planning Law; and that Feeney would, after some years in practice, become dean of the Common Law Section at the University of Ottawa Law School. But, as can be seen from the reminiscences covering this brief mini-Golden-Age, the students did not fail to recognize the worth of what they had got.

Here are some student appraisals of them individually. 'MacDonald was a constitutional lawyer of stature ... I recently found that the Dean's notes on the federal commerce power are surprisingly topical' and, as a lecturer, he would 'unroll one of his prepared summation pieces. And how those summation pieces would unroll. It was wondrously crafted stuff and he must have fashioned it with great care and erudition.' Feeney, just out of law school, 'whose memory was phenomenal,' 'taught his courses with clarity and exceptional command of his material.' Milner was 'a quiet man who had a keen interest in the evolving nature of law' and 'lived in a world of balanced probabilities ... Our first lecture opened with the word "Suppose," after which my notes recorded seventeen consecutive questions on which I waited in vain for answers. His mission was to make us think.'

'The first three were certainly extraordinary, but Moffatt Hancock was an unforgettable experience. Brilliant, eccentric, theatrical – none of the labels do him justice. It wasn't simply that he dramatized lectures in Property I – think of it, Property I! – it was the way he visualized and animated the subject ... You never knew what to expect except that from each dazzling hour would come some vivid and unforgettable impression.'

Here are the verdicts given on this little faculty group as a whole by two students who are now at the top of the profession. 'The faculty was small in numbers ... The teaching load was unheard of by modern standards. ... However, what the faculty lacked in numbers it certainly made up in quality. It included some of the finest legal minds I have ever met.' And 'the quality of all these men was exceedingly high. They were stars in their league; and, because each of us was exposed to all of them, and only to them, by today's standards their influence as law teachers on their students was inordinate. Even today, in retrospect, their image appears to have been larger than life.'

In preparation for the beginning of term in the fall of 1949 MacDonald added to the faculty yet another potential star – W.R. Lederman. But by early summer that year both Hancock and Milner had gone, Hancock to the University of Southern California because Dalhousie could not (or Kerr would not) pay him the salary he was worth, and Milner to Harvard to do his LLM because Kerr refused to give him a permanent appointment, the reason being that he had no Arts degree; MacDonald had, of course, wanted to keep both

of them. In this unhappy way ended the brief but memorable interlude that
we have just described.

Bill Lederman was a find. When he came to the School he was already on
the way to becoming a real professional: a graduate of the Saskatchewan Law
School and well trained in both law and political science, he had served overseas as an officer in the army, had been to Oxford as a Rhodes Scholar, while
there had won the coveted Vinerian Scholarship, and had for two short
periods taught both political science and law at Saskatchewan. For the next
few years he will be the scholar on the faculty – publishing, among other
things, two long, deeply founded, and imaginative articles (on classification in
the conflict of laws and on the independence of the judiciary);[15] he stayed at
the School until he became in 1958 the first dean of the new law school at
Queen's. He did not, by the way, come to the School by accident; he came via
'the Dalhousie family,' though not 'the Dalhousie Law School family,' network; it was R. MacGregor Dawson, a devoted Dalhousian and Lederman's
political science teacher at Saskatchewan, who suggested Lederman's name to
Vincent MacDonald and urged Lederman himself to give Dalhousie Law
School a trial.

To fill the gaps left by the departure of Hancock and Milner, MacDonald
was forced, in a shortage of law teachers more acute than it has ever been
since, to look for replacements among the School's own recent graduates. He
secured two promising juniors, one of them being Jim (J.M.) Hendry ('47).
Hendry was a Halifax boy who had been an officer in the navy during the
war, had already got his LLM at Harvard, and was studying at Michigan for his
SJD. He had the same instinct for scholarship that Lederman had and during
his eight-year stay at the School – he went to Ottawa, and eventually the
federal civil service, in 1957 – published a book and a prize-winning article.[16]
The other junior turned out to be just 'passing through'; he only stayed one
year and does not call for any mention.

These staff problems of the year 1949 – they turned out to be the last that
MacDonald would have to deal with – call for three brief comments. The first
is that one of the most enduring characteristics of Dalhousie's Little Law
School was that its faculty fell apart from time to time. The reader may
perhaps recall the trouble that Weldon ran into with the only staff he
had – his downtowners, especially at the beginning of the nineties – and he
will certainly recall 1934 when out of a faculty of four the two linch-pins,
Sidney Smith and Horace Read, both left, and 1945 when the Dean himself,

the unfortunate Vincent MacDonald, was the sole remaining survivor. Something of the same sort happens again to the unfortunate Horace Read when he comes as Dean in 1950. How fragile was the base upon which Dalhousie's Little Law School's 'solid reputation' rested!

The second comment is that even in the more settled days of 1950 to 1976 there continued to be, as happened with MacDonald's unnamed junior of 1949, a constant going and coming among the juniors. This constant going and coming is particularly marked in the period covered by this Part. Of a total of twenty-four full-time teachers who joined the staff between 1945 and 1966, six stayed only two years or less and six stayed more than two but less than five years; they were, as someone has said, 'in and out like flies.' The result was, of course, that the teachers who stayed found themselves constantly called upon to take on the courses of those who left and were so occupied in getting them up that they found no time to write – and write they did not.

The third comment is that the shortage of available law teachers throughout the whole of the same period made absolutely inevitable the recourse to 'old boys' – out of the twenty-four newcomers all except seven were old boys and of those seven 'outsiders' only two (Lederman, 1949-58, and Nicholls, 1957-77) stayed more than five years – and almost inevitable an intellectual atmosphere which was less stimulating than it would be in the seventies when the faculty was predominantly composed of people coming from every direction except Dal.

We have now arrived at what was, from the point of view of the School's future, by far the most important event in this post-war period – the coming of what may be called 'the Angus L. money' and of what may be called 'the Dunn money.' Without more money, especially for salaries, the School, with its authorized roster of no more than four full-time teachers, could not hope to keep up with the two Canadian schools which were making the running at this time – the University of British Columbia (seven in 1950) and the University of Toronto (eight in 1950). From these two sources, the government of Nova Scotia, of which Angus L. Macdonald was premier, and the Algoma Steel Corporation, of which Sir James Dunn was president and controlling shareholder, there came, as a result of negotiations by Dean Vincent MacDonald (with some finishing touches added by his successor, Dean Horace Read), enough, and more than enough, money to pay the salaries of three more teachers. In dollar terms there came from them a combined annual revenue of some twenty to twenty-five thousand dollars. To those whose eyes have become accustomed to the one and a half million dollar budgets of the seventies, this amount seems trifling, but it was a veritable lifeline to the School in the realities of 1950 when its budget was sixty thousand dollars, or of 1956 when it was one hundred thousand, or even as late as 1961 when it was two hundred thousand. What, be it noted, produced these benefactions was the affection felt for the School by the two old boys who provided them.

Angus L. Macdonald ('21) was, as the reader already knows, one of the 'names-to-be' intimately connected with Dalhousie's Little Law School in its golden age. A member of one of those remarkable post-war classes of veterans, he also taught there for six years before he left to go into politics. He was a friend of Vincent MacDonald and, while teaching at the School, had shared an office with Horace Read. The reader may perhaps recall that in 1885 the infant Law School asked the government of Nova Scotia for aid but was turned down and must now be told that at the time we are now writing about that government was still not giving one penny piece to Dalhousie University – with one exception, a small annual grant for the schools of Medicine and Dentistry. In 1948, as a result of discussions with Kerr and Vincent MacDonald, Premier Angus L. Macdonald expressed his willingness to arrange for an annual grant from the province to pay the salary of an *additional* full-time professor – additional, that is, to the four (including the Weldon and Bennett chairs) that the University was under a moral obligation to maintain. It was this new Province of Nova Scotia chair in Law that enabled Vincent to add the fifth man, Lederman, to the staff in 1949 as the first Province of Nova Scotia Professor of Law. Three years later the provincial grant was increased so as to render possible the addition of another junior teacher. Skipping the tiresome details, the upshot was that from 1949 on the province was giving to the Law School an annual amount that rose gradually from $10000 in 1949 to $20000 in the early sixties – not all of which, by the way, was expended, or meant to be expended, on the two teachers. Some of it, again skipping the tiresome details, was earmarked to establish and maintain in the library the Nova Scotia Collection on Public Law; the Premier was, as one would expect, himself interested in public law, wanted to foster the study of it at the School, and took a personal interest in the kind of books selected.

What inspired Sir James Dunn ('98) to procure the gift to the Law School from his corporation was what had a few years earlier inspired his fellow benefactor R.B. Bennett – his admiration for Weldon and his gratitude to

Weldon for having given him, as he saw it, his start in life. When he came to the School in 1895 he was a penniless young man from the North Shore of New Brunswick who had to put himself through by doing menial jobs, such as working as a deck hand on a Halifax tugboat and for the Halifax Electric Tramway Company. He proved to be an able student and, as the *Gazettes* of his day show, a fiery debater both in and out of class. To help him out Weldon gave him one of the student librarian jobs at $50 a year and at the end of his second year gave him a letter of recommendation which he treasured for the rest of his life; it is now in the archives of the library. By the end of the Second World War he was a multi-millionaire with two brilliantly successful careers behind him, the first in the field of finance as an investment banker in England and the second in Canada as an industrialist, at the head of Algoma Steel Corporation, a vast project of industrial development in the Lake Superior region.[17]

The immediate cause of the coming of the Dunn money to the School was the Dalhousie Law School family network. Dunn's executive vice-president at Algoma Steel was J. Gordon Fogo ('24), classmate and friend of Horace Read, and during the war Dunn himself had from time to time run into Angus L. Macdonald, then on his wartime stint of Navy Minister, and Vincent MacDonald, then on his wartime assignment as Assistant Deputy Minister of Labour, in Ottawa and had on each occasion mentioned his debt of gratitude to Weldon and Dalhousie. Sparked by Dalhousie's 1947 campaign for funds, Fogo, C.J. Burchell, and Vincent MacDonald (plus, of course, President Kerr) together took steps to interest Dunn in doing something for the Law School, their line being that, to counter the threat of competition coming from other schools, someone should do something 'to maintain the prestige' of the School. To their aid came also Angus L. Macdonald who – perhaps unfortunately – succeeded in converting Dunn to his own personal belief that a young Canadian should not have to go outside his own country to do post-graduate work in law but should be able to do it at Dalhousie. As a result of their efforts Dunn, who always gave generously to worthy causes and had in the past contributed to Dalhousie campaigns, arranged a gift from Algoma Steel to the University of $50 000, 'the income from which is to be used to meet the needs of the Faculty of Law and particularly to facilitate the undertaking of graduate instruction in that Faculty,' and also arranged for Algoma Steel to contribute to the University $10 000 a year for twenty-five years beginning in 1950, such sum 'to be fully expendable each year for the support of an additional professorship in law and for otherwise furthering the teaching and research programme of that Faculty.' This Dunn money gave to the School yet another full professor – who was to be known as the Sir James Dunn, Bart. Professor of Law – and an annual income of more than $12 000 which could be used in part for paying the salary of the new professor at the then current rate of around $5 000 and the rest in paying for such luxuries as adding to the library materials not provided for in the ordinary budget or financing the production of casebooks. There was however a sting in its tail; the School would have to start a graduate course – of which more later.[18]

Another, and rather different, manifestation of the Dalhousie Law School family network which occurred around this time deserves at least a brief mention. In the fall of 1948 Vincent MacDonald was retained as constitutional adviser to the Newfoundland delegation on union with Canada. Three out of the seven members of that delegation were graduates of Dalhousie Law School: A.J. Walsh ('28), later Chief Justice; F. Gordon Bradley ('14), later the first Newfoundlander to become a member of the Canadian cabinet; and J.B. McEvoy, the winner of the University Medal in 1935. On hand to meet the delegation when it arrived in Ottawa to sign the terms of union was C.J. Burchell ('99), the Canadian High Commissioner to Newfoundland.[19]

In February 1950 MacDonald was elevated to the Bench of the Supreme Court of Nova Scotia – the first Canadian law teacher ever to be made a Judge – but, with the co-operation of his judicial colleagues, he stayed with his Law School job until the end of the academic year. Of all the deans of Dalhousie Law School he had had the most demanding and the most thankless task, coping with the frustrations of the Great Depression and the Second World War and devising the scrambling improvisations that were necessary to meet the post-war veteran bulge. He did, however, have the satisfaction of seeing accomplished at the end of his time as Dean what were probably the most important of all the changes that came over the School in the period 1945-66: an increased and reasonably stable enrolment of students; and the reasonable measure of financial security provided by the Bennett money, the Angus L. money, and the Dunn money. Like his predecessor Sidney Smith, he never ceased to miss the School. Asked on one occasion by an ex-fellow-student of the twenties how he liked being a Judge, he replied: 'It's a lonely job. When I was Dean of the Law School, the boys would drop into the office after classes for a chat. There was always company. I was very happy there. But now there's always a barrier.'[20] He was, nevertheless, as successful at turning himself from a dean into a judge after 1950 as he had been in turning himself from 'practical man' into teacher and scholar after he went into academic life in 1930, so that when he died in 1964 Chief Justice Ilsley called him 'the most distinguished member of this Court.'[21]

SECTION TWO: 1950-1958

Innovations

The years 1950 to 1958 were years of innovation – nothing startling or dramatic, but innovation nonetheless. The changes came in two waves some years apart. The first wave began in 1950 with the coming of Horace Read as the new Dean; by the time it ended in 1957 or thereabouts (these time divisions are of necessity somewhat vague and artificial) the full-time faculty had increased to seven, the downtowners were receding into the background, and there had been significant changes in the academic offerings and in the curriculum; the most important 'event' in the period was the move from the Forrest Building to Studley in 1952.

The second wave came in the years 1957 and 1958; in 1957 the School's LLB degree became for the first time fully 'portable,' i.e., became recognized by all the common-law provinces as fulfilling all the academic requirements for admission to their bars; in that year too Professor George Nicholls, a newcomer from outside, set in motion a chain of events that resulted in a significant change in methods of teaching and in the library; and in 1958 at the ceremonies celebrating the School's seventy-fifth birthday the President announced yet another Dunn benefaction, money to support a librarian and a library staff (a 'first') and money for scholarships to be awarded to outstanding students for the study of law at Dalhousie (another 'first').[22] The effect of all these innovations – together with others that are not tangible enough to be included in this brief catalogue – was to raise the School to a new plateau.

The new Dean, Horace Read, was in himself an innovation, something new, at Dalhousie Law School. No newcomer of course – he had been both student and teacher there in the Golden Age – he was the first dean who could claim to be a 'professional' law teacher. All his predecessors were, in a greater or lesser degree, no more than hastily got up as law teachers when they became dean. He was already a pro. With two solid and imaginative books to his credit and with sixteen years of teaching at the high-ranking Minnesota Law School behind him, Dalhousie was lucky to get him; other Canadian schools had been angling for him, but had all been turned down.

The manner of Read's coming and his approach to the School when he came were both in the true Dalhousie Law School tradition. He was getting between ten and eleven thousand at Minnesota, but all that Kerr and the Board were prepared to offer was seven thousand, a figure well below that which the other comparable schools in Canada were paying their deans; so to make up the difference, that family stand-by, Premier Angus L. Macdonald, arranged for him to be appointed chairman of the Nova Scotia Labour Relations Board in succession to Dean Vincent MacDonald, now Mr Justice MacDonald. And he brought with him an affection and devotion to the School that was even more intense than was that of his two immediate predecessors and one-time colleagues, Vincent MacDonald and Sidney Smith. As a mere glance at the reports he made to the President during his deanship will show, the School was for him always bathed in a rainbow. In 1959, for example, he describes a little group of full-time teachers who were no more than O.K. by not very exacting Canadian standards as 'comprising teachers and scholars of national and international stature and some of the ablest of our recent graduates.' And the fact that in 1962-63 (called 'a typical year') there were among the 111 students more than the usual number from outside the Atlantic region calls forth from him the comment that 'It is clear that despite Dalhousie's high admission standards and the added costs of attending a school far from home, most of the students from outside Nova Scotia are attracted largely by the reputation which the School has established, and deserves, for high quality of professional education.'[23]

Also true to the darker side of the Dalhousie Law School tradition were the staff problems that met him when he arrived. The men he thought he had were: inherited from MacDonald, Lederman ('Oxford'), Hendry ('Harvard and Michigan'), and the unnamed old boy who had joined the faculty in 1949 ('London'); and an old Minnesota student of his own ('Minnesota') whom he had succeeded in luring to Nova Scotia as a replacement for Feeney who had resigned to go into practice. In rainbow mood he had written to President Kerr: 'With the influence of Oxford, Harvard, Michigan, London, and Minnesota ideas brought in contact with those of Dalhousie, we should have a stimulating and creative atmosphere; no danger of intellectual sterility through inbreeding.' Alas for the reality!

A few weeks before term began in the fall of 1950 'London' left ('I hear,' Read wrote to a friend, 'that ... said that my remark to him that a full-time law teacher should put in a minimum eight hour day at the law school influenced him to accept the ... offer, that if he was going to have to work that hard he might as well get more pay') and at the end of October 'Minnesota' had run into a drinking problem so severe that he had to be shipped home. Despite the assurance from the Angus L. money and the Dunn money that the faculty could soon be expanded to seven, there were now as a matter of hard fact just three, Read, Lederman, and Hendry. Inbreeding or no inbreeding, Read was forced, in order at that late date to fill 'London's' place, to look for an old boy; as for 'Minnesota's' classes two unselfish members of the Halifax Bar came, as usual, to the rescue and took them over. As it turned out Read was lucky in the old boy he found – R. Graham Murray ('40). Murray was by family tradition – it was his father, Judge R.H. Murray ('96), who founded the short-lived Dalhousie Law Association in 1922 – as devoted to the Law School as Read was, and was, after doing an LLM at Harvard and serving with the air force, practising law in Halifax, both privately and as solicitor for Halifax County. He proved to be a 'natural' for law teaching and in 1976 was still at the School, the most long-standing of 'the Old Guard.'

We will not bore the reader with all the details of the comings and goings of the full-time staff – let alone the downtowners – during the next few years. The problems were never again so severe as they were in the fall of 1950 but they continued to be considerable. Read was, for example, minded to fill the new and well-financed Sir James Dunn chair with a 'name' but, after corresponding with a 'name' he knew in Australia, seeking the advice of the dean at Harvard, and surveying the field in Canada, he had, in 1952, to settle for Lederman – who was then, of course, just a promising, though a very promising, young fellow. But the real loss caused by the constant comings and goings was the constant re-assignment of courses among the members of the little staff; in Lederman's nine years at the School, for example, he taught some ten different courses in various combinations of three or four a year, ranging over both private and public law. This may, as Lederman has said, have saved him from premature specialization in his early years of teaching but it was pretty hard on those who had less stamina than he had – and very hard on their students.

Notwithstanding these set-backs the full-time faculty slowly grew in numbers until by the fall of 1955 there were seven of them. Among them there were, in addition to Read, Lederman, Hendry, and Murray, one who stayed with the School long enough to make a contribution, Lorne Clarke ('51), and one who by 1976 would be the second most long-standing of the Old Guard, though by then on a part-time basis – Arthur Meagher ('36). Lorne Clarke came in 1952 and stayed until 1959 when he went into practice; while he was at the School he rescued the Mock Parliament from one of its recurrent bouts of being just a bear garden and after he left he continued for many years to act as its Speaker and keep it meaningful. Meagher was, also in 1952, induced to come to the School after sixteen years in practice, most of them with a good firm in Halifax; it was just because he had been in practice that Read wanted him; his main job was to revitalize the courses on Procedure. So that by 1955 Read had succeeded in gathering together a full-time faculty that had at least some teaching experience and that had in it the beginnings of a 'core.' It was not, however, as diversified as he had in 1950 hoped to be able to make it; they were all, except Lederman, old boys.

At this point we will break off for a moment to answer some present-day law teacher who is bound to object: 'Read did this, Read did that; 'I'm sick of all this talk about the Dean; was the Dean the only man on the faculty?' Yes, in those days, as little as only twenty years ago, he was still, effectively, just that. He still had from time to time to bear the whole weight of the School on his own shoulders. Read was the last dean who had to do it; but he did have to do it.

The years 1955 to 1959, the years when the full-time faculty was first seven and then eight, saw the end of the School's traditional dependence on the downtowners. In some ways this was 'a good thing.' Not all the downtowners were up to snuff – they never had been; and as the law grew increasingly more complex none of them had time enough for the preparation that they would have to do to make their lectures – and lectures it had to be – coherent to their students. In other ways it was 'a bad thing.' The downtowner brings to the classroom a sense of reality that no full-time academic, however uncloistered, can; and, that apart, who with any sense of the past can fail to regret the passing of those who in the beginning created the School and were for so long essential to its continued existence?

Sticking to just the bare facts – and forgetting the rumour that, whatever he said publicly, Read was, as nearly all American law teachers are, privately in favour of leaving law teaching to the law teachers – the following 'practical subjects' were transferred from the practitioners to the academics. Meagher had already in 1952 taken over from the downtowners what had, with the exception of the John Read interlude in the Golden Age, always been an exclusively downtown subject, Procedure. In the years 1955-59 there were the following take-overs. Murray took over from Mr Justice MacQuarrie the subject which ever since the early thirties had been regarded as the preserve of a Supreme Court Judge, Evidence. Edwards, to bring in a man who has not yet made his appearance, took over Criminal Law, a course which, although shuttled back and forth between full-timers and part-timers, had up to then always been regarded, and treated, as a nuts-and-bolts course that should be given by a hard-nosed practitioner and not by an academic; the academic might be tempted to stray from strict law into such 'irrelevant' things as history, philosophy, medicine, penology, civil liberties, and so on. And Harris, another man who has not yet come on to the stage, took over from an oft-changing series of practitioners the subject of Taxation, a subject that was in England until very recently excluded from the curriculum of all university law schools on the ground that it was 'too practical.' There will hereafter still be some downtowners teaching at the School but with the growth of the full-time staff they have ceased to be essential.

We have now finished dealing with what Read did, in this first wave of innovations, in the exercise of what is always the most crucial of a dean's functions, getting and keeping teachers. But before going on to some significant changes in academic offerings and curriculum for which he was directly or indirectly responsible we will merely mention three products of a new mood of 'reaching out' which seems to have come over the School at this time – presaging the extensive reaching out which will appear in the seventies. In the 'helping myself' aspect of reaching out were the more or less annual trips by Read and Lederman to the meetings of the new Association of Canadian Law Teachers – the beginning of the end of the isolation which had plagued all Canadian law teachers, and especially those at Dalhousie, for so long. And in 1952 Read began the practice of bringing to the School, for such stimulation as the students might be able to get from a one- or two-day visit, at least one or two authoritative visiting lecturers a year; a list of those who came from 1952 to 1963 will be found in Read's reports to the President.[24] There was not, of course, anything particularly new about the idea – the short-lived series of triangular exchange lectures between Osgoode, McGill, and Dalhousie in the early thirties was an earlier manifestation of it – and the visiting lecturers were certainly not as numerous or as contemporary as those which the students themselves bring to their weekly 'Law Hour' in the seventies; but they were a beginning and a much-needed beginning. In the 'helping others' aspect of reaching out was the inauguration at the School in 1954 of a two-day refresher course for practising lawyers in co-operation with the Nova Scotia Barristers' Society and the Nova Scotia branch of the Canadian Bar Association; it has convened there annually ever since. Although members of faculty have from time to time given papers at these sessions, the School has not normally done any more than lend its building. Once again, however, this small beginning does to some extent foreshadow the conferences which the Public Services Committee of the Faculty puts on in the seventies.

The most startling, but, as things turned out, the least important of the innovations made in the School's academic offerings during the Horace Read wave was the beginning of graduate work in 1950. It certainly startled, and amused, the members of the staff at the new and not yet fully recognized University of Toronto Law School which was reluctantly carrying on the graduate course – the only graduate course in common-law Canada – that it had a year earlier inherited from its predecessor, that university's non-professional School of Law; the writer was there at the time and well remembers how amused we all were. And Read himself was both startled and dismayed when, a month after he had been appointed Dean and was still at Minnesota, he learned that he was going to have to start a graduate course at Dalhousie. He had to because, as he later found out, some of the Angus L. money and all of the Dunn money (the major part of which was then still only in the offing) would not be forthcoming unless he did so. 'The general understanding between us,' wrote Dunn in a letter to him, 'is that the Chair in question [the Sir James Dunn, Bart. Chair in Law which would be bringing in $10 000 a year] embraces legal subjects aimed at making Dalhousie Law School a postgraduate institution.'

The pipe-dream, which, as we noted a few pages ago, came from Angus L., was that: Canadians ought not to have to go, as he and others had done, to the United States, or sometimes England, to do their graduate work in law; to start a post-graduate course at Dalhousie Law School would lend added prestige to the School; and the course would attract graduates from other Canadian schools. But the unfortunate Read was fully conversant with the realities, which were as follows. While he would, when all of the Angus L. and Dunn money became available in a year or two, have seven men, he now had only five, all of them juniors except himself (as a matter of fact, as we already know, he would actually lose two of them, add another, and end up with only four). The library was, if more or less adequate for undergraduate work, wholly inadequate for graduate work. And graduates from other Canadian schools would continue to go as they had always gone, to the United States, usually Harvard, where they could get substantial scholarships, an LLM degree that was everywhere in Canada regarded as 'the union card' for all intending law teachers, and in addition to all that a change of scene. Nevertheless, 'since further delay in entering the field appears unwise,' he wrote to Fogo, Dunn's executive vice-president, just two weeks before the beginning of his first teaching term in his new job, 'to avoid any other School pre-empting it we are going to offer graduate work this fall leading to the degree of Master of Laws.' Read had to do what he did, and if the writer and his colleagues had known in 1950 what the writer now knows they might still have laughed; for Read himself they would have had nothing but sympathy.

Before term began he had improvised what was going to be the new graduate program. It was based upon what were then the requirements for the LLM degree at Harvard – course work in three courses, plus a mini-thesis; for that was the course he himself knew most about. One course, Jurisprudence, was compulsory for all candidates; at this time 'Dalhousie was the only law school in Canada offering Jurisprudence' and it was hoped 'that most of the candidates might come from other law schools in Canada.' The other two courses were to be chosen from a list of subjects, which were all in the field of Public Law; one of the reasons for that was Angus L.'s own often-expressed interest in Public Law studies; another was that that field had 'gained greatly in importance in recent years owing to the increased concern of government with the economic affairs of the community.'[25] In other words, not only the establishment of the course but also its content were very much the product of the exigencies of the time. The details of that content – who taught the various subjects, who the candidates were, and what they wrote their thesis on – are all recorded in the three reports that Read made to the President in the period 1950-63; so also is the fact that in 1961 post-graduate work was suspended pending revision of the requirements, of which more later. All that need be said here is that, as Read had known would be the case, this post-graduate course did not attract many students: only seventeen in all during the eleven years it was in operation and of those seventeen all except three were the School's own graduates and of those three only one was from another Canadian law school. Those who did take the course did, no doubt, get something out of it, but the objectives that Angus L. and Dunn had in mind when they forced it on Read – attention-getting for Dalhousie Law School and providing for Canadian law students a Canadian graduate school – were not realized.

Another new venture, this time an imaginative and seemingly feasible one designed by Read himself with the co-operation, once again, of the Premier, was also begun in 1950, the Nova Scotia Legislative Research Centre. It was far in advance of its time, foreshadowing as it did in the field of government that now familiar institution, the law reform commission (there was at that date not a single one in Canada), and in the field of law school curriculum the now equally familiar 'learn by doing and help somebody else at the same time' kind of learning experience, such as Student Legal Aid courses (the Canadian law school curriculums of that date had not progressed beyond the occasional seminar). It too was destined never really to get off the ground.

While he was at Minnesota, Read had added to his classroom course in Legislation what he called 'laboratory work.' The classroom course itself de-emphasized that standard fare of all law schools everywhere, how the judges set about interpreting statutes, and emphasized the process of legislation it-self: what, step by step, someone, many 'someones,' has to do before a bill is ready to be put before the legislature. In order to render that part of his course meaningful, he put his class to work doing the necessary research and drafting on actual measures that actual groups and organizations wished to present to the Minnesota legislature – a device that proved to be so much in demand by 'customers' and so stimulating to his students that the laboratory was just about to become an institute with himself as director when he was appointed Dean at Dalhousie. With the endorsement of Premier Angus L. Macdonald the Minnesota institute-to-be became transformed in 1950 into the Nova Scotia Legislative Research Centre with Read as Director and Henry Muggah ('34), Legislative Counsel of Nova Scotia, as Associate Director.

Read's hope was that this modest experiment in both legal education (giv-ing his Dalhousie students some experience in using methods of research and drafting essential for effective legislation) and public service would relieve the civil servants of some of the research work that they have to do in prepar-ing their bills and would perhaps grow into an embryonic law reform commission, keeping the laws of Nova Scotia under continuous, objective, and politically disinterested study with the aim of discovering how to develop them best to fit the needs of the province. But by the time he came to write his 1955-59 report to the President he had become reconciled to viewing the work done by the students in the so-called Centre as no more than a valuable supplement to the classroom work of his course in Legislation. The students had done much of the purely scissors-and-paste work involved in producing the *Revised Statutes, 1954* and some of the groundwork for a few reform measures but that was all. Read had failed to realize that the government-sponsored measures on which his Dalhousie students would be working would normally be more complex and more of a rush job than the privately sponsored ones with which his Minnesota students had been so successful. What happened in Nova Scotia was that the needs of the civil servants did not usually mesh with the students' available time and capability, with the result that the Centre did not get many suitable projects to work on. Even as a purely educational device the Centre ran into problems: sometimes there were not enough projects; at other times the students were not sufficiently devoted to do the necessary 'bull work,' particularly the leg work involved in finding out how the present law was actually operating; and Read himself found that with his growing outside commitments he did not have the time to give them the day-by-day advice and supervision that all students in 'do it yourself' courses must have if they are to learn anything. By the early sixties the Centre had petered out into the name of the room in the Studley Building where the students worked on projects which the teacher in charge of the Legislation course had himself selected and himself regarded as no more than some practical work in legislation that would help them to understand the theory of the legislative process and statutory interpretation. Under less unfavourable circumstances Read's imaginative experiment might have developed into something worthwhile, but in point of fact it did not.

A few other innovations in the curriculum remain to be noticed. In 1950 Weldon's own broadly humane subject of International Law was revived after being in abeyance for ten years, the reason being that Hendry, who was doing his graduate work in it, was available to teach it. And in the same year Lederman, who had been trained by his political science teacher at Saskatchewan, by his dean at the Law School there (a Harvard man), and by his Oxford experience to take the broadly humane approach to law, introduced into the curriculum, for the first time ever at Dalhousie Law School, the subject of

Jurisprudence. That was not, as he himself has said, because he was qualified to teach it but because he thought – as John Read had thought twenty-five years earlier – that the students ought to be getting it from someone. Two comments. First: with Read's Legislation, Hendry's International Law, and Lederman's Jurisprudence, humane cracks are beginning to appear in the strictly professional MacRae curriculum that had governed the School for the last thirty years. There will be more of them in the next few years, e.g. Murray's Community Planning in 1956 and Edwards' Criminology in 1958. Second comment: how largely, in a School with a faculty as small as Dalhousie's then was, the shape of the curriculum had to depend on the special interests of the individual teachers who are at any given time on the full-time staff.

Yet another innovation was in the direction of making 'relevant,' intelligible, and coherent the nuts-and-bolts subject of Procedure. Breaking with an old tradition which had, save for the short and memorable John Read interlude, existed since the course was first established in the nineties – the tradition that it was a downtowner who gave the course and that what he did was merely lecture on the Rules of Practice, with cases – Arthur Meagher, a full-time teacher taken from active practice, in 1952 started a new one, covering the Rules by making the students solve problems, procedural problems, themselves. Put in a nutshell, what he did, and would still be doing in 1976, was to get each student to prepare in writing the forms required for carrying through the most commonly recurring kinds of court proceedings (e.g. debt collection, motor vehicle collision cases), thereafter discussing the problem assigned in class and correcting the answer the student had given. Comment: the laboratory work in Read's Legislation and the preparation of forms in Meagher's Procedure were the beginnings of the so-called problem or 'do it yourself' method which will in 1976 play so large a part in the work of the School.

The sharpest break with the past in the whole of the twenty-year period 1945-66 that we have called 'Changing' came with the School's departure from the north wing of the Forrest Building which had been its home for sixty-five years. In 1952 it moved to the Studley campus and into the Law Building, the first home of its own that it had ever had. The move came thirty years later than had originally been planned. The building, completed in 1922, had been built to house the Law School but, because of the financial difficulties of that time, had been lent to the Arts Faculty for temporary occupation, which became so permanent that everyone called it the Arts Building. The School's new home was an improvement on the cramped and squalid quarters it had left. From the outside, the charming stone, Georgian-Colonial, ivy-covered Law Building (now the Faculty Club) was – and still is – the architectural gem of the campus and, in the inside, the Reading Room of the Library, a cathedral-like hall with beautiful beams and windows, delighted everyone who saw it. It was, however, even in 1952, inadequate for the humdrum day-to-day uses that it was supposed to serve. Designed to accommodate a library of 17 000 volumes, 100 law students, and four full-time members of faculty, there moved into it more than 20 000 books, 130 students, and six full-time teachers – numbers which even then were expected to increase, and did increase, substantially over the next few years.

To the students who moved with the School from the terrible facilities of the Forrest Building to the Studley building the change was in every way a change for the better. But the traditionalists, to whom the real Dalhousie Law School was Dalhousie's Little Law School and the Forrest Building its real home, voiced some regrets. Here are two of them: 'most of us here [at the ceremonies held to mark the occupation of the new building] are probably nostalgic for the historic old quarters in the Forrest Building which will always hold hallowed memories for us all' (Dean Horace Read); and 'we had Spartan quarters in the old building and no student conveniences except the Library, yet the old quarters are still dear to my heart' (one of Weldon's old students).

A few weeks after classes began in the new building a symposium on 'The Role of the Lawyer in the Community' and a special convocation were held to mark the occasion. It was a very family affair. Every past dean – except, of course, Weldon, who died in 1925 – made his contribution to it. MacRae, during whose deanship (1914-24) the School was supposed to move into the Studley building – he was now retired, old, not very well, and living in Toronto – sent the following message: 'Sincere congratulations on the successful realization of the long deferred and cherished dream. I had hardly hoped to see it realized.' Sidney Smith ('20), Dean 1929-34 and in 1952 President of the University of Toronto, wrote a typically bouncing letter in the course of which he set forth in these words the approach that the School had always tried to take to legal education: 'the School has sought first to develop the educated man, then the responsible citizen, then the learned lawyer, and only then the skilful practitioner.' John Read, Dean 1924-29 and then a Judge of the International Court, gave a paper at the symposium on 'The Lawyer in International Affairs.' And Vincent MacDonald ('20), Dean 1934-50 and then Mr Justice MacDonald of the Supreme Court of Nova Scotia, gave the convocation address. He preached, as was perhaps expected of the most recent of the ex-deans, on the excellence of Dalhousie Law School; his address was not published but it has been printed at the end of this book, together with two other parallel pieces, under the heading 'What Dalhousie Law School says about itself when it is on parade' (Appendix III); we shall return to it in a moment. A very distinguished group: dramatizing the good fortune of the School in having had such men as these, in their dean days unrecognized, to preside over it; and dramatizing also the unusual strength of the School in what we have called the Golden Age, with which period in its history every one of them was connected.

It was originally intended that all the participants in the symposium except one should be members of the family – that one being Dean Erwin Griswold of the Harvard Law School, who was invited to be there in recognition of the debt that Dalhousie Law School owes to Harvard and spoke on 'Educating the Lawyer for New Responsibilities.' But Sir James Dunn ('98), who was invited to speak on 'The Lawyer in Industry and Commerce,' was unable to be present and his place had to be taken by one who was outside the family. Premier Angus L. Macdonald ('21), another star from the Golden Age, dealt with 'The Lawyer in Government Service.' 'Summation and Commentary' was done by George Curtis, a teacher at the School for eleven years and now dean, the founding dean, of the new University of British Columbia Law School. Presiding at the morning session of the symposium was J.L. Ilsley ('16), the universally admired federal finance minister in the years of the Second World War, by then Chief Justice of Nova Scotia. A roster of past deans and of other members of the family that any school would be proud of.

The tone of Vincent MacDonald's convocation address, 'A National Law School,' was such as to be likely to draw from anyone who was not of the household of the faith the jibe 'Horn-tooting has always been a good Maritime trait; Dalhousie has just made a tradition of it.' But we shall let that one go; a little boasting is everywhere *de rigueur* on ceremonial occasions. What we are interested in is, first, two statements of fact made by him and, second, a dream that he dreamed. He drew attention, as Dean Sidney Smith before him had done in the days preceding the School's fiftieth birthday in 1933, to the long honour roll of judges and political figures right across Canada who had been provided by the little School: 'the record – relative to numbers – is astoundingly high.' True enough, but by the time he spoke the School had ceased to be the factory for distinguished men that it had once been. By 1976 the School would still be able to point with pride to *some* distinguished graduates (for example, the premiers of Nova Scotia, New Brunswick, Prince Edward Island, and Saskatchewan, all of them Dalhousie Law School old boys), but 'you have to look for them now.' His second statement of fact, made merely in passing, was that 'the School had to draw students from outside Nova Scotia in order to survive' and he could have added (but did not) that while he was Dean and thereafter 15 to 20 per cent of the students would normally be from outside the Atlantic region. But he did not – please note, he did not – as Horace Read did in his 1959-63 report to the President, inflate that simple statement of fact into the dubious assertion that 'the Law School at Dalhousie continues to be a "national law school," more truly so than others in this country, in the sense that it attracts students from across Canada and elsewhere.' The title that Vincent MacDonald gave his address, 'A National Law School,' does not refer to any statements of fact made by him. It refers only to the dream he dreamed at the end of it: the dream that there would come into being in Canada a school 'of such excellence as will attract to it all who desire the best opportunity for legal education, or for research, which Canada can offer' and that Dalhousie would be that school. As of 1976 neither part of that two-part dream has been, or is on the opinion of the writer likely to be, realized: there is not in Canada any law school that stands out above the others.

Before passing to the second wave of innovations, which began in 1957, we pause to give a very brief sketch of what the School was like in the early and middle fifties. It was now in its own building at Studley. Its curriculum had, in addition to the innovations described above, undergone, at the instance of a standing Curriculum Revision Committee set up in 1950, changes which, although of significance, would be of little interest to anyone except a professional law teacher. A few, but very few, improvements had been made in the library – of which more later. To what we have already said about the full-time teachers – that there were now seven of them, that all of them except one were old boys, that they perpetually came and went, and that they had largely taken over from the downtowners – we shall here add some impressions gained from reading the reminiscences of those who were in the School at this time (they will be found in the second special issue of *Ansul*, December 1977).

The full-time teachers were, as a group, still what their predecessors had traditionally been – young, hard-working, overworked, with no opportunity to specialize and with little time available to see students, let alone write for publication. But 'there was good rapport between staff and students, and we had a goodly number of stags or smokers. Graham Murray and Sugar Jim Hendry came to all of them; Dean Read and Bill Lederman came often,' so that the atmosphere of the Studley building was, like the Forrest Building's, 'club-like.' As class-room performers they were as good a mix as their predecessors had been. One of them, for example, 'was regarded with special fondness by first year students because, being an accomplished scholar, he left little for the students to work out on their own' while another was 'very special to many of us. He challenged us to think ... Our reaction tended to be – you son of a gun, we will figure it out on our own in one way or another.' And as a counterweight to those who have suggested that before the second wave of innovations the School was not dynamic and that it was in danger of falling behind other Canadian schools, here is an evaluation made by an ex-student: 'In looking back I have often thought that Dalhousie Law School when I was there had great teachers in abundance ... I say this from a perspective of a year at Harvard Law School following graduation from Dalhousie where I was briefly exposed to some of the superstars in the United States legal academic world. They were great at Harvard but they did not in my opinion outrank Horace Read or Bill Lederman or Graham Murray.'

We come now to the students – about whom we have so far said nothing, the reason for that being that in most respects they were so like their forerunners that there is no history in them. They continued to be mostly men with the usual sprinkling of women, mostly Maritimers with the usual small contingent of outsiders and, as usual, a goodly number of them, sometimes as many as half, had to look for work outside the Maritimes when they were through. They continued to carry on in the same old way the traditional institutions of the Moot Court and the Mock Parliament (which continued to be noticed, and now even sometimes photographed, in the *Gazette*). Their subsequent career interests continued to be as diverse as they had always been. To take just one example: from the same class, the class of 1952, there have come a Liberal premier of Nova Scotia, a maverick Independent MP for Moncton, a man who successfully practised law in Calgary for twenty years before going into academic life, and the present Dean of Dalhousie Law School who is regularly called upon to take on important assignments in international affairs. In some minor ways, however, they did differ from their forerunners. There were, even after the veteran bulge was over, more married men and even a married woman or two in the student body; two new career opportunities were added to the traditional ones of law, the civil service, and business, i.e., law teaching and the provincial magistracy; and more of them went on after graduation to do graduate work in the United States or England, winning substantial scholarships to do it with (in 1956, for example, five students out of a class of forty-five were awarded such scholarships, and one of the award winners was the third Dalhousie law graduate to win the premier Canadian award, the Viscount Bennett Scholarship, since it was first awarded in 1951). To balance the evaluation of the teachers of this period – perhaps too rosy a one – by a student that we quoted earlier we quote the following recent evaluation – also perhaps too rosy – of the students of the same period by one who has been student, teacher, and Dean at the School and is now Vice-President of the University, Andy (W.A.) MacKay: 'The thing that made the Law School in my view was the contribution which the students made to each other. The faculty were good, they were interested, but I think the thing that made Dalhousie great in the old days, and I think it is still true, was the students.'[26]

And now for two widely differing evaluations of the School itself as it was at this time. Leaving aside as Dalhousie horn-tooting at its most blaring the article in *MacLean's Magazine* on 1 March 1954 by David MacDonald, entitled 'The Brainiest School in the Country,' there are in that article two flattering contemporary evaluations by two highly respectable authorities who knew the School only from the outside and from afar. In the very same year, 1952, Prime Minister Louis St. Laurent, a lawyer and a graduate of Laval, referred on a public occasion to 'Dalhousie Law School which we in Laval are inclined to regard as our only possible peer among the law schools in Canada' and D. Park Jamieson, a Bencher of the Law Society of Upper Canada, which was then still operating the largest law school in Canada, the Osgoode Hall Law School, referred to Dalhousie as 'Canada's most outstanding Law School.' But three men who were at the School at the time and so knew it from the inside describe it in terms that are, in varying degrees, the very opposite of flattering.

D.A. Soberman, who was a student from 1949 to 1952, a teacher from 1955 to 1957, and was later dean at the Queen's Law School, writes in his *Ansul* 1977 reminiscences: 'The combination of a small overworked staff, a large proportion of classes taught by part-timers, inadequate library facilities, and a compulsory curriculum was hardly conducive to a scholarly atmosphere. To the extent that quality prevailed, it was a triumph over adversity, aided by camaraderie and high spirits.' George Nicholls, who came, as we shall see, in 1957 straight from the editorial chair of the *Canadian Bar Review* to teach full-time at the School and is now Professor Emeritus, has recorded in his *Ansul* reminiscences the impression that it made upon him when he first arrived: it struck him as 'undynamic' and 'local.' And Lederman, who had been teaching at the School since 1949 and was leaving it to become the first and founding dean at Queen's, wrote this to Lady Dunn in 1958: 'In spite of the fine accomplishments of the past and present, I am uneasy concerning the future of the Dalhousie Law School ... exceptional and sustained efforts are necessary if Dalhousie Law School is to hold the position it has always had in the very front rank of Canadian law schools.' At the very best then the School was in the years before the second wave of innovations seen by the insiders as 'in danger of losing ground to the other Canadian schools' – a note that had been sounded by Vincent MacDonald in 1945 and would be heard again in the early sixties.

In 1957 there were three innovations, all of more than ordinary importance for the future well-being of the School. The first was the final removal – *only twenty years ago* – of the barriers erected by the various provincial law societies against students educated in 'outside' law schools. Putting it another way, in 1957 the Dalhousie LLB became for the first time fully portable in all the common-law provinces; it became, that is, for the first time recognized as fulfilling all the academic requirements for admission to their bars. It had been recognized by the Nova Scotia Barristers' Society ever since 1891, it had won partial recognition from the other law societies in 1952, but it was not accorded full recognition by them until 1957. What this innovation meant to the School was something that everyone now takes for granted. Using Ontario as an example (it is in practice the most usual one), since 1957 a Maritimer who wants to practise in Ontario can, without suffering any penalty, do his law school work at Dalhousie and an 'Upper Canadian' who is proceeding to the Ontario Bar does not have to go to an Ontario law school but can, again without suffering any penalty, come, if he wants to, to

Dalhousie. They could not do that before 1957. For Dalhousie Law School which, as has always been the case, 'must export or die,' this innovation is easily the most important of all those that came about in 'Changing,' the years 1945 to 1966. The story of what the position was before 1952 and how, by whom, and why that position was partially changed in 1952 and wholly changed in 1957 cannot therefore be left out of this history – particularly since Dean Vincent MacDonald, as well as others connected with the School, was the prime mover in it. That story is, however, too long and complicated to form part of the text: it has been relegated to a long appendix, Appendix V, 'How the Dalhousie LLB degree became "portable".'

The second innovation in 1957 was the raising of the standard for admission to the School. The reader may perhaps recall that it was Dean MacRae who in 1921 induced the Faculty to raise, beginning in 1924, the admission requirement to two years of Arts – he was a great believer in a good general education – and a year later was able to persuade the Canadian Bar Association to recommend that that be in future the standard in all the common-law provinces. The Dalhousie standard became, that is, on that occasion the standard for all Canada. In 1957 the Dalhousie standard was raised to three years of college work, but this time the shoe was on the other foot. Dalhousie was in effect forced to adopt the new standard because the Conference of Governing Bodies of the Legal Profession in Canada (the offshoot successor to the Canadian Bar Association in this area) had, after consultation with the Association of Canadian Law Teachers, so recommended. The new standard was a compromise between the requirement of a BA that some law societies had recently adopted (but Horace Read objected to that because it would, he thought, 'sever the study of the humanities and sciences on the one hand from the study of law on the other at a time when the best contemporary thought seeks to join them') and the old two-year rule. Because, however, most students feel that if they have to spend three years in college in order to get into law school they may as well spend another and have a piece of paper to show for it, 90 per cent of all students have since 1957 come to the School with a degree. Whether the higher admission standard had any effect in raising the quality of the students is hard to say. That they are in 1976 far better able to cope with the rigours of law, particularly first-year law, than they were in the fifties is indisputable but what probably brought that about was something quite different – the intense competition for places that began in the late sixties.

The third innovation of more than ordinary importance that took place in 1957 was the arrival of Professor George Nicholls: for it was he who injected into the curriculum the emphasis on legal writing that has ever since characterized the School's methods of teaching and it was he who was primarily responsible for rescuing the library from the low state into which it had been allowed to fall. In the same year, incidentally, Andy (W.A.) MacKay joined the staff as a junior; a graduate of Dalhousie in both Arts and Law ('53), he had done an LLM at the School and had spent three years in the federal civil service before turning to law teaching; he would become Dean in 1964 and in 1969 Vice-President of the University. But it is with Nicholls that this paragraph is concerned. Trained in the civil law, first at McGill and then in France, he was approaching middle age – with all the authority that that, when coupled with a varied experience, can give a man – when he came to the School to fill the place of Hendry, who had resigned. After fourteen years of various kinds of legal work he had for the last ten years been editor of the *Canadian Bar Review*, in the course of which he had got to know all the leading law teachers in Canada and had become familiar with the plans that some of them had for imposing higher standards on Canadian legal education. So that, as a civil lawyer who was not prepared to accept without reserve all the habits of thought traditional with common-law law teachers (e.g. case method) and as an outsider to whom Dalhousie was not 'the only' common-law law school, he came into the tradition-minded School as one who was prepared to question Dalhousie Law School standards and to re-think for himself Dalhousie Law School ways of doing things and was, because he was a man of middle age and wide experience, able to make himself heard.

'A factor in my own appointment,' says Nicholls in his *Ansul* reminiscences, 'was, I suspect, that I would be able to draw on my editorial experience to help in introducing a first-year course on Legal Research and Writing.' And that is what in the fall of 1957 he proceeded to do. It was not, as is sometimes claimed (but not by Nicholls), the first such course in Canada – the Alberta Law School had had a kind of one since 1944 and the University of Toronto had in the mid-fifties started one no less ambitious than Nicholls' but had almost immediately reduced it to no more than a rather useless pint-size on the ground that the students were having to spend so much time on it that their work in the other courses was suffering; but it was the first one ever at Dalhousie. All first-year students had had, it is true, in the thirties to write an essay on a legal subject (for the Carswell Essay Prize) and Lederman had since 1950 been requiring a paper from all the third-year students in his Jurisprudence class, which was a compulsory one; but writing an essay or paper on your own time and just handing it in for grading is something very different from what Nicholls made the students do.

Disregarding as unimportant the details, such as how many exercises and of what kind – those were, and still are, regarded as experimental and subject to change – the scheme of the new course on Legal Research and Writing was that every student had to give, *in writing*, and in the same form as a practising lawyer would, the reasoned 'solution' to a legal problem at which he individually had arrived after his own individual use of such books in the library as he individually considered relevant. But the nub of it was supervision and supervision on an individual basis: Nicholls, with some assistance from his colleagues, corrected, criticized, and discussed at a personal interview the written exercise that each student had produced. This was 'work it out for yourself' – the rationale underlying case method – with a vengeance and was, as a device for training students, far more effective than case method where all the student had to do was to take part orally – or, if he so chose, remain silent – in a classroom discussion that was almost always in practice imprecise, wandering, and inconclusive. The new course made, of course, enormous demands on the time and energy of Nicholls and his assistants, demands which would almost certainly have resulted, as at the University of Toronto, in its abandonment were it not for the lucky accident that in its first few years the first-year classes were abnormally small. And many, perhaps most, of the students, objected to the rigorous treatment they received. But it was from the beginning a success. According to MacKay, 'by Christmas the first-year students were showing the third year how to use the Library' and 'the bad old days' ('in all the three years I was at the School I never had to put pen to paper except in exams') were gone forever. All first-year students have ever since 1957 been subjected to Legal Research and Writing and in the years that followed a writing requirement was, again largely due to the influence of Nicholls, introduced into the other years also. This emphasis on legal writing by the student is, in the opinion of the writer, the most important change in curriculum in the whole history of the School – far more important than the much-vaunted expansion in content and optionalization that took place in the seventies.

A by-product, and very important by-product, of the new Legal Research and Writing course was the long overdue reform of the library. In his reminiscences Nicholls gives in a nutshell the story of how it came about; our account of it will have to be even shorter than his but we shall borrow from him and shall put the events in a wider and sometimes slightly different perspective. 'I remember,' says Nicholls, 'the shock when I first examined the law library in the Studley building. An adequate and efficient library is essential for the kind of course on legal research and writing I was planning ... it was probably adequate for courses employing the Case Method. For any other purpose it was a disaster.' He then proceeds to give particulars of the library's inadequacy – a very limited number of textbooks (most of them kept under lock and key or stored inaccessibly in the basement), no full-time professional librarian, no catalogue, and so on – and to recount the steps he and his colleagues took to render it just barely usable for a course 'one of whose chief objects would be to familiarize first-year students with the use of legal materials, *all* legal materials.'

We do not propose to rehearse all over again the long history of the library's trials and tribulations; we will only state baldly that the reality of the library in 1957 was a long way removed from the dreams that the School's founders had had for it nearly seventy-five years earlier. The School had started off with a full-time paid librarian; in 1957 there was only a part-time paid librarian, and that was a very recent improvement on the student-librarian system that had been in effect since 1884. As to the collection of books, the School had announced in 1884 that 'during the past year 3 000 volumes have been procured and it is the aim of the Faculty to make it the most complete in Canada'; in 1957 it ranked low among the very modest collections that the other schools had.

The state of the library was not, of course, the result of neglect but of lack of money, and in the early fifties Dean Read had managed, by his own contacts and his own persistent pressure on President Kerr, to make some slight improvements in it. From his contacts, Premier Angus L. Macdonald, Harvey Todd Reid (the president of the West Publishing Company of St Paul, Minnesota), and the late Gordon Fogo, there had come the Nova Scotia Collection on Public Law, a valuable collection of American reports, and a small sum to buy legal materials with. His pressure on Kerr had produced from the University an increased, but not yet adequate, budget for the library and in 1954 the school was given, for the first time since Bulmer, the School's first librarian, had had to be let go in 1884 (no money to pay him), the services of a full-time paid librarian; but the newly acquired librarian did not stay and by 1957 the School was back to a part-time one, with the traditional student 'librarians' to help her. Nicholls' discovery that the library was totally inadequate for his new course showed that more drastic action was needed and Read asked him to visit a number of libraries in central Canada and report on their methods. Armed with a monumental and blistering report from Nicholls – its conclusion was that 'the law library at Dalhousie is not at the moment a good library' – Read was able to persuade the University authorities to authorize a search for a librarian with training in both law and library science, which search was proceeding without much success (the University was not offering enough money) when Dunn money came, once again, to the rescue.

The Dunn money did not, of course, appear of itself and by magic. What started it on its way was a letter that Lederman, the Sir James Dunn Professor of Law, wrote to Lady Dunn, the widow of Sir James and the president of the Sir James Dunn Foundation, in 1958 when he was leaving the Dunn chair to become dean at Queen's. From something that Sir James had said when he produced the money for the chair a few years earlier the School had half-expected to get some more after his death, but he had by now been dead for more than a year and what had come to the University from the Foundation was not a gift for the Law School but a gift, a magnificent gift, to build a Sir James Dunn Science Building. In his letter, which was written to express his gratitude for what Sir James had done for him and for the School and to explain that he was only leaving the chair and the School to become the founding dean of a new school, Lederman took the opportunity to pass on to Lady Dunn the concern that he and his colleagues were feeling about the future of Dalhousie Law School. 'In the field of legal education, the most striking advances in Canada's history are now rather suddenly developing in other places [i.e., 'the minor revolution' in Ontario of which the reader has already been told something in the introduction to this Part and can find more in Appendix V] ... exceptional and sustained efforts are necessary if Dalhousie Law School is to hold the position it has always had in the very front rank of Canadian law schools.'

Lady Dunn's reaction to Lederman's letter was immediate, hard-headed, and forceful. In the negotiations which ensued with the University authorities she underlined her desire 'to rebuild the prestige and prominence of the Law

School': if competition was coming from other schools 'we must find,' she wrote in connection with the suggestion of a librarian for the library, 'a person of distinction that would in time become an attraction not being offered at other law schools.' She, personally, made detailed and searching inquiries into the School's problems and the School's needs and, after fully and carefully considering where help was most needed, she procured the Foundation to provide, until further notice, the following annual grants: $16 500 a year for the engagement of a highly qualified librarian, a cataloguer, and a stenographer; and whatever annual sums were necessary to provide seven scholarships, worth $1 500 apiece, for exceptionally promising young Canadians who wanted to study law at Dalhousie, such scholarships to be renewable for a second and a third year to any student who was able to maintain a very high standard of performance. The library gift, to which she annexed the condition that the University itself would allot an additional $10 000 a year for five years to build up the collection of books, was a godsend to the library. As for the scholarships, they were unique in Canada; no other law school in Canada had anything like them.

The new Dunn contributions were announced by President Kerr – 'a princely gift' he called them – during the symposium and convocation which was held at the end of October 1958 to celebrate the School's seventy-fifth anniversary. The celebrations were much less of a family affair than those which had been held six years earlier to mark the move to the Studley building. The Faculty had indeed, in what must have been a mood of 'reaching out,' formally resolved that one person be invited from each of Great Britain, the United States, and Canada to give special addresses to the gathering. So that those who in fact came and gave addresses were: from England, A.L. Goodhart, long-time editor of the *Law Quarterly Review*; from the United States, Mr Justice William O. Douglas of the Supreme Court of the United States; and from Canada, Professor Frank Scott of McGill – all 'names' and all well-known to all Canadian lawyers and law students. There was, however, still one family touch. Portraits of two former Deans were unveiled: one of the late D.A. MacRae (Dean 1914-24) – a group of his distinguished old students, headed by Sidney Smith (Dean 1929-34), MacRae's old student, one-time colleague, and life-long admirer, had clubbed together to have the portrait painted, and Mr Justice MacDonald (Dean 1934-50), another old student, paid a short tribute to him – and one of John Read (Dean 1924-29) who had recently retired from the Court of International

Justice after twelve years' service there; Frank Covert, an old student and a great admirer of his (see his reminiscences in the 1976 *Ansul*), paid the tribute.

There were also two features to the celebration which hinted of things to come. The students at the School – in the Weldon Building School it will come to be taken for granted that the students initiate – prepared on their own initiative and almost entirely without assistance a special supplement to the *Gazette* which contained, among other things, a short history of the School, miniscule histories of the law library and the Mock Parliament, and a long history of the Moot Court. And two old students, George Farquhar ('27) and John Barnett ('07), produced, with a view to their publication at the anniversary, two historical pieces on the School. George Farquhar's thirty-five-page 'The Dalhousie Law School 1883-1958' is interesting and lively on the very early days but soon peters out into the rather boring recital of 'events' typical of most histories of law schools. John Barnett's twenty-page 'Dalhousie Law School, Ideals and Traditions' is an appreciation of Weldon the teacher, Weldon the politician, and Weldon the man, plus some facts and comments about the wave of Dalhousie Law graduates who went West during the great wave of settlement. Neither was published – no money – and both still repose in 'the Yellow Book' into which Horace Read bound some of the basic writing and basic information that he needed for his projected history. They did, however, undoubtedly inspire Read to embark on that project and are therefore the seed-germ of the present volume, which will not be appearing until more than twenty years after that seed was sown.

The School's seventy-fifth anniversary coincides more or less with the ending of the second of the two waves of innovation that marked the years 1950 to 1958. But before we end this section, 'Innovations,' we must introduce three new faces who joined the staff in the years 1958, 1959, and 1960 – two of them because they would in 1976 still be at the School and would be members of 'the Old Guard,' and one of them because he and Nicholls together formed an 'outsiders' bloc' that in the course of the next few years questioned some aspects of Dalhousie ways, Dalhousie teaching methods, and Dalhousie curriculum. The two future members of the Old Guard will not receive in these pages the attention they deserve: they were too junior to make much impact in the years before the move to the Weldon Building in 1966; and after the move the School will become so big and there will be so many events that our story will of necessity cease to be individual and personal and will become general and impersonal. They were Eddie (E.C.) Harris ('58) and Bill (W.H.) Charles ('58). Harris was a qualified chartered accountant as well as a lawyer; as a student he had won everything in sight in both fields; although he went into practice after a few years, he remained at the School half-time (but was always regarded by his full-time colleagues as 'one of us'), inducting his students into the mysteries of Taxation and Corporate Finance and being a prolific practical scholar in both those areas. Charles' special interests when he came on the staff were the problem method of teaching – not long after he arrived he published an article on it which is the classic statement for Canada[27] – and the Legislation course, which he took over from Horace Read and was still teaching in 1976.

The outsider was John Edwards. When he came in 1958 to succeed Lederman in the Sir James Dunn Chair he came, like Nicholls, as a man of authority from the larger and wider world outside Nova Scotia and Dalhousie. With three law degrees (from Wales, Cambridge, and London), several years of experience as a law teacher in London and Belfast, and an already established reputation as a specialist and scholar in the fields of criminal law and criminology (he had published his well-known *Mens Rea and Statutory Offences* and was in the process of writing his almost equally well-known *The Law Officers of the Crown*), he was a strange bird to have strayed into a school where nobody was publishing much and few were disposed to leave well-trodden paths. He stayed only five years before going to the University of Toronto as the founding director of its new Centre of Criminology, but during his stay he and Nicholls together challenged some of the well-established patterns at the Law School.

We are now ready to pass on to Section Three, 1958-66: On a new plateau. That section will begin by recording the effect on the School of the Dunn Foundation's library grant and scholarships grant – both were immensely helpful at a time when help was needed but neither proved to be permanent – and will then explore some of the effects of some of the innovations that took place in the years 1950-58. It will end with the School readying itself for the great expansion of the mid-sixties.

SECTION THREE: 1958-1966

On a New Plateau

By the end of the innovating fifties the School had reached a new and higher plateau. It was now housed in a building of its own – not a very adequate one, but still its own. The staff had grown in number, had become more stable, and a little less 'old-boy': in 1960 there were eight full-time teachers, six of whom would still be connected with the School in 1976 and two of whom were men of authority from outside. The long-standing MacRae curriculum had been brought more into line with contemporary lawyers' needs by the addition of such subjects as Labour Law and Estate Planning, had been to some extent re-infused with the humane or Weldon spirit by the introduction of such subjects as Jurisprudence and Legislation, and had recently acquired, through the new first-year course on Legal Research and Writing, the beginnings of the emphasis on writing by students that would be so distinctive a feature in 1976. The student body was for the four years beginning with 1959 abnormally small, around 110 all told – which was not all loss, because, with twice the number of teachers to look after only a few more students than there had been at the end of the thirties, the ever-open door policy and the easy and natural relationship between teachers and taught that had been so marked a characteristic of Dalhousie's Little Law School came once more, briefly, into their own; but even in those years everyone knew that it was on the verge of an unprecedented expansion. The quality of the general run of these students was, again abnormally, giving their teachers some concern – the timing of the new Sir James Dunn scholarships plan, one of whose aims was to attract exceptionally good students to the study of law at Dalhousie, was just right – but everybody hoped that the recent raising of admission standards and the presence of Dunn scholars would soon bring it back to normal. And the library, the long-neglected library, was, due to the impetus given by the new arrangements sponsored by the Sir James Dunn Foundation, at the beginning of an era of transformation into one that would be in 1976 one of the best in Canada.

The effect on the library of the Dunn grant, and the condition annexed to it, was immediate and beneficial. Under the direction of Miss Eunice Beeson, the Sir James Dunn Law Librarian – she was qualified in both law and library science and had held responsible positions in good law libraries in the United States – organization of the collection was improved, much of it was catalogued, and good service was provided to students and staff; Nicholls' reproach that what books the library had were not readily available ceased to be true. Also improved by the $50000 special appropriation that the University had been forced to make by the condition annexed to the grant was the collection of books; over 12000 carefully chosen volumes, chiefly legal periodicals and British Commonwealth materials, were added to it, making a total of over 40000; and when the special appropriation ran out, the Board made that extra $10000 per year part of the School's regular annual budget. And Miss Beeson herself took an active part in forming the Canadian Association of Law Librarians, thereby helping to raise the sights of those who in the schools and in the profession were concerned with library matters. In 1966 Miss Beeson died prematurely and the Foundation decided not to continue the grant. By this time, fortunately, the government support of universities, to which we are all in 1976 so accustomed that we take it for granted, had come into operation and the end of the grant was not the disaster that it would otherwise have been. But finding another person who was qualified in both law and library science to replace Miss Beeson proved very difficult – such persons were hard to come by – and it was not until 1971 that he was found.

In the Sir James Dunn scholarship plan, and in the Dunn scholars themselves, Lady Dunn took from the beginning a close personal interest. It was so close that for the whole of the twenty years that the plan lasted she insisted on receiving for her personal inspection the file of every candidate whom the Faculty recommended to the Foundation for an award or renewal of a scholarship and expected – and got – reports on what prizes or post-graduate awards the graduating Dunn scholars had won. And for the first ten years she even instigated, and paid for, an annual party, held on the anniversary of Sir James Dunn's birth and complete with birthday cake and champagne, to which all the Dunn scholars then in the School were invited. The standard set, both for original award and for renewal of the scholarships, was, and was meant to be, exceptionally high. For original award the candidate who was proposing to enter first year was required to possess 'those qualities which are needed for the attainment of distinction in the legal profession' – which the Faculty and the Foundation interpreted to mean an unusually good academic record plus an 'all-roundness' approximating that required of a Rhodes scholar. To be eligible for renewal of his scholarship at the end of his first and, if he succeeded in keeping it, at the end of his second year, the student had to maintain a first-class average (75 per cent) and stand among the top ten in his class. That these standards were faithfully adhered to is shown by the fact that it was not until 1968 that all of the seven scholarships theoretically available in the first year were awarded and the fact that at the end of the first and second years there were always some Dunn scholars who, though good and well-motivated students, were not recommended for renewal because they failed to meet the exceedingly rigorous – and pressure-inducing – dual test of excellence.

The scholarships – worth $1 500 a year when they began in 1959 and raised to $2 500 in 1967 to meet increases in tuition fees and in the cost of living – were, of course, a heaven-sent gift to students who wanted to study law but had not enough money to do so. In the long list of Dunn scholars who carried off the top prizes at the School and won prestigious post-graduate awards, such as the Viscount Bennett Scholarship and scholarships to the Harvard Law School, there were many who without a Dunn scholarship would not have been able to go into law at all. The scholarships were also extremely helpful to the School itself. Because of them there were always present among the students a few top-performers to stimulate and raise the sights of their fellows – something that was very badly needed at the beginning of the sixties when the general run of students was below the normal level. Because of them too there came to the School from right across Canada many students (not only the Dunn scholars themselves but also those who came to be interviewed, did not get a scholarship, but liked the place and came anyway) who would normally have gone to the school in their home provinces – bringing to the Maritimers in the School their own regional viewpoints and taking back home with them some understanding of the Maritimers' point of view. And as to Dalhousie's need to meet the competition coming from other schools, the writer remembers at least one top student who was going to do his law at the University of Toronto but was, to that school's dismay, lured away to Dalhousie by a Dunn scholarship – an experience that must have been shared by many other schools. In the fall of 1977, however, the Foundation discontinued the scholarships: 'the results,' said the letter from the Foundation, 'have not been encouraging. In many cases, first year students have not attained the required standard for renewal of their Scholarships into the second year and even fewer students have completed the three year course under a Sir James Dunn Law Scholarship.' True enough, but the Sir James Dunn scholarship plan gave to the School itself in 1958 an encouragement that was at the time very badly needed and in the twenty years that followed produced for it results that were much more than merely encouraging.

The years 1958 to 1966 were quiet years. The only events were even less dramatic than the uneventful ones of the period 1950-58. They were, in order of time, a prolonged inquiry into the curriculum of the first year, a fundamental revision of the graduate program, the retirement from the deanship of Horace Read, and planning for the projected new building, the Weldon Building. There were, however, a number of minor events which foreshadowed the emergence of the new and very different kind of institution that would be inhabiting the Weldon Building in 1976.

No doubt partly because of the increase in numbers of the full-time staff but also because of the presence among them of the two men of authority from outside, there are the beginnings of what in the seventies will become the well-accepted concept of faculty control of the Dean and of the School. The School had traditionally been the Dean's School; he had, of course, always consulted his young colleagues before he made important decisions but what a young man will accept as sufficient consultation will not necessarily satisfy a man of middle age and experience. In his reminiscences in the 1977 *Ansul* Nicholls prefaces a biting description of the kind of consultation that Dean Read indulged in by saying that 'by modern standards, the faculty tended to operate in those days as something of an autocracy, the doctrine of the Divine Right of Deans.' By way of counterblast to the Divine Right of Deans, the full-time staff began in the fall of 1959 to hold frequent and regular meetings – traditionally they had met only twice a year, once in the spring and once in the fall, and then only to pass on examination results – and to record what went on at those meetings in voluminous and detailed minutes. These minutes are the precursors of the snowstorm of paper that would in the seventies afflict the members of a faculty whose communication with one another had traditionally been oral and informal.

The minutes of staff meetings have, however, helped the writer to form in his own mind a fairly objective picture of what was going on in these years; the contemporary reminiscences in *Ansul* tend to be somewhat subjective and Read's 1959-63 report to the President sees the School, as always, through a rainbow. Impressions worth mentioning include the following. Legal Research and Writing is again and again on trial for its life (it is 'over-burdening the students') but Nicholls' well-reasoned addresses in defence of it (some of them are in writing) ensure its survival. Nicholls and Edwards are as insistent on maintaining or raising standards ('we must challenge the students') as the old boys are on treating the student with humanity (a hangover from the days when the School was very small and staff and students knew each other as human beings). Edwards is experimental: he tries, without success of course, to get going in Halifax an interdisciplinary institute of criminology and brings into his class on Jurisprudence people like doctors, social workers, and theologians who can throw new light on the traditional wisdom current among lawyers. Read has become very conservative and is, as we can now see in retrospect, swimming against the tide; he is against a student law journal, he is not very enthusiastic about curriculum changes, and he does not want the School to become larger.

There are, we can also see, ventures afoot that will come to nothing but will in the Weldon Building become established realities and trends now barely discernible that will in the Weldon Building become well-settled traditions. Here are two examples of ventures afoot. Twice in the early sixties the students tried to start a law journal – there was nothing new about the idea, their predecessors in the mid-twenties had talked to Dean John Read about starting one – but they were not, it turned out, willing or able to do the necessary work; in the Weldon Building there will be two law journals, one a student affair (*Ansul*) and the other a faculty affair that welcomes, and gets, student contributions (*The Dalhousie Law Journal*). Sparked by the imminence of the annual meeting of the Canadian Bar Association scheduled to be held in Halifax in the summer of 1962, a committee of the faculty did a good deal of work exploring the possibility of forming a Dalhousie Law Alumni Association; there was, as the reader has been told earlier, nothing new about that idea either but, once again, all that effort produced nothing; in 1975-76 however there will be instituted in the Weldon Building an Office of Alumni Affairs. One further venture – which did come to something – positively cries out for mention because of the light it throws on the difference between the attitudes of 1976 and the attitudes (which were still the traditional attitudes) of the early sixties. In March 1961 there came into effect for the first time the mid-term lecture break which has become familiarly known as 'ski week' and regarded as just a holiday. In the minutes for 27 March 1961 appears the following entry: 'Dean Read reported that one first year student whose home was outside Halifax took advantage of his lecture break to go home and play hockey. A note to that effect appeared in his home town newspaper and was brought to the attention of Dr. Kerr. Dean Read expressed the opinion that this was an abuse of the lecture break and that precautions should be taken in future to avoid similar occurrences.'

As to trends then barely discernible that will become well-settled traditions in the Weldon Building, the minutes reveal both a student trend and a faculty trend. The students are beginning, it seems, to play in the operation of the School a part that foreshadows what will in 1976 be a deep involvement. To take just one example, in 1960 a Student Advisory Committee was appointed to assist a faculty committee which was conducting an elaborate inquiry into the first-year curriculum; appointed originally for the rather limited purpose of giving their views on the workload that a first-year man was bearing and their opinions on what he should be bearing, the student committee went far beyond that and 'volunteered general suggestions on curriculum ... [which] were discussed among the Faculty members and some interested practising lawyers.' And the faculty is beginning to exercise over the Dean a control that will in the seventies become so intense as almost on occasion to paralyse action. Examples are: the inauguration of the regular meetings of staff that we mentioned earlier; the appointment in 1963 of a committee of staff members to select a successor to Dean Read; and even, it seems, the establishment of the committee on first-year curriculum to which we referred a moment ago; for, as one who was at that time a member of the faculty has put it, 'the appointment of a committee to study the content of the curriculum was prompted by the desire of some members of the Faculty to develop the spirit of delegation of authority.' There is even, to conclude this overlong review of the minor events recorded in the minutes, yet another sounding of the tiresomely familiar theme of 'we are falling behind'; we are this time, it seems, even falling behind ourselves: 'under the terms of our Five Year Plan prepared two years ago, there should already be two more members on our Faculty than we have at present. ... our teaching staff [is] not keeping pace with that of other law schools, nor with that in other parts of the University' (7 November 1962).

We pass now to a chronological record of the 'events' of this period. The first in time – and the most time-consuming for the faculty – was what seems to have started out, in early 1959, as 'a three months study of the present curriculum' but became in actuality a three-year study of little more than the curriculum of the first year. It did, however, give some thought to the question of 'electives,' of which there were a few in the second and third year, and to the integration with first-year Legal Writing of the courses in second and third year, e.g. Legislation and Procedure, both of which had since the early fifties required some written work from the students. Nicholls, who was the instigator of the project, the chairman of the Curriculum Revision Committee, and the author of nearly all the long and comprehensive memoranda on which were based the voluminous discussions recorded in the minutes of staff meetings, has given in his *Ansul* reminiscences his own summary of what he thinks were the highlights of the inquiry. So that all that this historian need do is describe the inquiry in a line or two and put it in perspective.

Whatever it was originally intended to do, the inquiry did not, as the usual curriculum inquiry does, much concern itself with the subjects taught or with methods of teaching; its main thrust was on the nuts-and-bolts of the teaching process itself, i.e., on such matters as how many hours a week all told have we a right to expect the first-year student to spend on his legal studies, who among his instructors is unfairly poaching on the other instructors by assigning to his students more than his fair share of work to be done, etc. Useful as in some ways it undoubtedly was, it led, in Nicholls' own words, 'to no revolutionary changes in legal education at Dalhousie.' It was, however, the first serious inquiry into matters of curriculum at Dalhousie since 1915 when MacRae and his helpers (whoever they were) framed there the curriculum on which, the reader may remember, the Canadian Bar Association based its long-lived standard curriculum. Many modifications in and additions to the curriculum had, of course, been made since 1915 but they were all made on an *ad hoc* basis. The next serious curriculum inquiry, the Ontario-inspired one into optionalization, will not come until the seventies. And the present inquiry did have one crucially important side-effect.

This side-effect was a psychological one. The process of overview itself led the faculty to rationalize and be proud of – 'pioneering' is a self-bestowed accolade that will from this time on make regular appearances in the School's publicity on curriculum – the underlying basis of some of the step-by-step *ad hoc* innovations that had been made in the fifties. The originally unrelated courses in Legislation (with its written lab work), Procedure (with its form-drafting exercises), and Legal Writing became in their eyes transfigured into mere specific offshoots of a new teaching technique that they felt they had discovered for themselves: the 'writing requirement' or the 'do it yourself under supervision' method. In the Dalhousie Law School of the sixties – where the members of the faculty were publishing little or nothing and the School was certainly not what Sidney Smith had hoped it would be, 'a centre of legal research which is given expression by writing' – it was of crucial importance that the faculty should have confidence in what they *were* doing, i.e., teaching in a distinguished manner in a School that had always been, and prided itself on being, 'a good teaching School.'

In this connection a paragraph from Read's 1959-63 Report to the President is worth quoting in full. It tells us in very few words a great deal about the changes that were in this period taking place in teaching methods and, what is much more important, tells us what made such obviously desirable, and long-dreamed-of, changes possible.

The improvement of the library, both in its coverage and utility, the growth of the full-time faculty and a comparatively lower enrolment at Dalhousie, as at other schools over the past three years, have permitted the Dalhousie faculty to make a significant shift in educational methods. While retaining the case method as the principal teaching tool, there is a growing use of problem solving by students individually or in small groups under faculty guidance as distinguished from learning through discussion in large classes. Seminars, tutorials and comment upon student papers in small groups or individually has done much to improve the capacity and ability of our students.

This significant shift in educational methods – and in particular the slight decline in importance of the by now traditional case method – will be intensified by the advent of the lavish government funding which will begin in the mid-sixties and will make possible an immense increase in the number of full-time teachers and a huge enlargement of the library.

In 1961-62 a committee chaired by Edwards, who had himself earned two graduate degrees in England, gave critical examination to the Harvard-based graduate program which Read had in 1950 hastily put together to comply with the wishes of Premier Angus L. Macdonald and Sir James Dunn. The members of the faculty were all agreed that the existing requirements – three courses *plus* a thesis – had proved to be so heavy a load that the candidates were, generally speaking, unable to attain a satisfactory standard of performance and scholarship. Not all of them were agreed on a number of basic questions raised by the committee – for example, the capacities of present faculty members to guide students in doing graduate work and the level of scholarship that should be required of students seeking an LLM, questions that are still very much alive – but the faculty in the end decided to eliminate the course work and make the submission of 'a substantial and satisfactory thesis' the sole requirement, a step that was, in the opinion of the writer, as desirable as it was out of line with American practice at that time. They also took the opportunity to dispense with the requirement for which Angus L. had been responsible – that the student do his work in the field of public law – and left it open to the student to do his thesis in any subject in which both he himself was interested and a faculty member was sufficiently expert to be able to supervise him. The new requirements came into effect in the fall of 1962 but the occasional student who did enter the new program – there were only eight LLM degrees awarded between then and 1973 – was always one who had already done his undergraduate work at the School, not the kind of candidate that the faculty wanted and certainly not the kind of candidate, viz. a graduate of some *other* Canadian school, that the fathers of graduate work at Dalhousie, Macdonald and Dunn, had hoped to attract.

The years 1963 and 1964 are noteworthy for two separate but connected events: the method adopted in 1963 for selecting a new dean to take the place of Read who was due to retire from that position in 1964; and the appointment of Andy MacKay to succeed him. Like so much else in the period of 'Changing,' the method of selection was a sort of half-way house between that which had been traditional – no faculty input – and that which will have become *de rigueur* by the time when, in 1969, it next became necessary to find a new dean – selection (subject, of course, to veto by the President) by a committee of the faculty itself. What happened in 1963 seems to have been along the following rather hazy and hesitant lines. It having been suggested at a spring staff meeting that it was desirable that the University consult with the existing faculty in making the new appointment, Read 'got in touch' with President-Elect Henry Hicks (President Kerr had only a few weeks to go). 'Dr. Hicks,' Read reported back to the faculty, 'thoroughly agrees that consultation with the Faculty of Law should take place on this matter. However

Dr. Hicks proposes not to set up the necessary machinery until early in September.' But the faculty, fiercely asserting its own independence, formally resolved, on the initiative of Nicholls: '(1) That a Committee of three full-time members be established ... to be known as the Faculty Committee on the Appointment of a Dean, (2) That Dean Read will mention to Hicks that such a Committee has been formed,' plus four other paragraphs that are irrelevant to our present purpose. Over the summer the members of the committee discussed at length the kind of dean they wanted and why, and who out of a list of possible names they would prefer – one view being that the new dean should be an outsider, the other view being that he should be an insider (i.e., MacKay) – but when they met with Hicks in October 'the meeting was cut short [why, the minutes do not state] before much progress was made.' In the end, according to the gossip, it was Dean Read, and not the committee, who recommended to Hicks that MacKay be appointed, which was done. So much for the 'formal-informal' or 'half-way house' way in which the faculty in 1963 took part in the selection of their new Dean.

When Read ceased to be Dean in 1964 he did not cease, as all his predecessors had, to be connected with the Law School. He became in that year Vice-President of the University and continued for a while to carry a heavy teaching load at the School in addition to his new administrative responsibilities. When he retired from the office of Vice-President in 1969 he returned to his real love, the teaching of law. Even after he gave up teaching altogether, in 1972, he did not lose interest in the School. He was almost always to be found in the Weldon Building, working on 'the history' – the basic underpinnings of this book – and passing on with undiminished enthusiasm to anyone who would listen any and every detail that he had unearthed from the School's past; however uninteresting those details might be, to him they were all interesting because they were connected with the School and he loved the School. He was still working on his history when he died in 1975.

In his years as Dean he was, in one sense, Dean Vincent MacDonald in reverse. While he was Dean, MacDonald made himself over from 'practical man' into 'scholar.' Horace Read did just the opposite; he made himself over from 'scholar' into 'practical man.' When he came back to the School in 1950 he was well-known in the world of books; he had even acquired, somehow or other, the bowed and bookish look of the scholar. Although in his years as Dean he did write a little but not very much – which was perhaps a pity, because most of his staff were content to follow his example – what he spent most of his energy on were practical or scholarly-practical activities. Chairman of the Nova Scotia Labour Relations Board for more than twenty years; for many years chairman of the Educational Committee of the Conference of Governing Bodies of the Legal Profession in Canada; for many years a mainstay of the Conference of Commissioners on Uniformity of Legislation in Canada; for several years chairman of the Committee on Foreign Judgments of the International Law Association; and so on: in all those activities he prepared a host of practical papers designed to lead to practical action. But both he and Macdonald were in all that matters to the School – and this history is a history of the *School* – very much the same kind of man. To that the following tribute to both of them by Lederman will attest:

I have mentioned the two Deans with whom I served from 1949 to 1958, Vincent MacDonald and Horace Read. They were indeed friends and colleagues and treated us all as equals. Each was a fine scholar with a distinguished record of publishing, teaching, public service and loyal devotion to Dalhousie University. Moreover, each of them in his own way was a thoroughly kind and humane person with an abiding concern for other people, especially colleagues and students. In the summer of 1958, when I moved on to Queen's University at Kingston to become the first Dean of Law there, I was in no difficulty about the examples I should attempt to follow in discharging my new responsibilities.[28]

The new Dean, MacKay, has already been introduced to the reader. Like his three predecessors, Smith, MacDonald, and Read, he was an old boy, a Forrest Building boy and very conscious of the traditions of the School, especially the tradition that the teacher's overwhelmingly first duty is to teach, not write, and the tradition that the teachers and the students mix freely and easily with one another. He was not, however, afflicted by the excessive conservatism which had made Read so ready to fall in with the penny-pinching of President Kerr. On the contrary, he was, like the new President, the expansionist Hicks, ready to accept and deal with the coming unprecedented expansion of the School. And because he was by temperament more administrator than scholar – during Read's absences he had, although very junior on the staff, been Acting Dean ('I have always felt complete lack of worry with him as [my] Acting Dean') – he was well-suited to heading up the School at a moment when, with a move to a new building and an enormous increase in both students and staff impending, the School's chief problems would be administrative.

The last event that calls for any mention during this period is the planning for a new building. The Studley building, which was already too small for the needs of the School when first occupied in 1952, had by the summer of 1964 become so inadequate that the faculty was forced for the first time in the history of the School to refuse admission to a number of well-qualified applicants. By this time, fortunately, a new building had already been authorized, the big five-storey high-rise that will be known as the Weldon Building. A building of that size – designed to hold up to 450 students – had not been planned without grave misgivings on the part of some of the members of the faculty. Horace Read, for example, was dead against allowing the School to grow larger than 200; to limit enrolment to that figure was, he felt, the only way to preserve the traditional atmosphere. But MacKay, and others, felt that to do as Read suggested would deprive many Maritimers of the chance for a legal education. Notwithstanding their eventual unanimous decision – which was to expand and plan for a new big building – all the members of faculty were concerned about the potential loss of the traditional atmosphere, the close contact between teachers and students, between third-year and first-year, and between the individual members of each year. How, they asked themselves, are we going to retain in the new 'Big School' 'the relaxed but formal atmosphere' that has always characterized Dalhousie Law School? The next Part, 'In the Weldon Building,' will reveal how much of the traditional atmosphere was lost and how much preserved.

Should there not be a summary of the ways in which, as a result of the changes described in the present Part, 'Changing,' the School was in 1966 still like the School that it had been from 1887 to 1945 and the ways in which it was becoming like the School that it will be in 1976? No, there should not. This Part already smacks too much of the legendary sergeant-major's method of instruction – 'First I tells 'em what I'm going to say, then I sez it, then I tells 'em what I said' – and we will not insult the readers' intelligence further. All we are going to say is this. In 1966 the School stood with one foot in the past of Dalhousie's Little Law School in the Forrest Building and one foot in the future of the Weldon Building School portrayed in the brochure entitled 'The Dalhousie Law School' issued in 1975.

PART IV

In the Weldon Building: 1966-1976

At the end of Part I, 'Beginning,' we remarked: 'It could indeed be said that it was not until after the School moved to its fifth and present home in the Weldon Building that "anything really happened," so that this history might well end here in 1887 and begin again in 1966.' We have told the uneventful story of Dalhousie's Little Law School and have recounted the changes that slowly but surely came over it in the twenty years following the end of the Second World War. We come now to the last period with which this history will deal – the years 1966 to 1976. In this short ten-year period there are so many noteworthy events and the School becomes so obviously different from what it has always traditionally been that two separate and entirely different sections will be required to record those events and those changes.

In the summer of 1966 the School moved to its fifth and present home, the Weldon Building. At about the same time three things external to the School occurred that combined to make it in 1976 such a very different place. The first, and by far the most important, was money. For more than eighty years the School had limped along on what it got from student fees and, in more recent years, from the occasional munificence of grateful graduates like Viscount Bennett and Sir James Dunn. Now the two governments, federal and provincial, together began to supply to the University, and through it to the School, eighty per cent of operating costs; as to capital costs, the Weldon Building itself was almost entirely paid for by the government of Nova Scotia. There is now money, and what in comparison with the past seems money in abundance, for teachers, for the library, and even for luxuries like sculptures to adorn the entrance to the building. From the same source also began to come money, in the shape of small grants and generous interest-free loans, for students, with the result that there were in each of the three years prior to 1976 around twelve hundred applicants for admission to the first-year class instead of the one hundred and fifty odd that there were in each of the two years before 1966. The first change then is a change in size; there are so many more students and so many more teachers that Dalhousie's Little Law School is a thing of the past.

The second external factor combining to change the nature of the School was that world-wide phenomenon of the mid-sixties student activism. Student leaders are no longer relatively passive recipients of the traditional wisdom of their elders, patiently taking what comes until they can get their degree and go out into practice. They are self-starters, know what they want of their life at the School, say what that is, and do their best to get it. Those who were at the School during its first four years in the new building form an excellent illustration of this new trend. They organized and held at the School a cross-Canada student conference on the crisis in Confederation (on which no faculty member had written anything), started a journal of legal opinion, *The Ansul* (five years before the faculty's *Dalhousie Law Journal* got off the ground), secured (albeit at the instigation of the faculty) student representation on faculty committees, and were the prime movers in instituting what posterity will probably regard as one of the most important achievements of this period, the Dalhousie Legal Aid Service. The second change therefore is a change in the extent to which the School is shaped by the students.

The third factor was the ferment of ideas on legal education which began in Ontario in the mid-sixties and culminated in the relaxation of the control of the profession over the curriculum. To this third factor Dalhousie Law School owes the partial abandonment in 1969 and the total abandonment in 1974 – whether for better or for worse – of the rigid and narrowly professional MacRae or Canadian Bar Association standard curriculum to which it had been tied since 1920. So that the third change is a change of direction, and in the direction of the cultural mix with which the School started in 1883, in what is its central function – the subjects it teaches and how it teaches them.

Section One of this Part will describe in more or less chronological order the significant events of the last ten years. In reading about them please remember that all the time the teachers are continuing to teach and the students are continuing to learn – which is far more important in this, or in any other, educational institution than any 'significant event.' Section Two will be devoted to painting a general picture of developments in each of the three most important elements in the School – the faculty, the students, and the curriculum. Now that the School has ceased to be 'just a little family' with each of its members known, at least by sight, to all the others, the picture can no longer be individual and personal; it has to be general and impersonal.

SECTION ONE

Significant Events

The make-up of the three classes which started work in the Weldon Building in September 1966 was in itself a significant event. In striking contrast to the hundred-odd students who were at the School in each of the three years from 1959-60 to 1962-63, there were now more than two hundred of them; in less than ten years' time there will be all that the building can hold, four hundred and fifty, and there will be talk of expanding to take in still more. In striking contrast, again, to the class of 1963 which had thirty-two students in its first year, twenty-two in its second, and twenty-two in its third – so that, as Dean MacKay has said, 'the flavour was what it must have been like in the twenties and thirties and every class was a seminar' – there were in 1966 ninety-four in the first year, almost as many as there were in the combined second and third years. For the first time in the history of the School the first-year students were divided into two sections (in 1976 it would be three), so that henceforth their loyalties and their friendships are likely to be confined to the fifty-odd other members of their section, to the detriment of the traditional class solidarity. And the fact that they outnumbered the fifty-seven members of the third-year class meant that the tradition of the first year taking its tone from the leaders of the third year was probably broken; almost certainly it does not exist today.

Also in striking contrast to the past was the size and make-up of the faculty. For the last few years before the move to the Weldon Building there had been eight or nine full-time teachers, all but one of whom were old students of the School. In 1966 they numbered sixteen and among those joining in that year were two young teachers who had had no previous connection with Dalhousie and two returning old students who had been away far enough and long enough to feel that the School was in danger of becoming inbred and should recruit more outsiders. (In 1976 there were thirty-six full-time teachers, with the outsiders far outnumbering the old students.) It was fortunate for the School that the two returning old students, Arthur Foote and Murray Fraser, came back when they did. In the critical years which followed, each in his own different way played an important part in preserving a proper balance between the traditions of its past and the demands of its future. Foote, a graduate of 1954 and a Rhodes Scholar at Oxford who had taught for several years at the Ottawa and Osgoode Hall law schools, was conservative enough to carry on, as he still does, the 'ever-open door policy' of the Weldon tradition by talking to individual students about law, their problems, and themselves, but innovative enough to guide through its first three years the tradition-breaking partially optionalized curriculum of 1969. Murray Fraser, who graduated in 1960, took his LLM in London, taught for a while at Queen's Law School, and practised for a while with a firm in Halifax, was innovative enough to pioneer in 1970, together with Foote, an imaginative compulsory first-year course in Family Law but conservative enough to be, as Interim Dean, a stabilizing influence on the School after the sudden death of Dean Donald in the fall of 1971; he became in 1974 the first dean of the new law school in Victoria, British Columbia.

In the spring of 1967 ceremonies were held to mark the official opening of the new building and a plaque in honour of Weldon, the creator of the School, was unveiled with J.W. Weldon ('03) of Montreal, a son of Dean Weldon, assisting. The plaque, and close beside it a portrait of the Dean that shows his commanding presence, is one of the first things to strike your eye as you enter the foyer; the other things are the sunburst of a symbolical metal sculpture and the portraits of other past deans which are ranged along the semi-circular outside walls of a huge assembly room. Here again is a striking contrast with the past. For over eighty years, ever since the establishment of a School of Law at Dalhousie in 1883, both the teachers and the taught had had to endure facilities which by today's standards can only be described as rough, cramped, and primitive. In the Weldon Building their quarters can for the first time be described as 'commodious' – with a spacious students' lounge and a spacious faculty lounge-cum-library in addition to the usual library, class-rooms, and seminar rooms – and, what is more, some attempt has been made to beautify them. In the library, for example, there are soft blue carpets, handsome glass showcases, and a colourful portrait of Sir James Dunn.

At another ceremony on the same day the library was formally named the Sir James Dunn Law Library, in recognition of the generous support given to it by Sir James Dunn in his lifetime and by the Dunn Foundation after his death. It was not only formally but also fittingly so named: for when James Dunn was at the Law School in the late nineties he was hard pressed for money and took on the job of a student librarian at a small honorarium, in which office he became custodian of the five or six thousand books that then comprised the collection. The library is, it is true, a 'fulcrum, a pivot, a hub upon which the success of any law school is, and may fairly be, judged,' but it is not a very interesting topic to write about. George Nicholls, from whose brochure, *The Dalhousie Law School*, the words just quoted have been taken, is less boring on the subject than this hand could ever hope to be. Let him tell the story. After saying in the brochure that in 1957 'the library ranked among the worst of a poor lot in most essentials: staff, system – to venture an alliteration – space, size of collection, services provided' he goes on as follows:

A striking growth in library services has occurred over the past fifteen years or so at Dalhousie in common with the whole of Canada. Whereas the law library at Dalhousie had an estimated collection of 30,000 in 1957, a figure that itself was something of a padded one because of the high proportion of duplicates included, the collection is now close to 100,000. Whereas in 1957 the library staff consisted of one librarian assisted by eight students who received small honoraria for their part-time work, the staff now comprises a chief librarian, with training in law as well as library science, and a full-time staff of seventeen, including four librarians with library degrees and six others with a university education. The chief librarian is a member of faculty and has an active committee of faculty, the Library Committee, for consultation. Other improvements – in records like cataloguing, shelving, seating and all other aspects of a library intended for use – have kept pace. Two full floors in the Weldon Building out of the five are now occupied by the library.

Rapid expansion of curriculum, such as is occurring at Dalhousie, puts a strain on library services, but the Sir James Dunn Library is now among the best in Canada. It has an excellent collection of common-law materials, including a complete collection of legal periodicals in English. Here no doubt is one of the reasons why it has become the research library for lawyers throughout the four Atlantic provinces. As in other law-school libraries in Canada, there are limitations on its foreign-law materials and the specialized sources required by graduate students, but the Chief Librarian and the Library Committee have now the resources to look in those directions with improving eyes.

Every library should be of course a repository for the safekeeping of books, but, more important, the Dalhousie Law Library is a place where books can be conveniently used by students, faculty and sometimes by practitioners and the general public. It is a rewarding place to do research, and is certain to become more and more rewarding, for graduate students, undergraduates and others, as time goes on.

In this chronological record of significant events the fall of 1967 and the whole of 1968 belong exclusively to the students. In October 1967 students from every law school in Canada met in the Weldon Building and discussed such explosive and contemporary issues as 'separatism and Quebec,' 'an entrenched Bill of Rights,' and 'reform of the Supreme Court.' The idea of holding the National Centennial Conference of Canadian Law Students – a unique event, because for the first time in the history of Canadian legal education students from every Canadian law school came together to exchange ideas – was conceived, implemented, and brought to full fruition in the form of a printed report of the proceedings of the Conference, entitled *Confederation: A Look Ahead*, by a group of students at Dalhousie Law School. Three years later another group of them once again rendered themselves, and the School, visible nationally. At the annual meeting of the Canadian Bar Association, held in that year in Halifax, they gave concrete expression to the new spirit of social consciousness which was then at its height among law students right across the country by putting on what can best be described as a series of thoughtful antics derisory of the legal establishment; these antics received national coverage in the media. In the same spirit they also put out for that occasion a provocative special issue of their journal of legal opinion, *The Ansul: Dalhousie Law Forum*, with a photograph on its cover of the sleazily antiquated Full Bench courtroom in what was still at that date 'The Law Courts' on Spring Garden Road and underneath it the threatening slogan 'Thou Shalt Not Ration Justice.'

The first number of *Ansul* came out in December 1968. Stimulated by the successful publication of the papers and discussions presented at the National Centennial Conference, yet another group of students decided that the time was ripe to put an end to the reproach that 'Dalhousie has one of the few law schools in Canada that does not publish a regular law review.' Starting a student Dalhousie law review was not a new idea; in the fall of 1963 indeed it was so near to realization that the *Gazette* actually gave the name of the editor and the number of articles to be in the first issue that would appear in the following May. For various, and valid, reasons however, absolutely nothing came of the idea at that time but what came out of it in 1968 was, as one of the two founding editors told the writer, a 'student journal of legal opinion on things of interest to students and the practising bar, with hopes that it would turn into a regular law review.' Ansul is an old English name for what today we should call a balance or scales similar to those held by the familiar blind-fold Justice and symbolizing equality. The following two extracts from the editorial remarks in the first issue reveal the spirit in which *Ansul* was conceived:

The Ansul has been selected as the name of the new publication of the Dalhousie law students because it symbolizes the equality of worth, assigned by the first Dean of this School, Richard Chapman Weldon, to high academic standards and unselfish public service. To that principle it is dedicated. May it never represent anything less.

and

What we would like to achieve, and what we dedicate this forum to, is the fostering of a certain sense of social consciousness which seems so sadly lacking in today's institutions of legal training. If we can awaken, foster or promote even a minuscule amount of this precious commodity then we will consider our efforts a success.

The spirit in which *Ansul* was conceived has had, of course, to contend with the hard realities – among them the fact that not all the students want their journal to be a left-wing one, the fact that it is not always easy to get contributions for a journal that does not qualify as 'learned,' and the fact that student interest in having the journal at all fluctuates from year to year. So that its content and quality have from the beginning until today varied even from issue to issue and will probably continue to do so in the future. Sometimes primarily a house organ containing items of interest to those connected with the School, sometimes primarily a kind of 'broad picture' and unacademic law review on topics of contemporary legal interest, sometimes primarily a nakedly left-wing propaganda sheet on anything and everything that is even faintly legal, and sometimes a combination of all three, this off-beat publication is in the opinion of the writer nearly always worth reading and is in any event quite different from anything produced by any other law school in Canada.

In the fall of 1968 students began for the first time to serve on all standing committees of the Faculty. What was in those days of 'student power' regarded in some other schools as a controversial issue created no stir at all at Dalhousie Law School. To the faculty the taking of this step was no more than the natural outcome in the conditions of the late sixties of the close relations between students and faculty that had always existed ever since 1883; it was indeed from the faculty and not from the students that the new move came. By 1970 there would be students on the Faculty Council itself, with full voting rights on all matters except those involving an individual student – an exception requested by the students themselves – and by 1974 even that exception was removed. As to these further steps, neither the fears of the one or two more conservative members of the faculty nor the hopes of some of the more activist students have been justified; all one can say is that this totally new extension to the traditional close faculty-student relationship is on the whole working pretty well.

The year 1969 saw the disappearance of some of the last vestiges of 'the little family' and the beginning of a new era in curriculum. In both these changes Dean MacKay was the central figure. Because curriculum has been deferred for later description only two things will be said about it here. First, it was in this year that the first optionalization of the curriculum took place. And, second, it was MacKay who persuaded his colleagues to modify the much more drastic optionalization originally proposed by a committee of Faculty and who, in the year following, had, as President of the Conference of Governing Bodies, some influence on the decision of that organ of the profession to refrain from prescribing, as it had been feared they might, what the law schools should teach.

In the summer of 1969, and after only five years as Dean, MacKay was on short notice translated to the position of Academic Vice-President of the University. His lasting contribution is that he carried out, with the minimum of disturbance, what could have been a traumatic change from the little School to the big School. Because of his slow, gentle manner his colleagues were inclined to think of him as 'a delayer' and 'doing nothing much.' It was only after he left (though remaining to this day to lecture in Constitutional Law) that they realized what they had lost. His policy of delay was deliberate, to give everyone time to think sober thoughts and eventually reach a consensus;

and as to doing nothing much, he was spending, as the Law School files show, many lonely and inconspicuous hours in working out the tiresome details that were so vital to the success of all he undertook. In any event it was that slow, gentle manner of his which ensured the co-operation of students, colleagues, and downtown lecturers. To the question 'why on earth did you take it on?', one downtown lecturer replied, 'Because Andy asked me'; and one of his full-time colleagues still at the School has been described as 'being so high on Andy that no one else can ever be worthy of being Dean.'

For the purpose of this account of the last ten years in the history of the School, however, the most important thing about MacKay's departure is that he was the last in the long line of traditional deans. What ended the traditional dean was the vastly increased size and scope of the School. The old-time dean knew nearly all the students. In his anxiety to preserve the intimate atmosphere of the School – in which he was successful only as far as his own relation to students was concerned – MacKay still got to know most of them and made a deliberate effort to know the leaders in the third-year really well because he 'felt they set the tone of the School.' The old-time dean 'did everything,' from the comparatively high-level job of acting as a one-man admissions committee to the low-level one of helping to shift the books in the library. In continuance of this tradition MacKay was on one occasion found vacuuming the carpets in the Sir James Dunn Library so that all would be spick and span for the opening day of term. The old-time dean was in command, however veiled and benevolent, of his faculty. So, so far as his own temperament allowed, was MacKay. With MacKay's departure all that changed. In a year or two the dean will, to the students, be a somewhat remote figure in the recesses of the Dean's Office; an associate dean and a host of faculty committees will be doing the academic 'joe jobs' that he used to do; and he will in all matters of importance be subject to what is called faculty control.

Also a break with the traditions of the past was the manner of choosing someone to succeed MacKay. For the first time in the history of the School and in line with the requirements of that very recent phenomenon 'participatory democracy,' a committee of senior members of Faculty was set up to find a new dean. Meanwhile Robert T. Donald was appointed Acting Dean: of him in a moment. The committee were unable to find anyone on the Faculty who was both acceptable to them and willing to take on the deanship; on who from outside should be considered they ran into irreconcilable differences of opinion; they therefore disbanded. Another committee was then struck. Because it was now clear that getting a new dean would be a long job, Donald was appointed Dean retroactive to 1969. It was not indeed until two years after the departure of MacKay, in the fall of 1971, that the new Dean, Ronald St John Macdonald, then Dean of Law at the University of Toronto, was appointed effective 1 July 1972.

Robert Donald was only two years short of retirement age when he consented to take on the responsibilities of Acting Dean, and then only on the understanding that he was to be a caretaker dean merely. He had joined the staff in 1964 after a life spent in the practice of law and as a business executive. A Maritimer from Prince Edward Island, he graduated from the Law School in 1933 after leading his class in all three years and winning the University Medal. For a total of twelve years he was with a law firm in Halifax, interrupted by a three-year period of service with the wartime Department of Munitions and Supply; for the last fourteen years before he came back to the School as a professor he was secretary of Brazilian Traction in Toronto. In addition to his own fine legal mind he brought with him a special expertise in corporate finance and a habit of taking an active part in community affairs. It was therefore good fortune for the School that he, with his record of distinguished service at the Bar, to government, to business, to the community, and to Dalhousie, was prepared to take up the unrewarding load of caretaker dean. To quote from the tribute paid to him by the Faculty after his sudden and lamented death soon after the beginning of term in the fall of 1971: 'As Dean his qualities of personality, his sympathy and empathy with people, both young and old, and his gift for careful and patient planning, won the admiration, affection and respect of everyone.' What should also be remembered is the weight of the load he took up. After a life lived outside legal academia he had to cope – aided, it is true, by Arthur Foote, his Director of Studies – with all the problems raised by the new optionalized curriculum, and he found the innumerable student and other 'routine' problems, which at that time still landed on the desk of the Dean himself, much more disturbing than those which he had encountered in practice and in business. As to the self-sacrificing devotion with which he took the burden up and carried it, nobody has forgotten that.

In 1970 was born a new institution which has come to play an important part in the life of the School, the Dalhousie Legal Aid Service, or the Clinic as it is usually called. In its first beginnings it was the product of student idealism. A group of students, spearheaded by Dan Lapres (incidentally a Dunn scholar), were concerned at the number of people who, because they could not afford a lawyer, were appearing before Magistrate's Court in Halifax without legal representation; for it was not until two years later that the provincial legal aid system went into operation. They collected little bits of money from various charitable organizations in the city and, with the full co-operation of the Nova Scotia Barristers' Society and all the social service agencies, started giving, as far as the law allowed, legal advice and help to poor people who had, or thought they had, a legal problem. At this point two things happened which not only put the Clinic-to-be on its feet, but also determined the kind of activities it would engage in in the future: the federal government inaugurated a Canadian equivalent of the United States' poverty program and David Lowry came, fresh out of a graduate course at New York University that involved him in 'poverty law,' to the School as an assistant professor. Interested in finding out whether a 'neighbourhood law office' using the help of law students might be a way of delivering some legal services to the poor, the Department of National Health and Welfare produced a five-year grant and what had by that time become the duly organized, staffed, and directed Dalhousie Legal Aid service opened its 'store-front law office' in a poor district in the North End of Halifax. In line with the policy of furnishing innovative and law-oriented services to the poor on an experimental basis, other federal departments have since then provided it with a series of individual small grants to enable it and students connected with it to carry out short-term pilot projects in a variety of poverty law areas. And now for David Lowry. Had it not been for him, Dan Lapres' brainchild would never have amounted to anything more than a praiseworthy student activity like *Ansul*. For when he came as a 'new hand' in the summer of 1970 – for what turned out to be a stay of only two years – to prepare the classes he was to begin giving in the fall, he was able to persuade the Faculty to adopt Lapres' brainchild into the curriculum, thereby establishing the first clinical training course for academic credit in Canada.

With the able, hard-working, and supremely self-confident Lowry as the first of its directors and with the invaluable practically full-time assistance in its law office activities of Mr Justice Pottier, a retired Judge of the Supreme Court of Nova Scotia, the Service has become 'heavily involved in a variety of legal education and community service projects, including the training of paraprofessionals, major research into community problems, law reform, preventative legal education directed to the community at large, and the education of law students who are encouraged to become involved in all phases of office activity.'[1] In an unpublished address to law students Professor Innis Christie has given the following recent bird's-eye view of the Clinic and of its value to the School:

Each term the Clinic takes twenty Third-Year law students who earn six of the Year's thirty credits for their work in the Clinic. They are supervised and graded by [the Director and one other teaching member of the Faculty] ... their work covers a wide variety of matters, except indictable offences and divorce matters which, as a general rule, have been referred to Nova Scotia Legal Aid since it came into operation.

Not only does the Clinic provide a valuable community service and a vehicle for experiment and research in connection with the role of lawyers in society, it goes a long way toward alleviating the situation of Third Year students who might otherwise feel they were getting the 'bored to death' treatment. The clinical experience gives them a preliminary look at some of the realities of practice, brings the 'real world' into the ivory tower and gives that all too rare species, the idealistic law student, an outlet. For many law students it is the first and perhaps the last opportunity they will have to be sensitized to the needs, legal and otherwise, of that very large part of the population that does not customarily enter a lawyer's office.[2]

In the academic year 1971-72 there were three 'firsts,' each one of which is important enough to call for brief mention. For the first time there was an inrush of women; by 1976 they constituted about a quarter of the student body. For the first time the Faculty was forced by the ever-increasing number of applications for admission to make a deliberate decision on how 'national' the student body should be allowed to become; hereafter 60 per cent of the one hundred and fifty places in the first year will be reserved for Nova Scotians, 15 per cent for people from the Atlantic provinces, and 25 per cent for those from elsewhere. And the first-ever associate dean was appointed – to lift from the shoulders of the Dean the relatively trivial administrative details involved in running the School and to insulate him from the problems of individual students in such a way that he gets to know about them without having to see each student personally. In four years' time there would be 'the Dean's Office,' consisting of the Dean, the Associate Dean, a Course Counsellor, and a Placement Officer. The first Associate Dean, Professor Murray Fraser, was appointed at the beginning of September 1971, just before Dean Donald became fatally ill – with the result that he was there to bridge as Interim Dean the gap between the death of Donald in October and the arrival of the new Dean, Ronald Macdonald, in the summer of 1972.

Like all the deans before him, Ronald Macdonald has, although born and brought up in Montreal, deep family roots in the Maritimes, but he is the first since Weldon to have the horizon-expanding subject of International Law as his main interest. After taking his Arts degree at St Francis Xavier University he graduated from the old Forrest Building Law School in 1952 and then did nearly three years' graduate work, obtaining an LLM from London, an LLM from Harvard, and a Diploma in International Law from Geneva. For seventeen years he taught successively at the law schools of Osgoode Hall, the University of Western Ontario, and the University of Toronto, of which last school he was dean for the last five years before he came back to Dalhousie. Himself a prolific writer of articles for law journals, almost all of them on legal aspects of contemporary problems of international law, he was founding editor of the student-directed law journals at Osgoode and Western and was for ten years editor of the *University of Toronto Law Journal*, which, like the *Canadian Bar Review*, is a journal run by professionals for professionals. In his chosen field of International Law he has always played an active part in great affairs; he has, for instance, been a member of the Canadian delegation to the United Nations and a representative of Canada to an international conference on human rights. With his background of an upbringing in Montreal, study abroad, and teaching in Ontario, it is not surprising to find someone saying of him – with a measure of truth: 'The priorities of the School have traditionally been Nova Scotia first, the Atlantic Provinces second, the Dominion of Canada third, and the international community last. Macdonald's seem to be in exactly reverse order: first the international community, then the Dominion of Canada, then the Atlantic Provinces, with Nova Scotia last.' So be it, after disregarding the exaggeration. With a faculty that has come to have something of an international flavour, a student body that is more 'national' than it has ever been before, and a curriculum that is less concerned than it used to be with what Sidney Smith once derisively called 'the conveyancer from Liverpool, Nova Scotia,' the School itself has made a slight change in the same direction and had begun it before Macdonald arrived. Nor is it, with his background of extensive graduate work, editing law journals, and working on contemporary problems of international law, surprising that when he came to the School he had behind him assurance from the University administration that it would provide the financial input necessary to revive the languishing graduate program, start a law review, and set in train a novel venture in an area where international and domestic law and policy intesect, Marine and Environmental Law.

Post-graduate work leading to the degree of Master of Laws had been offered at the School ever since 1950. It was, the reader may recall, at that time practically forced on Dean Horace Read by Premier Angus L. Macdonald and Sir James Dunn who felt that Canadians should not have to go outside Canada to do graduate work in law. The School did not have during his deanship – nor indeed until very recent years – a library or staff adequate to the task and, what is more, as Read said at a Faculty meeting in 1960 'he never encouraged anyone to do post-graduate work here because he felt that the energy of the Faculty should be directed to the LLB students.' Dean Read's negative attitude was, by the way, shared – and is still shared – by most law teachers in Canada, but for a different reason: they feel that Canadians should continue to go to the United States (and to a lesser extent England) for their graduate work, as most of them still do, in order to expose themselves to the stimulus that can only be found at seminal centres of legal learning. In any event, until 1973 the School rarely had more than one or two graduate students registered in the same year and with only two or three exceptions they were people who had done their LLB there too.

By 1972 there was a library good enough and a staff large enough and enough interested in research in the area of public law – which is what most graduate students are looking for – to make a new start. Actively encouraged by the University administration because of the increased prestige that any graduate program is expected to bring, and aided by a substantial increase in the scholarship money it could offer, the School began to promote its LLM program more widely and more aggressively, both inside and outside Canada. In 1973-74 there was for the first time in the history of the School a sizable enrolment of registered LLM candidates – nine; in 1974-75 there were five; in 1975-76 there were again nine. Nearly all of them, however, were from outside Canada; the dream of Premier Macdonald and Sir James Dunn has not yet been, and in the opinion of the writer is not likely to be, realized. Now that the program seems to be stabilized, the Graduate Committee is making plans for its future. One of the Committee's hopes is that instead of being 'just another graduate school,' it will develop into an internationally recognized centre for graduate work in Marine and Environmental Law – of which more in a moment.

In September 1973 there came at last what has been described as 'the publication of Canada's most newly established legal journal by Canada's oldest established common law school,' the *Dalhousie Law Journal*.[3] As long ago as 1926 and only six years after the Faculty had ceased to be a merely one full-time man operation, Dean John Read 'brought up the question of the establishing of a Dalhousie Law Review and declared that several students of this Law School were very favourably interested in the matter' but, after looking into the feasibility of the project, proposed 'as a preliminary and experimental step to try to arrange for the publication of the work of our own student body in the *Canadian Bar Review*.[4] The student interest in having a law review and having it, at least in part, as an outlet for their own writings was therefore nothing new when, as we have seen earlier, they tried again in the sixties. So that when Dean Macdonald came to start the new law review the students assumed it was to be one in which they would have a major voice and in which they would publish their papers – in other words a training ground for students, which is what all the other law school law reviews in Canada are, with the exception of the *University of Toronto Law Journal*. Fresh from his ten-year tenure of the editorship of the *University of Toronto Law Journal*, Macdonald insisted that it was to be one run by professionals for professionals. Surprisingly enough in an institution that in these days is addicted to giving in to the students, Macdonald won the day. The editorial committee consists of Dean Macdonald as editor, four professors, and two students. Because it is 'run by professionals for professionals' the new *Dalhousie Law Journal* has so far been able to obtain worthwhile contributions from distinguished professors of law and related disciplines in many parts of the English-speaking world, but there have, of course, also appeared in it some excellent articles by Dalhousie law students, both undergraduate and post-graduate.

As to the new venture in Marine and Environmental Law, the University had begun with the seventies to develop multi-disciplinary and inter-disciplinary studies on the sea and the environment – the Halifax-Dartmouth district being a natural centre of marine studies and the Atlantic provinces having become increasingly concerned with the need to establish policies that balance the need for economic development against the need to preserve the natural beauty of their coasts – and in these studies law, and so the Law School, was expected to play an important part. In order to build up in the School a nucleus of staff members who would be needed for that purpose

Dean Macdonald brought with him from Toronto, to form the centre of that nucleus, a Scottish-born law teacher turned political scientist with a special interest in international law and policy related to the sea, Professor Douglas Johnston. Among the group in the academic year 1975-6 are professors interested in such non-traditional areas of law as those relating to the seacoast, to oil and gas, to environmental quality, and to resources management, as well as professors interested in the traditional admiralty law (among them one who has his master mariner's papers!). The members of this 'marine and environmental group' are offering no less than twelve full-year courses in that area and have been doing research in the law of the sea, energy problems, offshore resource issues, coastal zone management, and beach protection.[5] At the detailed proposal stage is a centre of marine policy studies involving specialization in law, economics, political science, oceanography, and other disciplines. So that, without diminishing in any way its loyalty to its own discipline of the law, the School is for the first time making a genuine effort to reach out to the other disciplines in the University of which it has from the very beginning been part.

Inspired by the driving energy of Professor Hudson Janisch, a native of South Africa who studied law at Cambridge and Chicago and came to Dalhousie in 1972 from teaching at the University of Western Ontario, the School has also begun to reach out to the legal profession, and even to the general public, through its ambitious continuing legal education program. This new venture, now three years old, is generally regarded as one of the best things the School has done in recent years. Week-end conferences aimed at the legal profession have dealt with problems in specialized areas – ranging from such familiar ones as sentencing to such esoteric ones as telecommunications regulation – into which the ordinary workaday lawyer in the Atlantic region is, in these days of rapid change, most likely to run; the audiences have been drawn from that entire region, not merely from Halifax-Dartmouth; the people giving papers have for the most part been Law School alumni or faculty members. In 'public legal education,' particularly well received was a series of Saturday morning sessions on the planning process attended by persons coming mainly from concerned citizens groups, with some from government and the universities. Very contemporary in its approach to this modern product of the Weldon tradition is the feeling of the Public Services Committee of the Faculty that it should as far as possible involve non-lawyers in all its programs; thus in the Sentencing Conference, which was aimed primarily at lawyers, 'there was a most valuable interplay between lawyers, parole board officers, prison service personnel, social workers and agency staff as well as between crown prosecutors, defense counsel and members of the bench.'[6]

Two other examples of the mood of 'reaching out' with which the School faces the future – and one sad event looking only to its past – will conclude this chronological record of significant happenings 1966-76. In 1974-75 the Faculty decided to foster a special relationship between Dalhousie Law School and the University of Maine Law School. In October 1975 four members of the marine and environmental group attended a workshop on Canadian – US coastal relations at Portland, Maine; the workshop was organized jointly by the two schools. A return engagement in Halifax, the second in what is expected to be a long series of meetings to discuss legal issues of mutual interest, took place in the fall of 1976 – a conference entitled 'Is the Common Law Dead,' in which judges, law teachers, and practising lawyers from both Canada and the United States participated. And in 1975-76 the School at last reached out to its own alumni by establishing an office of alumni affairs and by issuing in January 1976 the first number of what is planned to be a thrice-yearly news bulletin of what is going on, *Hearsay*. Like so many other things connected with the School, there is nothing new about the idea of what in the Faculty minutes for 1961 is ponderously called 'alumni liaison.' The reader may perhaps recall that as long ago as 1920 Dean MacRae made a trip to the principal cities of central and western Canada to meet with them and that in 1922 R.H. Murray actually succeeded in organizing a small group of them into the Dalhousie Law Association, which association soon died. What, like some other things that have happened during the last ten years, *is* new is that the idea has at last become a reality.

With the death of Dean Emeritus Horace E. Read early in 1975 there was broken a vital link with the past of Dalhousie Law School. When he came to the School as a student in 1921 Weldon was still living in retirement in Dartmouth, and MacRae, the man who made the School academically notable, was Dean. When he taught there as a young professor from 1925 to 1933, Dalhousie's Little Law School was in its golden age and he had as colleagues John Read, Sidney Smith, Angus L. Macdonald, and Vincent MacDonald. When he himself was Dean from 1950 to 1964 he was the central figure in that period of slow but sure change and, although promoted to be Vice-President of the University, he continued until the early seventies to teach in what may be called the new Dalhousie Law School of today. In the last two or three years of his life he was struggling to complete this history. Everybody who knew him, even those who did not particularly admire him, agrees that the School stood always first in his thoughts. An excellent teacher, a first-rate author, and an unaffectedly kind man, he will be long and deservedly remembered. In recognition of his contributions to legal education and legal scholarship the School has established an annual lecture, the Horace E. Read Memorial Lecture, that will be devoted in rotation to each one of the three principal areas of professional interest to him: legislation and the legislative process, witness his pioneering *Cases and Materials on Legislation*; conflict of laws, witness his trail-breaking book on *Recognition and Enforcement of Foreign Judgments*; and legal education. The inaugural lecture in the series, one on statutory interpretation, was given early in 1976 by a professor from the Columbia Law School.

SECTION TWO

Significant Changes: Faculty, Students, and Curriculum

This section will describe in broad outline what has been happening to the faculty, to the student body, and to the curriculum during the ten years leading up to 1976 where this history ends ('today'). It will reveal how greatly changed each one of them now is from what it traditionally was. It will also reveal how deeply those changes have affected the character of the School. We begin with the full-time faculty, disregarding the dean: about the change in his position all that needs to be said has already been said in the last section, in connection with Dean MacKay's departure in 1969.

The most obvious change in the full-time faculty has been, of course, one of size. From a level of eight or nine during the last few years before Horace Read retired as dean in 1964, it has gradually grown – with a sudden spurt at the time of the move to the Weldon Building to take care of the increase in enrolment and another spurt at the time of Dean Macdonald's arrival to permit the offering of a wider range of courses – to thirty-six today. In the days of the small faculty each one of the teachers was seen by all of the students in year after year and in class after class, so that not only did they get to know him through and through but they often came to see him – Weldon is the classic example – as larger than life. With today's large faculty the chances of a student ever seeing more than a small number of them are so great that devices, such as small seminars given by a revolving series of all the teachers to the members of each first-year class in their first week at the School, have had to be invented in order to introduce at least some of the teachers to some of the students. Gone too is the easy exchange of School news and the casual formation of School policy by colleagues as they happen to meet in the passage. Paper, masses of paper, and bureaucracy have of necessity become the order of the day. News about what is going on at the School now comes to each faculty member by way of written memoranda from the Dean's Office and also, since 1974, by a weekly newsletter consisting of six or seven pages of orange throw-away paper. As to the formation of School policy, that is now done – and has to be done, because in these days the students have to have a voice in it too – with all due formality by Faculty Council which must, since 1975-76, meet once every two weeks. At these meetings decisions will often turn on the 'true interpretation' of such 'authorities' as the 'Hutchins' Regulations' on the disposition of failures and the 'Christie Report' on curriculum; here, even here, bureaucratic labels reign supreme.

Fortunately this increase in size of the full-time faculty has not removed all traces of the atmosphere of the old School. The air is still warm and friendly; students respectfully josh teachers in the elevator; colleagues wrangle amicably in the faculty lounge. And size, coupled with diversity of origin and diversity of experience, has brought with it real gains. As recently as the first year in the Weldon Building, of the sixteen faculty members all but three were Dalhousie graduates and of those three two were just 'passing through.' Granted that these old boys loved the School, that they were conscious of its traditions, and that they wanted to continue them, the School was in danger of becoming inbred; as was said by a graduate of the early fifties who came back in that year to teach, 'we were still doing the same things that we did when I was a student.' At his instigation a policy of appointing outsiders was adopted, with the result that by 1976 the pendulum had swung so far in the other direction that the complaint now sometimes heard is 'what are all these Australians, Americans, and South Africans – you name it – doing on the faculty.' There are now twenty-two outsiders and only fourteen old boys. A few examples will do more than any recital of figures to show how diverse in origin and interests are the 1976 members of the group. Of the outsiders, one is a graduate of the Harvard Law School who worked three years in the Paris branch of a New York law firm and is now deep in research and writing; another is a graduate of law schools in South Africa, England, and the United States who has successfully organized a series of conferences on contemporary legal problems aimed primarily at lawyers in the Atlantic region; another is a graduate of the Osgoode Hall and Harvard law schools who is regularly to be seen on television in connection with legal and economic aspects of energy problems; and so on. (The reader should, however, be told that by the fall of 1978 the pendulum had begun to swing away from outsiders and back to old boys and that all the three outsiders singled out for special mention in the last sentence had left.)Of the old boys, one is chairman of the Nova Scotia Labour Relations Board and is writing a book on employment law; another is both a lawyer and a chartered accountant who practises tax law on the side in Halifax and has for many years written voluminously, and authoritatively, on the subject; and, once again, so on. One important result of this new-found diversity is that – as can be discerned from listening to what the teachers talk to one another about in the faculty lounge – the intellectual horizons of the group as a whole are now national, or even international, and not purely local, as they were not so long ago.

Another important result is an atmosphere of questioning and inquiry which is conducive to research and writing. Also conducive to it is the fact that, unlike his counterpart of a few years ago, the typical young law teacher of today thinks of himself as already a specialist and is actually encouraged to become one by being allowed to give, as one of his courses in what is in any event a relatively light teaching load, a small seminar on whatever corner of the law most interests him. So that, breaking sharply with what had during the deanships of Horace Read and Andrew MacKay become almost a tradition of teaching to the exclusion of writing, the faculty have in recent years been writing in a wide variety of fields. Read is said to have said that 'ninety-five percent of what is published in the journals is a waste of the reader's and the writer's time'; MacKay published nothing; their little faculty in what was still recognizably Dalhousie's Little Law School got the message and, with one notable exception, published little or nothing themselves. The influx of outsiders from places where a law teacher was expected to, and did, write and the advent of Dean Ronald Macdonald, a prolific writer who lets it be known that he expects others to do likewise, have changed all that. In the last year or so two books have come from the faculty, one on legal philosophy and the other on the law of criminal conspiracy; a third, on employment law, is in the making. As for essays contributed to collections in book form and articles published in legal periodicals, faculty members are now at last making themselves, and the Law School, visible in the following areas – to mention just a few: family law; tort law; administrative law; international law; and, as one would expect, in the contemporarily relevant fields of the law relating to natural resources, to the environment, and to the sea. After nearly a hundred years the Law School is, one hopes, now readying itself to make an addition to 'the Weldon tradition' – Weldon himself never published anything – that

Weldon's successors in the Golden Age dreamed of but were too overburdened with teaching to accomplish: a tradition of scholarly writing by members of the faculty.

Two other things of relatively minor importance should be mentioned to complete this brief sketch of what has been happening to the full-time faculty in the last decade. The first is that most of them are now very young, and, as is now *de rigueur* with youth, very vocal. Gone is the feeling of awe with which two old boys who came back to the School to teach soon after the move to the Weldon Building say they approached the core of old-timers who were at that time still in firm control of the future of the School. As with the other changes we have mentioned there are some gains and some losses. On the gain side the faculty is willing, as it would not have been ten years ago, to make the bold experiments called for by the rapid changes which are now taking place in the role of the lawyer. On the loss side, because the young teachers are inclined to empathize with the students – some of them go so far as to dress like them in order, said one of them, 'to relate to them' – the faculty as a whole is inclined in its discussion of any educational issue to ask as its first question, not, as it would have done ten years ago, 'is the idea pedagogically sound?' but 'do the students want it?'

About the second thing to be mentioned – the rapid turnover in full-time faculty that has taken place during the past ten years – there is nothing particularly new; in the more than fifty years that have elapsed since 1920 when the School first acquired a full-time faculty in addition to the dean, the periods of faculty stability have always been short and exceptional. What can, and should, be said is that, given its remoteness from where the action is, the School has been lucky to have got the bright young men it did and to have kept them even for the short time it did. Getting and keeping a competent staff at Dalhousie Law School has always been a headache. If in the future anything will tempt these bright young men to stay it will be the warm atmosphere of the School and the feeling, always general in the Maritimes but now spreading to the rest of the country, that 'there is more to life than being an intellectual sharpy in Toronto.'

And now for a few words about those who teach at the School but are not members of the full-time staff. Two innovations made during this period are sufficiently interesting to call for at least a mention: the occasional visiting professor, a teacher of some distinction who comes from another school, sometimes in another country, to fill for one year only the gap left by a regular member of the full-time faculty who is away on sabbatical leave; and the occasional 'airplane professor,' usually a teacher of rare distinction, such as Professor Frank Scott of McGill, who flies in for a few hours every week or so to conduct a seminar on a subject for which he is famous and flies back home again when he has done it. But what demands something more than mere mention is the changed position of the part-time faculty, the so-called downtown lecturers. A memorandum in the Faculty files dated 14 November 1966 and headed 'The Role of Part-time and Special Lecturers' is a formal recognition of the final end of their old role and the beginning of the new one that they have been playing ever since. In line with a trend that began with the gradual increase in their numbers in the fifties and early sixties and culminated with a sudden spurt to sixteen on the move to the Weldon Building, the full-time faculty had by 1966 taken over all the regular courses, and thereafter, as the memorandum proposed, the downtowner is only called in to provide an expertise that he and he alone possesses. As we have said so often before, in this there are some gains and some losses. Among the gains is the first-rate instruction that the students receive from the youngish practitioner who now comes up to teach a traditional subject, such as Trusts, merely because he loves it or to conduct a seminar in an area that no academic is capable of handling, such as Administration of Collective Agreements or Criminal Trial Practice, or to discuss on an individual basis the Legal Writing papers written by first-year students who are glad to rub shoulders with a real live lawyer. Among the losses is – quite apart from what may be merely this writer's sentimental regret at this final severance of the bond between the leaders of the Halifax Bar and the School which they in the beginning created and for so many years kept alive – the final disappearance from the daily life of the School of the figure of 'the wise old man' who, when he was not prevented from coming by clients' demands, came up at five o'clock and gave the students much more than mere law. The wise old men are still to be seen at the School on formal occasions, taking part in such events as the annual Smith Shield Moot Court Competition and the opening day of term each fall, but that is by no means the same thing.

Passing now to the student body, what has been happening to it during the past ten years? On the all-important factor of increase in size and the effect that that has had on what was left of Dalhousie's Little Law School, enough has already been said in the chronological record of significant events to give the general picture. All that remains to be done is to record some of the efforts that have been made to preserve at least a vestige of the intimate atmosphere. To compensate for the loss of the casual getting together that went naturally with the little family, the students created for themselves in 1967 a sort of social centre, called 'Domus Legis,' in a house on a nearby street; it is now an established custom for groups of them to go there every Friday afternoon to attend a weekly gathering, called Weepers, at which they are supposed to cry into their beer over the tribulations of the past week. They have also taken steps to bridge the communication gap that size has brought with it. In 1968 they found it necessary to invent the *Law Student Handbook* to do a job that in the past had always been done by word of mouth or just plain osmosis: this mimeographed booklet, issued annually since then to each member of the incoming first-year class, tells 'all you need to know about the Law School.' And in order, as one of them put it, 'to keep the School from becoming more of a rumour mill than it is' they started in the early seventies the *Weldon Times*, a news-sheet which appears sporadically to disseminate news and opinion on matters of more than casual interest to them – for example the controversial announcement made in 1974 by the President of the University that the School might have to be expanded by as much as fifty per cent. The most recent drive to bridge the gap brought about by mere size, between students and faculty as well as between student and student, was designed by the faculty and began operating in the fall of 1975 – the division of the first-year class in Contracts into eight small groups with the idea, among others, that each of the twenty students in each group should get to know at least nineteen fellow students and one professor fairly well.

Apart from two changes of significance, one major and the other minor, that will be mentioned in a moment, the composition of the student body has remained much the same as it was before the move to the Weldon Building. In continuance of a trend that had in the last few years before that date become established, there are students at the School with origins in all provinces. The School can now when on parade describe itself without any dishonesty as a 'national law school,' in the narrow sense of not being one attended only by Nova Scotians or Maritimers; indeed, as has been recorded earlier, it took a deliberate decision of the Faculty in 1971 to keep the Nova Scotian (60 per cent) and Maritime (15 per cent) element as high as it now is. The students continue to come from a great variety of academic backgrounds, but mainly, of course, from general arts and the social sciences; as before, nearly all of them have a first degree. The Dunn scholars continue to 'leaven the lump' by their presence and Lady Dunn (now Lady Beaverbrook) continues to take a personal interest in the selection of them; it took indeed her own personal decision, made at the urgent request of the Faculty, to open the scholarships up to women in 1975. (As the reader already knows, however, the Dunn scholarships were discontinued in the fall of 1977.)

And now for the change of major significance – the in-rush of women students. Ever since Frances Fish, Emelyn MacKenzie and Carol McInnes came to the School in the middle of the First World War, there had always been a sprinkling of women, but it was not until the fall of 1971 that they began coming regularly and in such numbers that by 1975-76 one in every four students was a woman. In these days of 'Women's Lib' the writer does not dare to predict what effect their presence is likely to have on the life of the School. It is, however, quite clear that in things academic they are more than holding their own with the men; in both 1974-75 and in 1975-76 one of the two members of the winning team in the Smith Shield Moot Court Competition was a woman, and in 1975-76 a woman was the editor of *Ansul*. In this connection it should also be recorded that during the last two or three years women graduates of the School have for the first time figured in the success stories that deans of the past used, when on parade, to love to tell: in 1974 Melinda MacLean ('69) was elected to the Nova Scotia Legislature; and in 1975 Bertha Wilson ('57) was appointed to the Ontario Court of Appeal, the first woman ever to be appointed to a court of appeal in Canada. The change of minor significance is that there will now be found among the students three kinds of people who would almost never have been found there ten years ago: two or three blacks; a handful of 'mature' men and women who have already been out in life and have decided to go back to school in order to become lawyers (for example, an ex-oil driller, an ex-professional librarian, an ex-helicopter pilot); and more than a handful of unmotivated refugees from other disciplines, people who do not really want to become lawyers but have drifted into law because of the disheartening job prospect for products of the graduate schools where they would really like to be.

Academically, the student body of today comes in better qualified, works harder, and does better than it did ten years ago. A few dry figures will help to give the picture. In 1966 an average of 60 per cent in your college work would have been enough to get you in. Today, because of the increased competition for the one hundred and fifty places in the first year – since 1972 the number of candidates has ranged around twelve hundred per annum – you will need an average of around 70 if you are a Nova Scotian, of around 75 if you are from the rest of the Maritimes, and of around 77 if you are from outside the Maritimes. As to working harder, the failure rate has dropped to almost nothing and, as to doing better, the percentage of students who succeed in maintaining a B average or better is much higher than it used to be: even after allowing for the recent continent-wide inflation in marks, there has been a marked improvement since 1966. Some downtown voices have been heard to say that the student of today may come in better but he comes out worse, meaning that as an embryo lawyer going into the articling stage of his legal education he is less competent than he used to be. However that may be – and 'less competent' may mean only that he is more ignorant of the nuts and bolts that no modern law school anywhere any longer aims to teach – his teachers make him work harder and expect more of him today than at any time in the School's history.

In each and every course the student of 1976 takes he is faced by a specialist with whose sophisticated handling of intricate problems he must keep up and is confronted by a xeroxed volume of cases and materials which he *has* to read in order to follow the discussion at all. Quite a contrast from the not so distant 'good old days' when the typical teacher was a hastily got-up generalist whose only materials were a mere syllabus of cases which he hoped, but did not expect, that the student would read in the library *if* he could lay his hands on a copy of the report! To compensate for the heavy burden thus laid on him, however, the student is pampered or mollycoddled, to use the words of two older teachers still at the School, in ways he was not ten years ago. In his first year he is no longer given the 'scare them to death' treatment; he is gently eased into his new life by a program called Orientation Week. In his second and third years he is no longer faced with a list of prescribed courses; since 1974 there has been for those years an *à la carte* menu of courses and he can choose the ones he wants to take; he can even choose his teacher. If he doesn't like the grade his teacher has given him, he has had since the fall of 1975 the *right* to have his paper re-read by someone else. In the spring of 1976 he was given class time to fill in a form evaluating his teacher, the results to be made public, although for several years now his teachers have been debarred from revealing to anyone his own grades and class standing.

The latest instance of pampering occurred in connection with the Moot Court, the oldest of the educational activities now run by the students. Because, as a number of times before in its history, the fun element was sometimes almost eliminating the educational element, a faculty committee (with students on it, of course) was appointed in the fall of 1975 to look into the matter and make recommendations as to what should be done to preserve the usefulness of what has ever since 1883 been an integral part of the curriculum. In the early spring of 1976 the committee came up with a recommendation that the faculty exercise greater control over the program, but the Faculty Council decided to defer action on it for a year 'because the students don't want it.'

Mention of the Moot Court leads naturally to the Mock Parliament and the Law Hour, the two other educational activities run by the students. The Mock Parliament has, with a few brief interruptions, been held every year since 1886; it has always belonged to, and has always been entirely run by, the students; it has never formed part of the curriculum. Here too in the last few years there had been too much fun. 'The whole thing had become a circus' – so it was dropped in 1974-75. In 1975-76, however, it was revived, this time with the new and untraditional name of 'Model Parliament,' 'to show that we mean it to be a serious affair.' The Law Hour is something new; it seems to have been started in 1967-68, and has from the beginning made a great contribution to the life of the School. It takes place at 11:30 every Thursday morning during the school year, and in recognition of its value in broadening everyone's horizons – faculty as well as students – no classes are scheduled for that hour. To it come speakers ranging from, say, a minister of the Crown who is in charge of a controversial piece of legislation to the president of the Flat Earth Society, to give two actual examples. First comes the address, then the questions, and then a free-for-all of a discussion – a great success.

We have reserved until last, and then only for very brief record, the most striking change that has taken place in the last ten years – the change in student attitudes. In line with the movement that in the mid-sixties swept across all universities on the continent, the students at Dalhousie Law School have become, with an intensity that varies from student to student and almost from year to year, critical, reformist, and very conscious of their 'rights.' Articles in *Ansul* – which cannot of course be taken as representing what all students, or even most students, think – berate the Faculty for what are made to seem their many deficiencies: the criticisms range from the self-serving and trivial, e.g. Faculty Council's refusal to change the name of the degree from Bachelor of Laws to Doctor of Law, to the unselfish and fundamental, e.g., the lack of social awareness in the curriculum. Most of these articles appeared around 1970 when both student protests and student idealism reached their highest point; both have since declined. As to student protests, there was never anything even approaching a confrontation. Law students, particularly law students in the Maritimes, have always been very conservative people and the study of law tends to make them ever more so. To quote a teacher who knows the students very well: 'the social reformer of the first year wears a business suit in the third.' As to student idealism, another teacher reports as follows: 'Before 1968 most of the students came to get a law degree so that they could make money with it; from 1968 on they wanted it so that they could go out and reform society; now (1976) they seem to be becoming like what they were before.' The reason is, of course, the present scarcity of jobs which has also, by the way, made them more competitive with one another than they were during the period of intense social idealism. Not only are they more critical and more idealistic than they were in 1966, they are also very conscious of their 'rights' and aggressive in pushing for them. They are no longer willing to accept as the roll of the dice the minor mishap that any student is likely to encounter sometime at the hand of some teacher – which is what they did in the past; they are quick to suspect injustice, are deeply resentful of it, and are not slow to do something about it. But here, to be fair to them, it should be said that they are equally resentful of what they consider to be the injustice done to what they call oppressed minorities and that to be quick to do something about it is a prime requirement in anyone who is going to be a lawyer.

Coming now to the curriculum, what has been happening to it during the past ten years? Before embarking on a very brief review of this area two things should be said. First, the striking changes made in the curriculum of the School during this period are not peculiar to it; they are similar, with local modifications, to those made in all the other common-law schools in Canada; they belong more to a history of legal education in Canada than to a history of Dalhousie Law School. Second, they are, in the opinion of the writer, much less important in this educational history of Dalhousie Law School than the introduction in the fifties of the 'do it yourself' method of teaching, a method on which more emphasis may have been laid than at any other Canadian law school. In continuance of the trend then established, each student was a few years ago for the first time required to write a major paper in each of his second and third years.

In order to avoid going into a mass of confusing details that would have little interest, or even meaning, except to the professional law teacher, the striking changes will be dealt with under three broad headings: a change of spirit, aim, or approach; proliferation of courses; and the replacement of what was throughout all three years a rigidly prescribed curriculum, mitigated by one or two options, by one where each second- and third-year student can, subject to taking Civil Procedure and Constitutional Law, design, with faculty guidance, his own course. In the result the rigid MacRae or Canadian Bar Association standard curriculum of 1920 that aimed to equip the student with a thin veneer of the narrowly professional knowledge needed by the general practitioner of those days has gone by the board. In its place is one better adapted to the changed, and still rapidly changing, role of the lawyer of the seventies: one that tries to familiarize the student with the part that law plays in society and with the effect of social change on law; one that enables him to dig deeper and range more widely than he could under the old curriculum; one that allows him to design for himself the course best adapted to what he sees as his own future, be it that of a general practitioner, a potential specialist in a large firm, or one of the many other kinds of lawyer that are now coming into existence in these days of rapid change.

The change that has taken place in the spirit, aim, or approach of the curriculum can be seen in the courses of all three years, but it is best illustrated by comparing the first-year curriculum of 1976 with the first-year curriculum as it was before the move to the Weldon Building. Because this is the year in which the mental lawyering skills have to be acquired, all courses are still compulsory and among them are the same 'Big Four' – Contracts, Torts, Property, and Criminal Law – as in 1966. But the spirit in which the Big Four are taught is much less purely professional than it was then. In the course description for Contracts in 1973-74, for example, we find the following: 'Students are encouraged to evaluate the utility of existing doctrines and precepts in the context of changes that are occurring in commercial practices and social concepts.' Similarly with Criminal Law: 'Students will also be given a brief introduction to questions of morality and the criminal law, with the purpose of examining the criminal law as an instrument of social control.'

Even more striking examples of this change of spirit are two new courses that have been added since 1966 to first year which is, as it always has been, supposed to lay the foundations of the lawyer-to-be – Legal Process and Family Law. Legal Process is historically the outgrowth of Introduction to Law which in 1963-64 supplanted the largely irrelevant and in general aridly taught History of English Law that had been given ever since the middle of the First World War. This sophisticated 'perspective course' on the processes of decision-making throughout the legal system – not only judicial but also legislative, administrative, and private – is first and foremost an attempt to make the first-year man see the law and the legal system as a whole. It is also an attempt to correct two false impressions that he is likely to gain from being drilled in the Big Four in analysing, synthesizing, and distinguishing cases – a drill that he *must* undergo if he is ever to think like a lawyer: the impression that 'only the judges matter' and the impression that thinking like a lawyer consists of nothing more than 'chasing little legal concepts round a stump.' Family Law, the law relating to husband and wife and parent and child, did not appear in the curriculum at all until 1966-67; up to that time the only course given in that area consisted of a few lectures given by a special lecturer from downtown on the only part of it that was then thought to be of any interest to lawyers, the law of divorce. First introduced as one of the very few electives then available in third year, it was made in 1970-71 a class that had to be taken by all students in their first year. The idea behind that was, once again, in part liberal and in part practical: liberal because this area of the law is 'an excellent demonstration of social problem solving through law,' and practical because 'it forces first year students to come to grips with statute law.'[7]

The other two changes – the great array of courses available to a student after his first year and his right to choose what combination of them he will take – are both in the main the result of the move to an optional curriculum which was begun in 1969 and was carried still further in 1974. The move drew its inspiration from Ontario, where there had been a positive ferment of ideas on legal education ever since universities in that province were in 1957 for the first time allowed by the Law Society of Upper Canada to enter the field of professional legal education. Having been a university law school since 1883, Dalhousie Law School had no such new wine to become intoxicated with and made its own move with some caution. Let Professor Christie tell the bare bones of the story.

The most significant change in the Law School curriculum came in 1968 when the move was made from a compulsory curriculum, mitigated by a couple of options in third year, to an optional curriculum in second and third years subject to the requirement that every student take Administrative Law, Civil Procedure, Constitutional Law, Legislation, one course from the 'commercial area' and one from the 'property area.' In 1974 the process of optionalization was carried further. Now after first year, the only compulsory courses are Civil Procedure and Constitutional Law.[8]

At the heart of the great array of courses available to the second- and third-year student still lie, it goes without saying, the traditional subjects – those that are designed to produce the general practitioner. To them, however, have been added courses that reflect both the specialization that is going on in the legal profession and the feeling of many law teachers that coverage is less important than sinking a shaft and sinking it deep. In the field of public law, for example, the student can go beyond the traditional Administrative Law to Advanced Problems in Administrative Law, Regulated Industries, and Civil Liberties. A man who has acquired a taste for labour law in the traditional Labour Law I can go deeper in Labour Law Problems and wider in Negotiation and Administration of Collective Agreements and in Employment Law. A man with an interest in the traditional International Law – taught continuously, with approximately ten-year interruptions during both world wars, at Dalhousie Law School ever since 1883 – can progress to Advanced Problems in International Law, International Institutions, and International Business Transactions. Similar clusters have developed in the traditional areas of Commercial Law, Corporation Law, Marine Law, Property Law, and Taxation.

But the curriculum of today is not confined to mere extensions of traditional subjects. There are courses that focus on the relation of the law to serious social problems, such as Poverty Law (Law and Social Problems), Law of the Sea, and Law of Environmental Quality – what some members of the profession deride as fringe courses but most faculty members applaud as a return to the cultural mix with which the School started in 1883: the supreme example is the Marine and Environmental Law program described in Section 1. This kind of a course has two main objectives: first, to teach the student how to do what in this day and age a lawyer is so often called upon to do – apply principles derived from a wide variety of fields to the solution of a new problem; and second, to encourage discussion of the 'great issues' in connection with specific problems where such discussion is meaningful and has practical results instead of taking them up in a broad background course such as Jurisprudence. And then there are one or two reflective courses, such as Jurisprudence and Quebec Law (Comparative Law) – only one or two, and they very poorly attended; alas for poor Weldon, the teacher of what in his day and in his hands were the reflectively cultural subjects of Constitutional History, Constitutional Law, and International Law! And finally, to complete the broad general picture, there are what are sometimes called practical courses – courses in skill development. Not the least important of the changes that have taken place in the last ten years is a renewed interest in the inculcation of practical skills; instance the following courses, nearly all of which have been introduced since the move to the Weldon Building. Reflecting the role of the lawyer as a man who goes into Court, there are courses in Trial Practice and Administration of Criminal Justice, where the student has on a 'do it yourself' basis an opportunity to go through the whole sequence of the stages of a piece of litigation. Reflecting the role of the lawyer as a man who provides a legal framework within which individuals and corporations can run their affairs, there are nuts-and-bolts courses in Corporate Finance, Estate and Tax Planning, and Real Estate Drafting and Negotiation. And reflecting the role of the lawyer as a man who is a general holder of hands for those who have or think they have a legal problem, there is the Clinic (Clinical Law), a 'course' which is taken by about one in four of all the third-year students every year.

The third change, the right of the second- and third-year student to design, subject to faculty guidance, for himself his own course, has been severely criticized by some traditionalists. Here are some of their comments: 'a helter-skelter curriculum'; 'this curriculum was not drawn up by a lawyer'; 'we have abdicated our responsibility in permitting so wide a range of courses.' At a more serious level, the Nova Scotia Barristers' Society has recently expressed its concern by deciding at its semi-annual meeting in February 1976 to 'constitute a Committee who, having discussed the matter with the Law School, would recommend ways and means of devising a system whereby students could be advised of the courses they ought to take. Or, in the alternative the Committee would study the matter and stipulate what courses must be taken for admission to the Bar in Nova Scotia.' In other words the future of the optional curriculum, as it now stands, is not by any means assured. Here, meanwhile, is what Professor Christie has to say about it in the May 1976 issue of Hearsay:

Experience at Dalhousie and right across North America demonstrates that an optional curriculum in second and third years does not result in students flocking to 'bird' courses. There are exceptions but the law course actually taken by ninety-five per cent of next year's graduates will differ only peripherally from what everybody had to take ten years ago. Most students permit themselves something like one 'luxury' course each term and are careful to keep their options open by taking most of the courses at the core of the curriculum. There is a paradox in this, of course. You may say, 'Well then, why bother with all those option courses?' The answer lies in the value of freedom of choice. The student who has been allowed to choose his courses will work harder and get more out of what he is doing. For the Faculty it is important to be able to explore new areas and new depths for students who are with us in that endeavour by choice.

To complete this account of what has been happening to the curriculum during the last ten years and also to explain the attitude of the Nova Scotia Barristers' Society recorded above, some mention has to be made of bar admission courses, courses put on by law societies for students who have graduated from law school and are in the final stage of their legal education, the old-time and still surviving apprenticeship to a lawyer in his office. A bar admission course is supposed to teach the young graduate-apprentice what everyone knows – except him – about the 'how we do it' of the transactions that regularly recur in a practising lawyer's life: simple litigation, selling a house, closing an estate, etc. The more thorough its bar admission course, the more indulgent can a law society afford to be to the kind of law school curriculum that we have described. The Law Society of Upper Canada has had a very thorough one since the early sixties and was therefore able to accept without demur from the Committee of Ontario Law Deans their proposals for the kind of optional curriculum which, as we said earlier, inspired the move made by Dalhousie Law School in 1969. Not blessed with such ample resources as the Law Society of Upper Canada, the Nova Scotia Barristers' Society did not have one at all until the early seventies, and even the one it has now is less than thorough. It is therefore forced, in fulfilment of its duty to ensure that incompetents are not foisted upon the public, to keep on the School's optional curriculum the watchful eye shown by its decision of February 1976.

EPILOGUE

How am I supposed to end this history of Dalhousie Law School? Do I just cut it off as of 1976 and leave the School hanging in the air? That offends my sense of the literary proprieties – according to which, I have always been taught, everything must have a beginning, a middle, and an end. Or do I gaze into the crystal ball and try to guess what the future holds? That is at the best of times a risky business and in these days, when some of the most basic underpinnings of the School – even Confederation itself – are seen to be shaky, it is positively dangerous. I have decided to compromise. To satisfy the literary proprieties I shall write something but, to avoid the dangers of the crystal ball, what I write will be no more than brief reflections on the School and its history. And because I have already made in the Introduction – and, indeed, throughout the book – all the generalizations I want to make about the pre-1966 School, most of what is new in my brief reflections is likely to be concerned with the period 1966-76 and the School as it has become in the Weldon Building.

There were, of course, many things – perhaps the most important things – about the pre-1966 School that I already knew before I began digging into its past. I knew for instance that it had always had going for it three things that most of the other common-law schools in Canada did not have. Its university wanted it and was proud of it; it was not, as in some other places, just a poor relation; it was 'the jewel in Dalhousie's crown.' The local Bar did not, as in some other places, resent it or look down on it; as a group, and as individuals, they were tolerant of its shortcomings and did what they could to help it. Why, even the local community felt that in a kind of way it belonged to them; until very recent times Dalhousie Law School, and what went on there, was 'news' and even rated editorials in the Halifax papers. I knew from my own personal experience that those scruffy quarters in the Forrest Building housed teachers and students who, despite all faults and notwithstanding the rather painful horn-tooting that seemed to be required of the dean on ceremonial occasions, were unpretentiously trying to do a solid job. And I knew in a vague sort of way that the family network – not only the family of students, but the family of old boys, old students, alumni, call them what you will – was a vital part of the School's traditions.

What then have I discovered that I did not know before? Many things; I will mention just three of them. I had no idea what a struggle the pre-1966 Dalhousie Law School always had just merely to survive, and, correspondingly, no idea of the ingenuity and sheer doggedness of those who worked to keep it alive – Weldon taking on at fifty-six a subject that was entirely new to him because he couldn't get anyone else to do it, Vincent MacDonald in the thirties having to go downtown begging for the three hundred dollars(!) that was needed to keep the current law reports coming in, and so on. I had no idea how many Law School products took part in that great saga of Canadian history, the settlement of the West, and, correspondingly, no idea why my western friends always spoke so respectfully of Dalhousie Law School. And I had no idea what an interesting lot of people – people into whom I had no time to look – I should run into.

Weldon, for example. How come that a man who had gone to the then premier founts of public law at Yale and Heidelberg (not Oxford or Cambridge, where a man with his deep devotion to the British connection would have been expected to go) was content to live out his life as a law teacher at a little struggling law school in Halifax? It was well for Dalhousie Law School that he did, but how come? And 'dear old Shannon' – as the contemporary *Gazettes* and R.B. Bennett's letter of congratulation to the fiftieth anniversary dinner in 1933 call him; what led that old man to take up unpaid arduous teaching chores at age sixty-seven? And the returned-men students of the First World War, so many of whom later became 'names'; what if anything, had the School to do with their becoming 'names'? Was it the 'working with pick and shovel on a railway to get enough money to go to college' or their hardening in the war that did it? And so on and so on.

Assuming always that a school with a small student body, a small faculty, a barely adequate library, and less than adequate premises *could* be a great law school, has Dalhousie Law School – in, for example, the palmy days of the

Golden Age of Dalhousie's Little Law School – ever been at any time a great law school? The little school had among many outsiders, e.g. Sir Lyman Duff, a Chief Justice of Canada (in 1936, p. 5), and Louis St Laurent, a Prime Minister of Canada (in 1952, p. 184), a good, even a great, reputation. And some of its students at some brief and favoured times have said that as a *teaching* school it was much more than merely good: look back again in these pages and see for example the compliment of compliments that a student in the Weldon-Russell period paid it in 1906 (p. 60) and the glowing praise which some of the students in the 'mini-Golden Age' that followed the Second World War lavished upon their teachers (p. 163). But nobody, even its most ardent admirers, will dare to claim that it ever was, to use the words of Sidney Smith, 'a centre of legal thought which is given expression by writing.' In all its long history only one book – a few articles in legal periodicals, yes, but only one book – had until the 1970s ever come from the pen of one of its faculty: half-time Benny Russell's *Bills and Notes*. Can a school whose teachers do not write books be called great? I think not. Perhaps the Big School in the Weldon Building, the post-1966 School, will one day produce the books that the pre-1966 School did not.

And now to the period 1966-76, in which the School finally ceased to bear any resemblance to the Dalhousie Law School which moved into the Forrest Building in 1887. The most obvious thing about that period is that more has happened in the last ten years than happened in all the years between the move to the Forrest Building in 1887 and the move to the Weldon Building in 1966. That is why it took so many pages to give what was clearly no more than a mere outline of significant events and significant changes in 1966-76. The next most obvious thing is that the School in 1976 is very different from what it was in 1966: faculty, students, curriculum, library, and 'plant' are all very much changed, and changed for the better over what they were then. In 1966 the School was a pretty staid place with nothing much going on; in 1976 there is lots of action, and more to come, on all fronts.

Has the School, with all these changes, become 'just another law school'? I do not think it has. Its claim to fame among 'outsiders who know' has always been that it takes its students very seriously, in the sense that it spends more time and trouble on its teaching than do most other Canadian law schools. It still does. Its claim to fame among its old students is that they – or most of them – enjoyed their time there: witness the reminiscences in the two special issues of *Ansul*. Despite the vast increase in size, the atmosphere of the

School is still warm and friendly and even in these hard-boiled days most of today's students will admit, if asked, that 'given I have to go to law school at all, I quite like it here.' In any event, it is not 'like a jungle,' which is what some other Canadian law schools are reputed to be.

Now that so many of the faculty and, so many of the students come from outside Nova Scotia, has the School lost its affection for, and its hold on, the local Bar on which it so long depended? I am not so sure about the answer to that one. So I evade it by saying that the tie between them is still closer than it is at most other Canadian schools.

And finally – to have recourse to the comparatively recent but now well-accepted slogan – how stands the Weldon tradition in 1976? High academic standards? Faculty, students, and curriculum are all better than they were in 1966 – better indeed than they have ever been. Public service? What in earlier times seems sometimes to have meant no more than getting into politics and making a go of it has in the last ten years come to mean giving such unselfish service to others as the Dalhousie Legal Aid Service and the Continuing Legal Education Program. The 'ever-open door policy'? That, alas, is not what it was in 1966. But the dream still lives on and, as has been recorded in 'In the Weldon Building,' strenuous efforts have been made, and are still being made, to bridge the gap between teachers and students inevitably brought about by mere size.

APPENDICES

APPENDIX I

Weldon

'Richard Chapman Weldon' was written by Benjamin Russell, Weldon's life-long friend and co-founder of the Law School, soon after Weldon's death in 1925; it was published in 4 *Canadian Bar Review* 197. Anyone interested in going more deeply into Weldon's life should read the following passages in Benjamin Russell's *Autobiography* (Halifax, NS: The Royal Print & Litho Ltd.; 1932), a book which is worth reading for its own sake: First Meeting With 'Dick' Weldon, A Literary Guide, Richard Chapman Weldon, Weldon at Yale, Return from Yale, pp. 69-79; and Dalhousie Law School, pp. 136-57.

'An Appreciation of the Late Dean Weldon' is by President A. Stanley MacKenzie, who was successively a science student, professor of physics, and finally president at Dalhousie at a time when all the students and all the teachers at 'the little college by the sea' were housed in one building, the Forrest Building; so he knew Weldon well. It, and a number of other tributes to Weldon, will be found in *Dalhousie Alumni News* for December 1925.

RICHARD CHAPMAN WELDON
by B. Russell

The advent of the late Dr. Weldon to the city of Halifax was indirectly the outcome of the movement initiated by the late Dr. J. Gordon MacGregor to consolidate the colleges of the maritime provinces. The direct results of that movement were to stimulate the denominational colleges to greater exertions for the maintenance of their individuality. Thus Sackville, the Alma Mater of Dr. Weldon, all its existing buildings being of wood, erected a central building of stone. St. Francis Xavier received a splendid endowment with which a new engineering building was erected in brick. Acadia sought the assistance of Rockefeller, whose purse was generously opened to such an extent that from this and other sources Acadia has become so prosperous that she is now more averse than she ever was to the surrender of her 'splendid isolation.' Kings made no move to leave Windsor for many years, nor until a disastrous fire inclined its governors to enter into association with Dalhousie in Halifax.

In this state of matters it was a brilliant conception on the part of the late Mr. Justice Sedgewick and a number of associated Dalhousians to bring Dr. Weldon from Sackville and make him the Dean of a Law Faculty in connection with Dalhousie, which would attract students from all other colleges, incidentally enhance the prestige of Dalhousie and create a spirit of fellowship among the patrons and students of the various colleges, which was one of the purposes of the consolidation contemplated by Dr. MacGregor.

Dr. Weldon was well fitted to be the instrument of such a movement. 'A boy's will is the wind's will,' says Longfellow, and as a boy young Weldon was somewhat reluctant to enter upon the career of a student. He thought he would prefer to be a farmer, a taste for which wholesome occupation he never altogether lost. His father was a wise man and permitted him to choose his own career, prescribing, however, a morning's work with the scythe, with the use of which, as a country lad, his boy was quite familiar. But on this occasion he was not a volunteer, appointing his own hours of beginning and ceasing. It was now and henceforward to be the work of his life and he must go at it in earnest. The result anticipated by his wise old father was realized. After a single morning with the scythe the boy chose the vocation of a student and was at once sent to Sackville, where he was duly matriculated.

As an undergraduate at Sackville he was easily first in all his classes. ...

It cannot be said that at Sackville Weldon had any specialties. He was equally excellent in every department of his work. It was after he left Sackville and, having taught school long enough to save the money requisite for a course at Yale, that he began at that institution to develop a special taste for the study of International Law and Political Science. The President of Yale, Dr. Theodore Woolsey, it will be remembered, was one of the high authorities on International Law, and Weldon was one of his favourite students. He graduated at Yale as a Ph.D., the youngest but one, (named, I think, Nelson), to take this high degree from this famous University. From Yale as a Doctor of Philosophy Dr. Weldon came directly to Sackville as Professor of Mathematics and Political Science. As a teacher of Political Economy it was his method to change his textbook every few years, so that his classes and himself should become familiar with the variant views presented by the authorities on this bewildering subject. After some years at Sackville he crossed over to Europe to take a post-graduate course at Heidelberg, where he studied International Law under the renowned Bluntschli, a name familiar to every reader of this REVIEW; but he was not permitted to complete his post-graduate course, and not long after his return to this country a distressing and disabling illness suspended his intellectual career for a full twelvemonth or more. His recovery, however, was complete, and he thereupon resumed his work as a Professor at Sackville. Among his students at this time, if I am not mistaken, was ..., who soon became a fellow-student with him in the subject of Constitutional Law, reading together, discussing and criticising the decisions on the British North America Act. He was the guest of the writer for several months before the opening of the Law School, and the valuable practice of reading and criticism just described was continued at Prince Arthur Park, where Weldon also prosecuted his studies in Conflict of Laws.

When Dr. Weldon came to Dalhousie as Dean his subjects were, therefore, International Law, Constitutional Law and Conflict of Laws, otherwise termed Private International Law. There was no difficulty in finding competent associates to teach the other branches required to fill out a complete three years' course of study. But it would not have been possible to fill the place that he occupied in the subjects on which he lectured. The late Sir John Thompson lectured on Evidence, the late Mr. Justice Sedgewick lectured on Equity, the late Sir Wallace Graham gave a course on Marine Insurance. After the school had been established a full year it became possible to appoint a permanent Professor of Contracts, who also lectured on Bills and Notes, Sale of Goods and Equity Jurisprudence, after the volunteer lecturers in some of these subjects became tired of their work.

The school attracted students from every section of the Dominion as far west as British Columbia and from British Colonies outside the Dominion, such as Newfoundland and the West Indies. Its graduates are to be found in the courts of almost all the provinces, all of them in fact outside perhaps of Ontario and Quebec. Of the Supreme Court Bench of Nova Scotia five of the seven judges now constituting the court were students in the Dalhousie Faculty, and all but one of the five are graduates.

It was while Dr. Weldon was a Teacher of Law at Dalhousie and Dean of the Faculty of Law, that the invitation came to him to accept a seat in the

House of Commons for Albert County, New Brunswick. He was elected without difficulty for the sixth and seventh parliaments and in the earlier of these two parliaments he moved the address in reply to the Speech from the Throne. Some of the phrases of his speech were so striking that they still linger in the memory of those who heard or read them. As a member of Parliament he was an independent Conservative. He had the highest possible esteem for the statemanship of Sir John A. Macdonald, and hardly less high in his estimation stood the late Sir John Thompson, with whom he had been so pleasantly associated in the Dalhousie Law Faculty. When Sir Charles Tupper, Prime Minister, presented his policy of a Remedial Bill for Manitoba he was among the dissentients with Clarke Wallace and the rest. He greatly admired Edward Blake, describing him as a man of 'regal intellect,' and was glad to accept his assistance in promoting the private bill known to this day as the 'Weldon Act,' designed to prevent Canada from continuing to be a shelter for wealthy scoundrels from the United States. He actively engaged with Sir George Foster, Dr. G.M. Grant, Dalton McCarthy, Alex McNeil, Colonel Denison and Sir George Parkin in the Imperial Federation movement, and heartily supported all other measures that tended to consolidate the Empire and secure its position as the bulwark of freedom and order throughout the civilized world.

There was a time when it seemed as if he might become the Prime Minister of Canada. *Dis aliter visum.* His name and fame remain secure in the hearts and minds of the hundreds of graduates throughout the Dominion on the Bench and at the Bar, who will evermore cherish his memory and say of him with all the deep reverence and sincerity with which Hamlet said of his honoured father: –

'He was a man, take him for all in all, I shall not look upon his like again.'

AN APPRECIATION OF THE LATE DEAN WELDON
by A. Stanley MacKenzie

Dalhousie has been conspicuous for the number of men of eminence whom she has been able and fortunate enough to attract to her teaching staff, notwithstanding her relatively small proportions in the academic world. There is no doubt that much of the reputation which Dalhousie acquired in her days of small beginnings was due to the high quality and distinction of her teachers. Of this group of notable men the late Dean Weldon was one of the most outstanding; perhaps, indeed, the greatest of them, if all the factors which constitute greatness are considered. He probably exerted a more profound influence on a greater number of students than any of his colleagues on the staff of Dalhousie. His direct impress will be found on every graduate of the Law School who passed through his hands during his deanship of over thirty years. But his influence was in evidence not only in the classroom and in the university councils. Though for only a short time in active political life he directly took a prominent part in initiating sound legislation; but, what is more important, he had a definite, if indirect, influence on his contemporaries in political life. His speeches, his presence and example were bound inherently to elevate the tone of political conduct. So many of the leaders of the bench and the bar of Canada were trained by Dean Weldon in his lofty conceptions of the broad principles and ethics of the law, that he is in no small measure responsible for the high standards and character of the legal profession, and for the steady progress in legal education and in a proper understanding of the constitution. And then he was beloved by all who came in contact with him and had all the influence upon them which love for a man of the finest character inevitably produces. It is quite impossible to analyse or calculate to a nicety the influence of a great leader upon his generation; but how great was Dean Weldon's influence may be measured from the fact that it is still very evident in the generation following his own.

Weldon's was a striking and inspiring personality. Nature had cast him in her noblest mould. In his palmy days his large, well-proportioned, erect figure, handsome leonine head and flashing eye commanded immediate attention. One instinctively felt here was a great man. His intellect matched his exterior. Few men of his day were mentally so well trained and so widely read as he. It was not only that he had been educated in Canadian, American and German Universities; he was a profound student and thinker. And he was not only a student of history and economics and of constitutional and international law, but of life and philosophy in their broadest aspects. As a consequence he was a conversationalist almost in a class by himself among his friends and contemporaries. But he did not monopolize the conversation, for his sympathies were too wide and his kindliness too great for him to be egotistical and selfish. His heart was big, and each student who went forth from the Law School recalled him as the friend as much as the teacher and inspiring chieftain. He was not only a clear and brilliant lecturer in the class, he was also a fine platform speaker with a mastery of pure English diction. But perhaps his most outstanding characteristic was his pure-mindedness and his lofty idealism. Possessing no guile in himself, he suspected none in others. And seldom did he discover it; but when he did, it was with a heavy heart that he was forced to believe it.

No wonder, then, that this man impressed his fellows, and influenced everyone who came in contact with him. Able as were his associates on the Faculty, including his colleague and close friend for thirty years, Benjamin Russell, recently retired Justice of the Supreme Court, the Law School was Dean Weldon's creation. Is it too much to say that Dean Weldon was the Law School and the Law School will always stand as his monument and his incarnate spirit?

APPENDIX II

The Weldon Tradition

'What is the Weldon Tradition about which people speak so often?' asks Professor George Nicholls in a brochure called *The Dalhousie Law School* that was issued by the School in 1975. As will be seen from the three statements of it printed below, different people give different emphasis to each of the several elements that compose it. The first statement, made under the heading 'The Weldon Tradition,' is that of Professor Nicholls; it will be found on the second page of the brochure. The second statement, given under the heading 'The Kind of Educated Person the Faculty is Seeking to Produce,' is that of the late Dean Horace Read in 'Aims and Practices of University Education in the Faculty of Law at Dalhousie,' a paper delivered to an inter-faculty symposium at the end of 1962 and published in 1 *Canadian Legal Studies*, pp. 3-4. The third statement, again under the heading 'The Weldon Tradition,' is that of a student speaking to fellow-students; it is taken from pp. 4-5 of the 1975-76 version of the mimeographed *Law Student Handbook* which the Orientation Committee has for the last few years been handing out to the members of each incoming first-year class for their information.

THE WELDON TRADITION
by George Nicholls

No one person or group of persons, human or divine, created the Dalhousie Law School. It is no bad thing, however, for an institution to possess some name, or motto, or concrete thing as a symbol to express its worthier aspirations. Richard Chapman Weldon was the first Dean, and his thirty-one years in that office represent by far the longest tenure of any of the eight deans the School has had. The building now housing the School, the most recent of its five addresses, is called the Weldon Building. If any one person is to be regarded as its creator, Dean Weldon would have to be the person ...

What is the Weldon Tradition about which people speak so often? No doubt some of it is the accretion added by the many who have followed later, teachers and students, men and women. In any event, those who for the moment happen to be the Dalhousie Law School believe that the Weldon Tradition is composed of three elements mainly, and that Richard Chapman Weldon presided at their birth: (1) high scholastic standards; (2) unselfish public service; and (3) the open-door policy, by which is meant that every member of the faculty is ready to discuss anything, at any time, with any student. These are the three articles of faith. As the size of the school grows, at least the third one becomes no easier to observe.

THE KIND OF EDUCATED PERSON THE FACULTY IS SEEKING TO PRODUCE
by Horace Read

Speaking at the opening ceremonies on the 30th of October, 1883, Dean Weldon, after a glowing tribute to the academic attainments of the Law School at Harvard, declared: 'In drawing up our curriculum we have not forgotten the duty which every university owes to the state, the duty which Aristotle saw and emphasized so long ago – of teaching young men the science of government. In our free government we all have political duties, some higher, some humbler, and these duties will be best performed by those who have given them most thought. We may fairly hope that some of our students will, in their riper years, be called upon to discharge public duties. We aim to help these to act with fidelity and wisdom.' During his thirty-one years as Dean, and the only full-time teacher, Dean Weldon saw his hopes for his students richly fulfilled. That the students of the School have been well prepared for professional life has been demonstrated over the years by the unusual success which has attended their efforts in every province, in practice, on the Bench, in political leadership and in academic life.

Dean Weldon's concept of the educational function of a University Law School was far in advance of his time. It has only recently become generally accepted in this country. In 1947 George H. Steer, Q.C., then a leader in legal education in Alberta and in the Canadian Bar Association, restated Dean Weldon's declaration of educational policy in modern terms. He said: 'The time has gone by when it can be argued with any degree of plausibility that law schools do all that should be required of them by turning out technically trained craftsmen. The lawyer, more perhaps than the member of any other learned profession, owes a duty to society to equip himself as a policy-maker. For no matter in what niche he may ultimately find himself, whether as practitioner, judge, teacher, legislator, civil servant or business man, he finds himself dealing with matters of high public policy. The skill acquired as the result of his training should equip him to decide upon that supreme question of policy, viz. the ultimate aim and basis of the organization of the state in which he lives and, having made his decision, he should, if adequately trained, find many ways in the course of his career of influencing policy to achieve his objective. He ought to be, as Dean Roscoe Pound has suggested, a member of an organization characterized by learning and imbued with the spirit of public service.'

Justice Oliver Wendell Holmes of the Supreme Court of the United States once declared that: 'The business of a law school is not sufficiently described when you merely say that it is to teach law or to make lawyers. It is to teach law in the grand manner and to make great lawyers.' By teaching law in the grand manner, Dean Weldon, and a succession of professors of law at Dalhousie in the context of a strictly professional curriculum, have succeeded in educating students who in after life assumed the role of legal statesmen as well as becoming ever-better legal craftsmen. Today the Faculty is seeking to continue to develop lawyers who are the living embodiment of the Weldon tradition of high academic and professional standards and unselfish public service.

THE WELDON TRADITION
from the *Law Student Handbook*

Although it is a tradition at Dalhousie Law School to have close student-faculty relations, that is only part of the often referred to, seldom defined Weldon Tradition.

The Weldon Tradition is also one of public service. It implies that graduates of this Law School are more than ordinarily willing to work and serve to improve the communities in which they practise as lawyers. It implies that one of the essentials of being a lawyer is the ability to make an effort to improve the system under which he lives. It is, in brief, a tradition of concern, of change and of humanity. Living the Weldon Tradition means having the ability to participate not only in the affairs of the Law School, but also the willingness to take part in the activities of the university and of the community.

Our participation is required in the larger community as well. In the past four years, this Law School, under the initial impetus of two of our students, has made possible a vigorous Legal Aid system that has become a Canadian model. It has given students attending this School a concrete opportunity to involve themselves in the community, allowing them to leave their ivory towers to see the world as it really is and to apply their theoretical notions of what law is all about to the daily problems of those less fortunate than themselves. That is an exemplification of the Weldon Tradition.

APPENDIX III

What Dalhousie Law School Says about Itself When It Is on Parade

'Fifty Years of Legal Education at Dalhousie' was written by John Read in 1933 to mark the fiftieth birthday of the School and was published in 11 *Canadian Bar Review* 392. From his boyhood John Read was a friend of the Weldon family. A 1909 Arts graduate of Dalhousie in the days when all the university faculties were in the Forrest Building, he would be familiar with the Law School at a time when Weldon and Russell were still the heart of it. A law student for a year at Columbia and a graduate in law of Oxford, he was uniquely qualified to view in proper perspective Dalhousie Law School, of which he became in 1920 the first full-time professor to be appointed in addition to the Dean (then MacRae) and from 1924 to 1929 the Dean. All of this accounts for the informed, evocative quality of what he has written.

'A National Law School' is Mr. Justice Vincent MacDonald's address to a special convocation held in 1952 to celebrate the move of the Law School, at last, into the building on the Studley campus which had been built for it in 1922 but had been temporarily occupied by the Arts Faculty for thirty years. The address was not published; a few passages that deal with a problem which no longer exists have been omitted. Vincent MacDonald was more deeply committed emotionally to the School than was John Read: he had been successively student, part-time lecturer, and full-time teacher during the School's fifteen-year period of growing self-confidence which led up to the birthday celebrations in 1933; and it was his faith and his courage, as Dean from 1934 until his elevation to the Bench in 1950, that kept it going during the difficult years of the Great Depression and the Second World War. Hence come, perhaps, what to some may seem a slightly over-rosy picture of the Law School's past and a slightly over-golden dream of its future. In any event he could have cited in support of any bragging – if bragging there was – that best of all authorities for Nova Scotians, Joseph Howe: 'Boys brag of your country. When I'm abroad, I brag of everything that Nova Scotia is, has, or can produce; and when they beat me at everything else, I turn around on them and say "How high does your tide rise?"'

'Reminiscences,' by Howard Epstein of the class of 1973, was never intended by its author to be an on-parade exercise. It is inserted here as an example of what an intelligent and articulate student might, in this age of the anti-hero, conceivably have said in a tongue-in-cheek celebration of the School and its past. The following extract from the Editors' Notes to the April 1974 issue of *Ansul* in which it will be found sufficiently explains the circumstances under which it came to be written. 'In this edition, the Ansul takes great pride in commemorating the 90th anniversary of the Dalhousie Law School. To celebrate this occasion, the Ansul presents a glimpse at this venerable institution ... Nor do we wish to over-indulge the narcissistic tendency to pat ourselves on the back. Such considerations contradict or undermine the dignity of the School ...' Included in the April 1974 *Ansul* are President A. Stanley MacKenzie's reverent 'An Appreciation of the Late Dean Weldon' (see Appendix I above) and reminiscences by Norman MacKenzie ('23) and Moffatt Hancock (Professor 1945-49) of what the School was like when they were there. Referring to these reminiscences the Editors' Notes continue: 'Lest it be forgotten that Dalhousie is continuing to grow and adapt to changing circumstances, the Ansul has asked Mr. Howard Epstein ... to give us the benefit of his opinions.' Ranging as they do over the School's past, the contemporary Mr. Epstein's irreverent glimpses at 'things of a scurrilous nature,' as he calls them, seemed to John Willis to positively demand admittance to the category of 'What Dalhousie Law School says about itself when it is on parade.' One or two passages, irrelevant to the School and its history, have been omitted.

FIFTY YEARS OF LEGAL EDUCATION AT DALHOUSIE
by John Read

To talk about the Law School, one needs the intimacy of the camp-fire and a circle to whom 'the Dean' and 'Benny' are unequivocal expressions requiring no interpretation section. In such a group it is possible to stir an old memory here, and to stimulate a long-forgotten emotion there, thus inducing the listeners to paint their own pictures.

It is impossible, on the cold, white pages of the CANADIAN BAR REVIEW, to convey to a generation that knew not Weldon, to whom 'Benny' is merely a jurist, the heart and soul of an institution vibrant with life. The readers are familiar with the general story of the School. They know its graduates; they have observed its general influence upon legal education in Canada; but they have not been initiated into its mysteries.

The foundation of the Dalhousie Law School in 1883 was an experiment. In the Eighties the conception of a university school of law was an innovation in British institutions. It is true that the study of law, as an element in a liberal education, was no novelty, but the idea that universities should undertake the project of training men for the public profession of the law was even further from acceptance in England than in Canada.

On the other hand, the need for a law school was obvious. The old regime of legal education was even then crumbling. Indigenous to England, where it was co-ordinated with the professional system and founded upon broad and liberal public school and university education, it fulfilled the needs of the community. In different circumstances, where the two branches of the legal profession were merged and where its members were too busily engaged in the struggle for existence to devote the time that was necessary for the development of the junior ranks, the need to supplement the practical instruction of the office was recognized. It was a need, not only for strengthening professional training, but also for giving to law students the elements of a liberal education.

Bearing in mind the character of the need and also the fact that, at the time, the University Law School in the United States was reaching its modern form under the leadership of Langdell, it is not surprising that the founders incorporated the law school as an integral part of the university.

As a result of the generosity of George Munro, a Professorship was established, and Richard Chapman Weldon was appointed Dean of the Faculty of Law, and George Munro Professor of Constitutional and International Law. Closely associated with him was Benjamin Russell, later the Hon. Mr. Justice Russell, who was appointed Professor of Contracts and who devoted a large part of his time to the School. Associated with Weldon and Russell were the Rt. Hon. Sir John Thompson, the Hon. S.N. Shannon (Judge of Probate), James Thompson, Q.C., Sir Wallace Graham (later Chief Justice of Nova Scotia), the Hon. Robert Sedgewick (later a Judge of the Supreme Court of Canada), John Y. Payzant, Q.C., and the Hon. S.G. Rigby (a Judge of the Supreme Court of Nova Scotia).

In this manner was established a policy which has been followed even to the present day, namely that of combining within the school two groups, the one including men who devoted the whole, or a substantial part of their time, to academic matters; and the other, including a number of leaders of the bench and bar, primarily engaged in the practice of their profession. An even balance between the cultural and professional sides of legal education is thus insured.

In its content, the curriculum was based upon the balancing of two principles. On the one hand, its scope was sufficiently extensive to give to the student an adequate foundation for his professional needs. On the other hand, the curriculum included the cultural elements in legal education. The relationship of law to the other elements in human knowledge and in life was not forgotten. It demonstrated that it was possible to make the study of law a liberal education and, at the same time to place the student in a position where he could readily learn to cope with the difficulties of practice after his graduation.

At Dalhousie, as in the case of most educational institutions, the influence of personality has been at least as important as that of ideas. The corporate entity is the product of two groups of personalities: the faculty and the student body. Weldon and Russell and the group of distinguished lawyers and judges who formed the original faculty, were followed by other scholars and lawyers who are worthy to rank with their predecessors. It would be invidious to refer to individuals, and tedious to set forth the entire list. It is, perhaps, possible to mention the work of the late Sidney Harrington, Q.C., the late Judge Wallace, Hector McInnes, K.C., and Judge Patterson, whose efforts on behalf of the School extended over many years and are so largely responsible for its reputation. It is also desirable to refer to the work of Dean Weldon's successor, Dr. D.A. MacRae, who was dean for a period of eleven years from 1914 to 1924. His contribution to the School was fairly comparable to that which he rendered to legal education in Canada generally. The School had established its prestige and its traditions when he took over the deanship, but it required organization. He transformed it into an institution with the standards and methods which are essential to permanent progress and which insured the perpetuation of the development and traditions which had already been achieved.

Not less important than the influence of the teaching staff has been the character of the student body. From the beginning the Law School has been fortunate in attracting students of exceptional character and ability. Further, geographical considerations have restricted the numbers of its student body so that its classes have been small groups partaking largely of the character of a seminar or tutorial group. This has given an intimacy to the relation of teacher and pupil that would be impossible in a larger institution and has made it possible to incorporate into the teaching technique some of the elements that have characterized the tutorial system of the English universities. At the same time, the exceptional industry and capacity of the student body have insured that there would always be, in the instructional groups, a high general level of intelligence, and a sufficient number of intellectual leaders, to make the best type of instruction possible. The writer, in a period of teaching extending from 1914 to 1929, had the privilege of working with the members of thirteen different classes, and of teaching, at different times, ten different courses. The School may be regarded as the teacher's paradise, which is so rarely found in real life. There is never any occasion to prod reluctant students into activity. Most of the instruction consists in the discussion by the classes of legal principles, and their members teach themselves under the leadership of the instructor. The latter is merely their guide, philosopher and friend. His function is to preserve the *esprit de corps* of the corporate group, and to continue the traditions of the institution.

It is inevitable that one should dwell largely on the past record of an institution in marking the conclusion of its first half-century of existence. It is more difficult to speak of the present and of the future, but it would be misleading to ignore them. The tendency to encourage and develop devotion to public service is as strong today as it was under Weldon and Russell. Further, largely as a result of the influence of Dean MacRae, a strong impetus has been given to legal scholarship. This is evidenced in the admirable case books that have been published in recent years and in the scholarly articles and notes, originating in the School, which have appeared in this and other law publications. It may be suggested that Canadian jurisprudence is being, and is likely to be, influenced by the kind of scholarly work which is exemplified in the Law Quarterly Review, and the writings of such scholars as Dicey, Anson and Pollock. Such work will, inevitably, come from the Canadian Law Schools and it may safely be predicted that the Dalhousie Law School will be one of the principal sources. Further, there is a fruitful field for research which requires combined efforts of economists, political scientists, and lawyers. At Dalhousie, where the Law School is in intimate association, day by day, with the departments of Economics and Political Science, there are exceptional opportunities for such research, and the foundations of this development are now being laid. Bearing in mind the present opportunities and the present personnel, it may be confidently predicted that the next half-century will be even more fruitful than the last.

A NATIONAL LAW SCHOOL
by Vincent MacDonald

When the Law School opened its doors in October, 1883, it was a pioneer step in British institutions for a University to undertake the systematic training of men for the legal profession.

The Law School began its career with a staff of great excellence and varied talents; for the first Dean (Weldon) was a scholar of spacious gifts, and his assistant, Russell, was a magnificent teacher; and the others were to rise to great distinction in the professional, judicial and political life of Canada.

That the students of the School have been well trained for professional life has been demonstrated over the years by the unusual success which has attended their efforts in every Province. In terms of service on the Bench, the record – relative to numbers – is probably unmatched in the whole country. Thus the School has provided a member of the Court of International Justice, members of the Supreme Court of Canada and of the Exchequer Court of Canada; six Chief Justices of Provincial Supreme Courts; and over 60 Supreme and County Court Judges spread through every Province.

In political leadership the record – again relative to numbers – is astoundingly high. For from the teachers' and students' benches have gone forth two Prime Ministers of Canada and more than 20 Federal Ministers (of whom 5 held office in the vital years of the last War), and numerous Members of Parliament. In provincial politics the story is similar; nine ex-students have been Premiers of Provincial Governments whilst dozens of others have been members of Provincial Ministries, and of Provincial Legislatures; and two have been Lieutenant Governors of this Province. In the sphere of Government service, our graduates have held high offices in the Civil Service of Canada and of Nova Scotia and the other Provinces.

In industry and commerce, graduates have reached exalted positions as executive heads of great corporations; and many students have sought our training as direct equipment for ways of life distinct from law as a profession.

In terms of scholarship, the record is marked by a very considerable output of legal literature from the Faculty; and from the School have gone forth many Rhodes Scholars to Oxford, and numerous post-graduate students to

Britain and the United States, who have made the name of Dalhousie honored in great institutions abroad. The School has supplied teachers to Law Schools in Canada and the United States; a Dean to the new School in British Columbia; and Presidents to the Universities of Manitoba, New Brunswick, British Columbia and Toronto, and to Memorial College in Newfoundland.

It was of such things as these that Sir Lyman Duff was thinking when, on an occasion similar to this, he said:

the contribution of the Law School of Dalhousie to the education of the lawyers of Canada, to the elevation and maintenance of professional standards in point of mastery of legal principle, and otherwise, cannot be over-emphasized or exaggerated ...

Graduates of this School have won renown in public and professional life, and have exercised high influence upon the course of public affairs in critical periods.

I venture to think that this record has seldom been equalled by any institution of comparable size and age on this continent.

The greatest single factor in the career of the School has been its constant awareness of its function as a University Faculty. As a University Law School it was founded and developed on the conception that it had three main objectives:

(1) to give thorough training in the principles and processes and spirit of the law so as to prepare men for the competent and ethical practice of a learned profession with great duties to the public and to the law itself;

(2) to teach Law for its cultural value and in all its relations to life and other branches of knowledge, and particularly as a living instrument of human government; and

(3) to teach it (in both these aspects) in an atmosphere of free inquiry controlled only by the demands of inflexible integrity.

In its application this conception translated itself into a teaching tradition of which the two great elements were Devotion to Public Service – always to be associated with Dean Weldon and his group – and Devotion to Legal Scholarship – which owes so much to Dean MacRae. To this conception and this tradition the School has always remained true. In its career it has drawn eager students from every part of Canada. It has also had the constant good fortune of attracting able professional teachers to its Faculty, who have been aided immeasurably by leaders of the Bench and Bar who have brought their great wealth of practical experience to the classroom. With this happy wedding of the Career-Teacher and the Practitioner-Lecturer, the School has secured an equally happy blending of academic and practical instruction.

More recently has come the realization that the environment and work of the lawyer have changed in many ways which require radical changes in legal education. This realization has encompassed the need of wider professional education, including more emphasis on legislative and administrative processes, and on the ultimate purposes of Law.

In a life full of paradox, it is notable that in all matters pertaining to curriculum and admission to practice, the School has been subject to the control of the Nova Scotia Barristers' Society. Had that Society been possessed of a narrow vocational approach to legal education, it could have aborted or warped the growth of the School. Fortunately it never sought to keep the School in thraldom to such an approach. On the contrary, it has been eagerly cooperative in the attempts of the School to provide a broadly based education which – without despising professional 'know-how' – sought to embrace knowledge of law in all its implications and particularly as an agency of government. In the result, the School has been able to pursue the true purposes of a University Law School; and has been able to make many experiments in curriculum and in methods which have tended to improve its efficiency, such, for example, as its exceptional development of the tutorial method of instruction. Without endowments of any significance in its first 60 years, the School had to draw students from outside Nova Scotia in order to survive ...

... it can be said with confidence that Dalhousie has attained national standing as a great Canadian Law School. Indeed this country is much in its debt for the constant stream of well-trained lawyers it has poured into every province to give guidance in professional, business, and public affairs.

It remains for it to achieve status as a National School of Law in the true sense of an institution devoted to providing legal education according to its own ideas ...

Wherever situate, it is incontestable that this federal country requires the nation-building services of a National Law School, if for no other reason than the necessity of establishing a Centre of Legal Research in which great problems of Canadian Law and Government can be explored exhaustively. In the race for that position Dalhousie can summon to her aid a history of constant adhesion to a worthy tradition, and a long pageant of successful graduates who have made its name honoured in the professional, educational, commercial and public activities of the whole country.

Accordingly, it is not fanciful to hope that in the measurable future Dalhousie will be the home of a National School of Law renowned both as a great teaching institution and as a great centre of legal research.

by Howard Epstein

As any legal scholar (me, for example) will tell you possession is a concept basic to the law – or at any rate it is a concept capable of being grasped by lawyers.

Now Dalhousie Law School is 90 years old – an age at which a lawyer would be doddering, but at which our institution is nowhere near its last gasp.

Ninety is a mature age for a school and a time for remembering one's first wise lessons in the importance of possession: what, then, does Dalhousie possess?

The cynic would say that our chief possession is our reputation. The late Dean (but not only of Toronto) C.A. Wright once said 'Horn-tooting has always been a good Maritime trait; Dalhousie has just made a tradition of it.' The gratuitous assumption of the learned Dean is that there is no more to the tradition than talking about it. He may be pardoned for his confusion, since some of the facts we cherish sound more like fiction.

Our reputation may be left to fend for itself: it is no delicate flower. What we are more concerned with here are a few of the notable facts about our alma mater; legend, tradition, or history – call it what you will, those of us who have enjoyed it here will take pleasure in learning of associations with the place, particularly one assumes, those things of a scurrilous nature, such as this: It is said that the first librarian of the Law School, a man without a law degree and therefore probably unacquainted with the meaning of felonious conversion, amassed a collection of some 3000 volumes within a year of the School's opening partly by absconding with them from local law offices. He would wear his academic gown and smuggle the books out underneath.

Whether the possession of these books may ever be of benefit to our scholars is open for discussion. In any event the oral tradition is much prized at Dalhousie and is happily exercised at the annual Model Parliament, in debates, and in Moots. Naturally enough, the inclination has been to produce politicians from all of this. Four of the present provincial premiers – Honourable Alan Blakeney of Saskatchewan, Alex Campbell of P.E.I., Honourable Richard Hatfield of N.B. and Regan of N.S. – are Dalhousie Law grads.

And this occurrence is not unusual. Like much else, historically, it is associated with Dean Weldon who was himself a Conservative M.P. and who changed the dates of the law School semester to leave him time to sit in Ottawa. In 1883 in his Inaugural Address Dean Weldon said:

In drawing up our curriculum we have not forgotten the duty which every university owes to the state, the duty which Aristotle saw and emphasized so long ago, of teaching the young man the science of government ... we may fairly hope that some of our students will, in their riper years, be called upon to discharge public duties.

From Sir John Thompson to R.B. Bennett to Angus L. Macdonald this part of the Weldon tradition has been maintained.

The emphasis on quick wit has not produced only polished politicians ... In the school itself ... were Dean Sidney Smith (later president of the University of Toronto) and his chief assistant and later Dean Vincent MacDonald. The two of them hit upon a good idea for encouraging classes to do their own thinking: feuds. In a lecture, MacDonald, say, would give an opinion on some point. In his next lecture to the same class, Smith would pointedly contradict him, implying that MacDonald must have cheated to get his degree. Once when the class took up Smith's opinion with him MacDonald told them: 'I'm sure you must have misunderstood him. Not even the dean would say such a damn fool thing as that.'

The spirit of joshing is infectious and may be seen at its best in the Moot Courts. The Supreme Moot Court of Dalhousie, bound by no precedent, has met annually to decide cases since 1883. The cases have always been argued by students but it is only since after the Second World War that the Moots assumed their present structure of a third year bench with second year counsel. Though there is no special moot court room in our new building, as there was in each of its predecessors, the spirit of the Moots has not been lost.

The Gazette used to carry reports of the Moots, and we find this in October 20, 1920: 'The court consisted of McNutt B. and McKeen J. (MacQuarrie C.J. being absent on circuit somewhere in the city.)'

One fine tradition has been that of counsel congratulating the judges on their appointment. We find this report in *The Gazette* of October 12, 1945: 'Before the case got underway, the Junior Counsel made fine speeches of flowing congratulations to their Lordships on their elevation to the Bench. Some smarted of insincerity. Some even derided the money-making capabili ties of their Lordships while at the Bar but all were received with equanimity.' The members of the Bench had presumably mellowed with experience, for a scant four years earlier we were told: '... of much more interest was the speech, congratulating the Justices upon their appointment, of Junior Counsellor Cohen. Cohen was asked by the worthy judges to stop the apple-polishing and sit down. Lawyer Cohen sat.' *The Gazette*, October 10, 1941.

In more recent years at the Law School the flowing eloquence has been emphasized in an active debating society where competition for the Angus L. Macdonald Debating Trophy, established in 1968, has been keen. Who will forget Geoff Fulton's 'Little Red Robin Hood – a tale of rampant feminism' speech, or the numerous occasions on which he made it? Who will forget the annual student triumph at the faculty-student debate (the vote invariably being the two student judges over the one faculty)?

Being fast on your feet is hardly the only thing the law school teaches, but it is a useful skill and one of the most pleasant ones to practice. From lectures to moots to model parliament to debates to Domus Legis, talk fills our school. What comes of all of it, who knows? But judging by precedent, all should be well.

APPENDIX IV

What the Law School was Like in 1883

A formal history of the Law School is all very well in its way, but what did it *feel* like to be a student or a teacher there, particularly during the more than sixty years when it was Dalhousie's Little Law School and 'we were all like a little family'? The reminiscences by former students and teachers in the two special issues of *Ansul* dated January 1976 and December 1977 give, for the relatively short period 1916-60, a full and vivid answer to that question. But what about the period 1883-1916?

It would have been possible to dredge out of the *Gazette* little snippets – from the voluminous reports of mock parliaments, class histories (there are a few of them), 'Law School Facetiae' (little 'in' jokes about fellow students, there are a few of them too), and descriptions of such social events as the Christmas tramp of the middle eighties, the Law Dinner of 1899, and the sleigh ride to Bedford of shortly before the First World War – but it would have meant a great deal of work for not much of a result; so we did not attempt it. We did, however, come across a piece so similar to the *Ansul* reminiscences and, because it tells us what it felt like to be at the School in the very first three years of its operation, so intrinsically interesting that we could not bear to leave it buried in the columns of the *Gazette* for 1886 (pp. 147-50). It is a long extract from the Law Valedictory given by A.G. Troop at the 1886 Dalhousie Convocation.

Troop came to the School as a first-year student in 1883 and graduated three years later. So, although he does not tell us anything about such commonplace matters, you must think of him as: having spent two years in the 'two commodious rooms' in 'the new High School' which were the School's first home and one year in the Halliburton House that Weldon and Russell bought and fixed up, which was the School's second home; and as delivering his Law Valedictory in the original Dalhousie College Building on the Grand Parade, the site where City Hall now stands. Troop belongs, that is, to the pre-history of Dalhousie Law School; for, as far as the writer is concerned, the real history of the real Dalhousie Law School does not begin until the move to the Forrest Building in 1887.

by A.G. Troop

What trials and tribulations law students had to endure before the establishment of the Law School! We recall today the opening before us when we first thought of entering upon the pursuit of legal studies. We were told then that the difficulties in our way were insurmountable, and that it would require a determined perseverance in a course of systematic study to make ourselves familiar with the principles of the law. We were informed that it would be necessary to construct and follow a plan of reading, that the great writers must be studied, that text-books must be perused and re-perused, that cases without end and decisions without parallel must be digested, that we must adopt the Revised Statutes as our Bibles, and withal that we should master the complicated practice of the Courts.

We commenced to advance with slow and cautious steps. We soon found ourselves enveloped in a cloud of volumes whose titles no mortal man could remember, and there were a thousand reports from the tribunals of both hemispheres, and all of them authoritative. We discovered that the great writers were partly obsolete, that there were a dozen text-books on every subject, no two agreeing, and each one better than the other, that cases were continually over-ruled and decisions were constantly explained away, that the Revised Statutes, not exceedingly interesting, were frequently amended, and that it would take a life time extending through the ages of eternity to read through the volumes on the practice of the Courts.

There was then no course of instruction to attend, except in American colleges. The student groped in the dark. He generally became acquainted with office work, sometimes learned a point in practice, was told how to issue a writ, and once in a while emancipated some unfortunate debtor. It is marvellous yet instructive to us that so many lawyers, in spite of their difficulties, have attained celebrity in the Maritime Provinces.

After a time the Law School of Dalhousie University was founded. We immediately enrolled ourselves amongst its students. The innumerable text-books were superseded by the lectures of eloquent and learned professors.

Under their direction useless and obsolete law was left upon the shelf. A large and valuable library was placed at our disposal; at our hand were the reports cited constantly and appropriately. Every department of law was embraced in the curriculum and we travelled over the whole realm of jurisprudence with the certainty of definite and invaluable results.

This afternoon we recall to our minds the line of study we have followed. We recall the beauties of Anson, the wit and wisdom of Bigelow, the peculiar phraseology of Williams, and the long and exciting footnotes of Taswell-Langmead. How eagerly we dived into the mysteries of the criminal law in Canada! Most unfortunate will be the Stather or Cadby who falls into our hands! Never did authors have more earnest readers than Snell and Cartwright. Our silver-tongued lecturer on Evidence in the midst of his parliamentary duties will sometimes, we hope, recollect the days when we puzzled him with unanswerable questions. The banks of our cities will be astonished to hear that Bills of Exchange and Promissory Notes, forged or unforged, are familiar to us as the faces of our watches. We believe that under the guidance of Benjamin we could effect a sale which would cause our friends to sew up their pockets. We would be happy to accept a retainer to prove that the steamship *Oregon* is not actually a total loss. We long ago settled the international fishery trouble and have decided that Canada deserves an extra indemnity for the illegal and unsupportable assertions and demands of our Southern neighbours. It has been proved to our satisfaction as a moral demonstration, that Blackstone knew nothing about Adam and Eve and the family compact, that Abraham was a despot under the guise of a father, that Isaac was nothing more than a slave, that the story of Ruth becomes infinitely more beautiful when we understand that she was the daughter of her husband and that by the ties of agnation and cognation we are all closely related.

The development of amateur eloquence in the debating clubs has led to deep inquiry into the perplexing questions of social and political life. Woman's rights and manhood suffrage, the faults and failings of judges and juries, imperial federation, and inter-provincial relations, we have dogmatically discussed. We recall these debates today, the struggle of the hour, and a hundred pleasant evenings. Moot courts, sleigh drives and lectures, midnight dinners and speeches, examination papers and reading-room athletic performances, are all incongruously mixed together in our reminiscences.

APPENDIX V

How the Dalhousie LLB Degree Became 'Portable'

In 1957 the School's LLB degree became for the first time fully 'portable' in all the common-law provinces of Canada – became recognized, that is, as fulfilling the academic (but not, of course, the practical training under apprenticeship) qualifications required by the law societies of those provinces for admission to their bars; it had, the reader may recall, been so recognized by the Nova Scotia Barristers' Society ever since 1891. What this meant to the School was that thenceforth a resident of any of those provinces could, without suffering any penalty, come to Dalhousie for his law school work, bringing with him to what has always been a predominantly Maritime student body the viewpoint of the region where he was brought up and to which he would return on graduation. What it also meant was that thenceforth a Maritimer could on graduating from the School migrate, again without suffering any penalty, from the hungry Maritimes to the rich legal pastures in, say, Ontario, Alberta, or British Columbia.[1]

'Without suffering any penalty' – what penalty? At the risk of gross oversimplification and of some unfairness to those law societies whose policies were a little less parochial, the historic position of Ontario's Law Society of Upper Canada on what may be called 'extra-provincial study' can be taken as typical; in any event it was from Ontario that the Dalhousie Law School had always looked for, and got, most of its handful of students from outside the Maritimes and it was to Ontario that most of its would-be emigré Maritimer graduates wanted, since the beginning of the thirties, to go. The penalty, and it had since the beginning of the thirties become a severe one, was not, as one might have expected, educational but financial, purely financial. What the Law Society of Upper Canada said was, in effect, as follows: 'If you want to become a member of the profession here you must go to *our* Law School, the Osgoode Hall Law School; that is the only one we recognize. We do however allow those who are already members in good standing of the profession in other common law provinces to transfer here upon taking a rather perfunctory oral examinaton and upon paying, first, the same admission fee that we charge our own graduates and, second, a "transfer fee" for the privilege of being allowed to "transfer." ' From the 1890s on, therefore, a student who had done his law school work at Dalhousie and got his degree there but wanted to practise in Ontario (or in any province other than Nova Scotia) would first get himself admitted to the Bar of Nova Scotia (paying Fee no. 1, the admission fee) and would then, as a fully-fledged (!) member of that Bar, transfer immediately to the Bar of the other province (paying Fee no. 2, the admission fee, and Fee no. 3, the transfer fee).

The purely financial penalty thus imposed on students who wanted to do their law school work at Dalhousie but practise in Ontario was always indefensible in principle – as also was the odd back-door method of getting into the Ontario profession without going to its law school – but nobody seems to have thought of challenging it until after the Second World War. It was something that the students, and the Law School itself, felt they could live with. Early in the depressed thirties, however, some of the provincial law societies, including Ontario's, took protective tariff action against outside lawyers – including, of course, the impecunious newly admitted lawyer who was coming in by the back door – by raising the transfer fee to what was meant to be a prohibitive height. Ontario raised its transfer fee to $1 500, or about one-third of the annual income of a full professor at the Law School, and in those hard days law professors were doing much better than most lawyers.

The first voices to be raised in public against the prohibitive money barrier thus erected against the student who wanted to do his law work in one province and practise in another – both voices came, be it noted, from Dalhousie Law School – did not question the odd, but long established, back-door method by which the student was able to do it. The first of the two voices was a student voice. In 1946 the Student Veterans of Dalhousie Law School asked, in a brief submitted to and approved by their cross-Canada parent association, for an exemption special to veterans: that in the case of veterans the transfer fees be reduced to a nominal amount. In addition to other reasons, as valid for all students as for veteran students, they stated that 'having been members of the armed forces of Canada during the recent war [they] had as their object, not service to any particular province, but to all provinces alike.'[2] They did not get what they asked for. To quote from the reminiscences of an ex-navy member of the class of 1948 who transferred to Ontario after graduation: 'Eventually, about one-third of us followed the well-worn path of Dalhousie graduates who made their way to other parts of Canada. Reciprocal admission was not the order of the day and we had to pass a rather stiff financial examination, which took the last fifteen hundred dollars I had.'[3]

The second of the two voices was the voice of Dean Vincent MacDonald. In 1949 at a symposium on legal education put on by the University of British Columbia and participated in by such luminaries as Dean Griswold of Harvard, Professor Hughes Parry of London, and Dean Wright of Toronto, MacDonald made a stinging public attack on the 'high protective tariff' set up by 'certain of the Law Societies' for the transfer of barristers which created quite a stir in the Ontario newspapers. He did not, however, venture to attack the back-door transfer-as-a-barrister method that had so long been the only avenue open to the extra-provincial student or to suggest that it be replaced by what we have called the 'portabliity of degrees' system; that would, in 1949, have seemed a step so revolutionary as to be quite impractical. The main thrust of what he said was that 'there is cause for regret that the prerequisites to admission [of extra-provincial barristers] are of a fiscal rather than of an educational character.'[4] And six months later, in his capacity of chairman and prime mover of a special committee of the Conference of Governing Bodies of the Legal Profession in Canada which had been appointed to devise a reasonable and workable system regarding transfer of lawyers from one provincial Bar to another – he was one of the representatives of the Nova Scotia Barristers' Society to the Conference, which consists of representatives of each of the provincial law societies – he presented to the Conference a report recommending a system under which the prerequisites to admission of the extra-provincial barrister would be 'of an educational rather than of a fiscal character.'

Educational rather than fiscal though the new prerequisites were meant to be, they did not make any distinction between the extra-provincial barrister with experience and the extra-provincial barrister who had just graduated. This was too much for the Benchers of the Law Society of Upper Canada, who, to be fair to them, had always taken very seriously their duty to protect the public against the inexperience of the young. When Vincent MacDonald's report came up for discussion in 1952, therefore, their representatives at the

Conference announced that they would have none of it and that their Society was going to distinguish between extra-provincial barristers as follows: those who had been in active practice for six years; those who had been in active practice for three years; and those who had been in active practice for less than three years. Those who had been in active practice for less than three years would have to begin all over again in Ontario – enrol themselves as students at law, attend the Osgoode Hall Law School, and pass the examinations and pay the fees required of students at law.

Dean Vincent MacDonald's attempt to improve the position of the student who came to Dalhousie Law School from Ontario and of the student from the Maritimes who wanted to go to Ontario when he was through – for that is the real reason why, as early as 1939, he had persuaded the Conference of Governing Bodies to appoint the special committee – had only, it seemed at this moment, succeeded in making it immeasurably worse. Those students had escaped from the frying pan of having to fork out $1 500, but they were now in the fire of having to treat as wasted the three years they had spent at the Law School; what was the point of coming there at all if at the end of it they had to start all over again in Ontario? Or, putting it another way, the serious financial barrier to the access of Dalhousie Law School graduates to the practice of law in Ontario had been removed but in its place there was now an educational one that was, in terms of expenses to be incurred and time to be spent in law school, absolutely insurmountable. It occurred to Horace Read, however – who had by this time succeeded Vincent MacDonald both as Dean of the Law School and as one of the Nova Scotia Barristers' Society's representatives to the Conference of Governing Bodies – that there might be a way round the barrier. This round-about way would, as things turned out, become in a few years' time a main road through it, resulting in the recognition by the Ontario Society of the LLB degree from Dalhousie – and from all the other 'approved' law schools in Canada – as fulfilling all the academic requirements for admission to their Bar.

Read knew that the Law Society was already giving partial recognition to the LLB degree from another law school in Ontario, the one at the University of Toronto. In the wake of a controversy of which a brief account has already been given in the introductory paragraphs to Part III, the University of Toronto had in 1949 established a new three-year full-time professional law school on the Dalhousie model and the Law Society had reorganized the course at its own Osgoode Hall into a four-year one. The new Osgoode course, a compromise between a three-year full-time course plus a year of apprenticeship, which some of the Benchers were prepared to accept, and the traditional three-year course to be attended part-time by students working the rest of the day in law offices, which a majority of the Benchers wanted, was organized as follows. The first and second years were spent in full-time attendance at the Law School (the 'academic' input); the last two years were to emphasize the 'practical' input, the third year being spent in full-time apprenticeship in a law office and the fourth year being spent in attendance at lectures at Osgoode Hall while concurrently serving as an apprentice in an office. The Benchers had been asked by the University to admit the graduates from its new school to the profession after service as apprentices for a year – once again on the Dalhousie model. Committed as they were to emphasizing the importance of the last two 'practical input' years of their own new course, they denied the request but did accept the University's three-year LLB degree as equivalent to the first two 'academic input' years at Osgoode Hall. To the student at the University of Toronto Law School this meant that it would take him a year longer to get to the Bar than if he had gone to Osgoode Hall and that he would have to do all over again in Osgoode's fourth year work that he had already satisfactorily completed at the University – a situation that was, of course, nearly fatal, and meant to be fatal, to the success of the new school.

But to the students at Dalhousie Law School a similar partial recognition of his LLB degree by the Benchers would be better than the total disregard of it with which he seemed to be about to be faced. So, with the support of the Law Faculty at Dalhousie and of the Council of the Nova Scotia Barristers' Society – support which was absolutely necessary to counterbalance the wrath that his old friend and colleague, Sidney Smith, now president of the University of Toronto, was bound to heap on him for condoning the inferior position to which the Benchers had relegated his new school – Read made to the Benchers a formal and well-argued request that graduates of Dalhousie Law School be granted equal recognition with law graduates of the University of Toronto for the purpose of admission to the Bar in Ontario. Coming as it did from a school that had for many years been 'an institution' throughout Canada, Read's request could not be denied; nor, on the other hand, could the Benchers single out Dalhousie Law School for special treatment. In the result what a spokesman for the Law Society of Upper Canada called 'these Osgoode Hall privileges' were in the fall of 1952 extended to the graduates of Dalhousie – 'no doubt Canada's outstanding law school,' he termed it – and to the graduates of all other approved Canadian law schools.[5]

The partial recognition thus accorded to the Dalhousie LLB did little to encourage the Ontario resident to come to Dalhousie for his law school training: he would be adding an extra year to his course. Nor did it relieve from all penalty the Maritimer who wanted to go to Ontario on graduation: he had been relieved of the financial penalty but he was still faced with the educational one of having to do all over again at Osgoode Hall the academic work that he had done in one of his three years at Dalhousie. It did, however, serve as a precedent for the total recognition that came five years later.

By 1955 the Benchers of the Law Society of Upper Canada had woken up to the fact that enrolment at their Osgoode Hall Law School had become established at a level approximately double that of pre-war years and was probably going to climb some more. Faced with the prospect of having to provide legal education and training for many more Ontario students than their building space and their financial resources could cope with, they decided in 1957 to give up the monopoly to which they had clung so long and established a new plan for legal education in Ontario. Reserving to the Law Society its undoubted prerogative, and duty, of providing the practical training – an apprenticeship of fifteen months after graduation from law school plus a six-month bar admission course – they threw open to all Ontario universities possessing adequate facilities and following an acceptable curriculum (including, of course, the Osgoode Hall Law School) the provision of the academic education, which was to be a three-year full-time program that would earn the student a law degree.

Following the precedent established at the instance of Read in 1952, graduates of Dalhousie Law School – and of other approved law schools across Canada – were thereafter 'granted equal recognition with law graduates of [Ontario universities] for the purpose of admission to the Bar of Ontario' and, bringing their now fully recognized degree with them, could without any penalty, financial or academic, become qualified to practise in Ontario by taking the practical training required and provided by the Law Society there. In a word the Dalhousie Law School's degree was now 'portable' to Ontario and, in a few more words, the School had now become as regular an avenue of approach to the Bar of Ontario as it had since 1891 been to the Bar of Nova Scotia. As for the other common-law provinces, their law societies had in the years following the adoption, with some amendments, of the MacDonald Report by the Conference in 1953, already given to the Dalhousie LLB degree recognition similar to that now given to it by the Law Society of Upper Canada. Thus in 1957 the School's degree became for the first time fully 'portable' in all the common-law provinces of Canada.

Why, the reader may ask, has so much space been devoted to the history of what is, after all, only one of the innovations in the period 1950-58? Because the story, properly understood, brings into sharp relief some of the most enduring characteristics of the School.

Why, for instance, was removal of the protective tariffs so important to it? First, because as a matter of hard fact the School was, and always had been, an exporting school; it had to export a goodly number of its students from the Maritimes or just die. Second, because from Weldon ('The light must come from the East') through the realistic MacDonald ('A national law school') to the unrealistic Read ('the law School at Dalhousie continues to be a "national law school," more truly so than others in this country, in the sense that it attracts students from across Canada and elsewhere'), those who ran it had always been dreamers, dreaming of it becoming a Canadian Harvard; but that could never be so long as the law societies in the other common-law provinces imposed on their law students artificial restraints that prevented them from coming to it.

And how come that MacDonald and Read, mere academics at a school at the eastern extremity of Canada, were able to play so central a role in resolving a national problem that only the leaders in the practising profession across the country had the power to deal with? Because of the close relationship that existed, and had always existed, between the School and the Bar of Nova Scotia. The aspect of that close relationship which was of importance in the story we have just told was that at least since the early thirties the Dean of Dalhousie Law School had been *ex officio* a member of the Council of the Nova Scotia Barristers' Society and was, as such, eligible to be sent to the Conference of Governing Bodies by the Society as one of its representatives. It was as representatives of the Nova Scotia Barristers' Society and not as teachers at Dalhousie Law School that MacDonald and Read were able to deal face to face and on cosy terms with those in whose hands lay the resolution of a problem which, though national, was of vital importance to the School. The same thing would be true in 1969 when Dean Andy MacKay, as representative of the Barristers' Society and also, as it so happened, president for that year of the Conference, would help to dissuade the Conference from standing in the way of the radical optionalization of the curriculum that all the common-law schools in Canada, including Dalhousie, were at that time proposing to undertake.

NOTES

INTRODUCTION

1 *Dalhousie University, Special Convocation, August 19th 1936*, p. 11.
2 Some of the language in this paragraph is borrowed from Bora Laskin, *The British Tradition in Canadian Law* (London: Stevens and Sons, 1969), pp. 75-6 and 84.
3 A.Z. Reed, *Present-Day Law Schools in the United States and Canada* (New York: Carnegie Foundation for the Advancement of Teaching, 1928), pp. 346-7.
4 (1957), found in Horace Read's files; unpublished.
5 Quoted in the *Atlantic Advocate* article referred to earlier.
6 In an article in the *Evening Mail* reprinted in his *Autobiography* (Halifax, 1932), p. 151.
7 See Brian D. Bucknall, C.H. Baldwin, and J. David Lakin, 'Pedants, Practitioners and Prophets: Legal Education at Osgoode Hall to 1957,' 6 *Osgoode Hall Law Journal* 141 (1968).
8 per Laskin, *The British Tradition* (note 2), p. 84.
9 The law school in Saint John, New Brunswick, although founded in 1892 as a faculty of the University of King's College in Windsor, Nova Scotia, and taken over in 1923 by the University of New Brunswick as one of its faculties, was until 1950 a very rudimentary practitioner-operated affair. For its history see McAllister, 'Some Phases of Legal Education in New Brunswick,' 8 *University of New Brunswick Law Journal* 33 (1955).
10 Letter from M.M. Porter KC ('17, later Mr Justice Porter) to Dean Vincent MacDonald, 30 November 1935.
11 *Gazette* 14 March 1889, p. 164.
12 Vincent J. Pottier, *Ansul*, January 1976, p. 9.
13 Letter from Sidney Smith to Horace Read, 3 February 1929.
14 J.W.E. Mingo, *Ansul*, January 1976, p. 86.

I BEGINNING

1 *Report of Committee on Legal Education* (Cmd 4595, 1971), pp. 8-10.
2 See Laskin, *The British Tradition in Canadian Law* (London: Stevens & Sons, 1969), pp. 81-2.

3 Printed by Joseph Howe (Halifax, NS, 1832), p. 7.
4 'Legal Education,' Address by Mr Justice Russell, 3 *Proceedings of Canadian Bar Association* 118-19 (1918).
5 See *Debates and Proceedings of the House of Assembly* for remarks made in the course of the debates on the Law Students' Bill in 1872 and on the Halifax Law School Bill in 1874.
6 See 'A Retrospective Glance,' *Dalhousie Gazette* 13 February 1895; *Dalhousie University Bulletin No. 2, Munro Day Bulletin*, pp. 1-2 (1928); and more generally D.C. Harvey, *An Introduction to the History of Dalhousie University* (Halifax, 1938), esp. pp. 77-102.
7 Harvey, *Dalhousie University* (note 6), p. 101.
8 Russell, *Autobiography* (Halifax, 1932), p. 148.
9 R. St. J. Macdonald, 'An Historical Introduction to the Teaching of International Law in Canada,' 1974 *Canadian Yearbook of International Law*, 67, 93.
10 Charles Morse ('85), editor of the Canadian Bar Review, in 11 *Canadian Bar Review* 402-3 (1933).
11 See J. Castell Hopkins, *Life and Work of the Right Honourable Sir John Thompson* (Brantford, Ontario, 1895), pp. 66-7; and an article in the *Dalhousie Gazette*, 30 November 1897, pp. 86-7.
12 See Russell, *Autobiography*, and an article in the *Alumni News* for June 1939, 'The First Law Dean.'
13 The biographical details on Sedgewick and on the people mentioned in this paragraph have been culled from such books of reference as *Canadian Who Was Who* and from scattered notes in the *Dalhousie Gazette*.
14 Transcribed by Professor Peter Waite of the History Department at Dalhousie from Volume 288 of the Thompson Papers in the Public Archives of Canada.
15 The assertion, made by R. St. J. Macdonald in 'An Historical Introduction' (note 9), p. 90, was, Macdonald tells the writer, made to him by Horace Read. But the writer has been unable to find any direct evidence to back it up. As to indirect evidence, the writer has discovered, to his surprise, that the Dalhousie curriculum of 1883, with its heavy infusion of non-technical subjects, was more closely allied to the markedly cultural Columbia curriculum of the day than it was to the strictly private-law Harvard one. See on the whole matter: letter signed 'Senex' in *Gazette* 4 March 1892; *Centennial History of Harvard Law School, 1817-1917*, pp. 75-6; and *History of the School of Law, Columbia University* (1955), p. 90.
16 *Gazette*, 23 November 1883.
17 For an entertaining and appreciative description of Bulmer see Russell, 'John Thomas Bulmer,' 9 *Dalhousie Review* 68, esp. pp. 71-3.
18 *Morning Chronicle*, reproduced in *Dalhousie Gazette* for 10 November 1883.
19 Cited by E.A. Corbett, *Sidney Earle Smith* (University of Toronto Press, 1961), p. 13.
20 Russell, *Autobiography*, pp. 137-8. They are in Volume 287 of the Thompson Papers in the PAC (per Professor Peter Waite).
21 *Gazette*, 24 November 1884.
22 This memorandum is reproduced in Horace Read's draft of the history, but J.W. has been unable to discover where he got it from.

23 See *Gazette*, 28 November 1885; 7 May 1887, p. 151 (Valedictory); and 7 May 1888 (Valedictory).

24 See Denis Healy, 'The University of Halifax 1875-1881,' 53 *Dalhousie Review* 38, esp. pp. 46-9 (1973), and 'University of Halifax, Regulations relating to degrees in Laws,' February 1877 (copy in Law School Files).

25 This compressed description of the affiliated-student system has deliberately sacrificed completeness and absolute accuracy of detail to ease of comprehension.

26 Russell, *Autobiography*, pp. 139-43; Law School Calendars for 1884-85, 1885-86, and several later years.

27 Shipping is excluded because it was dropped from the curriculum after only one year and was not given again until 1893.

28 *Gazette*, 12 December 1885, p. 35; 7 May 1887, p. 151. A tattered, mimeographed, historical description of the Nova Scotia Barristers' Society, apparently written some time in the 1920s and found among the late Dean Horace Read's papers, gives 1891 as the date; see N.S. Statutes 1891 c.22, s.4. The wording of 'the recent Act,' N.S. Statutes 1887, c.24, s.1, gives some, but in the writer's opinion insufficient, ground for the Valedictorian's statement.

29 *Gazette*, 13 March 1890.

30 For the information contained in this paragraph see Harvey, *Dalhousie University* (note 6), pp. 105-7, and *Gazette*, 18 November 1887.

31 *Gazette*, 13 February 1895, pp. 196-200.

32 8 *Canadian Law Times* 71.

33 16 *Law Quarterly Review* 227 (1900). Other comments of his will be found in 2 *Law Quarterly Review* 118 (1886) and 15 *Law Quarterly Review* 241-2 (1899).

II DALHOUSIE'S LITTLE LAW SCHOOL
SECTION ONE 1887-1914: WELDON

1 per J. Chisholm Lyons ('51), *Ansul*, January 1976, p. 91.

2 F.M. Covert ('29), *ibid.*, p. 41.

3 F.A. McCully, *Gazette*, 7 May 1887.

4 Editorial, *ibid.*, 14 March 1889.

5 Covert, *Ansul*, January 1976, p. 41.

6 A.J. MacIntosh ('48), *ibid.*, p. 83.

7 *Gazette*, 31 December 1886.

8 *Ibid.*, 29 December 1899. The menu has for some reason or other been preserved in the Law School files.

9 The Law Yell deserves at least a footnote. This is how it went:
Lindley, Anson, Pollock, Beven,
All good lawyers go to Heaven,
Odgers, Thayer, Blackstone, Snell,
All the rest can go to hell.

10 *Gazette*, March 1912, pp. 224-5.

11 See *Report of Proceedings of 1st-3rd Annual Meetings* (Canada Law Journal Company, 1898; reprinted Toronto: Carswell, 1969).

12 See *Gazette*, 28 February 1906, p. 153 ff. and p. 165 ff.

13 2 *Law Quarterly Review* 118 (1886).

14 See Gloria Read, 'The History of the Moot Court,' *Gazette*, Law Supplement, 5 November 1958. This full and interesting account overstresses, of course, the fun and games element.

15 per J. Chisholm Lyons, *Ansul*, January 1976, p. 92.

16 per Peter O. Hearn ('47), *ibid.*, p. 80.

17 See *Gazette*, Law Supplement, 5 November 1958, for an excellent brief history of the Mock Parliament.

18 See *Gazette*, 29 August 1952, for a description of the functions of the Society at that date. For a description of its functions today see the most recent issue of the *Law Student Handbook*, a mimeographed vademecum furnished by the Society to each member of every incoming first-year class. For those who are interested in such matters, the first Law Dance to be held outside the Forrest Building seems to have been in 1919 (see *Gazette*, 18 December 1914; 27 October 1920; and 10 November 1920). The annual Law Dinner or Banquet, which was an important event in the School's social year when the writer was there in the thirties and early forties but is now a thing of the past, seems to have started some time between 1905 and 1911, to have been suspended in the First World War, and to have been revived in 1922 (see *Gazette*, 22 October 1914; 15 March 1922).

19 *Gazette*, 1 March 1895.

20 *Ibid.*, 13 March 1890.

21 *Ibid.*, June 1913, p. 372.

22 *Ibid.*, 22 November 1895; 13 November 1896; 28 February 1906.

23 See the following *Gazettes*: 14 March 1889; 13 March 1890; 15 October 1891; 4 March 1892; and 10 October 1894. See also Regulations of Nova Scotia Barristers' Society, 1899.

24 Letter from Weldon to New Brunswick Barristers' Society, 30 October 1907. As to missed lectures, the attendance record kept by the downtown lecturers and several comments in the *Gazette* during the years 1911 to 1914 reveal an astonishing number of them.

25 See the following *Gazettes*: 15 February 1887; 6 April 1888; 3 May 1893; 17 May 1894; and 11 May 1896. And see N.W. Hoyles, 'Legal Education in Canada,' 19 *Canadian Law Times* 261, 265 (1900). See also the following Law School Calendars: 1912-13, footnote on p. 7; and 1914-15, p. 11.

26 In his review of Russell's *Autobiography*, 11 *Canadian Bar Review* 68, 69 (1933).

27 per Emelyn MacKenzie ('19), *Ansul*, January 1976, p. 5.

28 *Gazette*, 19 November 1886.

29 *Ibid.*, 27 September 1935.

30 *Alumni News*, June 1939, p. 5; January 1938, p. 10; *Gazette* 1912-13, p. 372; and Lord Beaverbrook, *Courage: The Story of Sir James Dunn* (Fredericton NB: Brunswick Press, 1961), p. 51.

31 per R.H. Murray ('96) in *Alumni News*, December 1925.

32 per President A. Stanley MacKenzie, in a communication to the Herald Office on Weldon's death, 27 November 1925.

33 See J.P. Martin, *Dartmouth Free Press* 22 March 1967; Russell, 'Richard Chapman Weldon,' 4 *Canadian Bar Review* 197; House of Commons, *Sessions Papers*, Volume 35 (1901), Return of the Ninth General Election for the House of Commons of Canada, Province of New Brunswick, Albert County; and *Canadian Annual Review*, 1906, pp. 551-3, esp. p. 553. For an account of the Manitoba School Question see Arthur R.M. Lower, *Colony to Nation* (Toronto: Longmans, Green & Company, 1946), pp. 394-5.

34 In a letter to Russell, 5 September 1914.

35 *Gazette*, 22 December 1896.

36 John Barnett, 'Dalhousie Law School – Ideals and Traditions' (unpublished).

37 *Alumni News*, June 1939, p. 5.

38 The notes were taken by S. Edgar March ('93); the paper on which they are written is, alas, falling to pieces.

39 *Ansul*, May 1974.

40 *Alumni News*, December 1925.

41 Arthur Morton, *Alumni News*, June 1939.

42 R.B. Bennett ('93) in a letter to L.P.D. Tilley read at the banquet held in October 1933 to celebrate the fiftieth anniversary of the founding of the School.

43 In a review of Russell's *Autobiography*. Read quotes this passage in his first draft of the history, but J.W. has been unable to locate the review.

44 L.H. Fenerty ('05) in a letter to *Ansul*, February 1971.

45 The words in quotation marks come from *Gazette*, 14 October 1903.

46 *Gazette*, 17 February 1932, gives the names and the courts, as well as the names of those who were on county or district courts. The *Gazette* is wrong about the Sedgewick on the Ontario Supreme Court; he was a Dalhousie Arts graduate, but not a graduate of Dalhousie Law School.

47 Nova Scotia: E.N. Rhodes ('02), from 1925 to 1930 and Gordon Harrington ('04) from 1930 to 1933. New Brunswick: L.P.D. Tilley ('93) from 1933 to 1935. Newfoundland: Sir Richard Squires ('02) from 1919 to 1923 and from 1928 to 1932.

48 See Roy St George Stubbs, 'Lord Bennett,' 29 *Canadian Bar Review* 631, 634-8 (1951).

49 Beaverbrook, *Courage: The Story of Sir James Dunn* (note 30), p. 54.

II DALHOUSIE'S LITTLE LAW SCHOOL
SECTION TWO 1914-1924: MACRAE

1 *Ansul*, special issues, January 1976 and December 1977.

2 36 *Canadian Law Times* 85-6 (1916).

3 *Gazette*, 22 October 1914; a letter to an unidentified Prince Edward Island newspaper from M. McKenzie, Canoe Cove (MacRae's birthplace), 22 November 1955; and letter from A. Stanley MacKenzie to Judge Russell, 11 September 1914.

4 Letter from A. Stanley MacKenzie to Judge Russell, 11 September 1914.

5 See, *inter alia*: letter from Russell to MacKenzie, 14 April 1913; letter from MacKenzie to MacRae, 14 September 1914; letters and other material concerning honoraria to members

of part-time faculty from 1911 to 1915; and 'A Hitherto Unwritten History of the Class at Law '13' in *Gazette*, June 1913, pp. 371-5.

6 See Law School Calendars for 1912-13 and 1914-15; Law School Faculty Minutes, 5 April 1914; and letter from President MacKenzie to J.L. Barnhill, Secretary of the Nova Scotia Barristers' Society, 4 December 1920.

7 See letter from R.S. Deane to Judge Russell, 13 August 1913; Faculty Minutes, 13 October 1913; and Council of the Nova Scotia Barristers' Society's Minutes for 12 March, 27 March, and 9 April 1914. The 'mysterious entry' in the Calendars is a statement – the first in any Calendar to say anything whatever about what credit, if any, the Barristers' Society gives for work done at the Law School – to the effect that the Society gives credit for the particular subjects there specified. The inference is that the Society is no longer giving – or is thinking of no longer giving – the credit so long given for all subjects covered by the School's degree.

8 A.Z. Reed, *Present-Day Law Schools in the United States and Canada* (New York: Carnegie Foundation for the Advancement of Teaching, 1928), p. 344.

9 per Emelyn MacKenzie in *Ansul*, January 1976, p. 5.

10 per Vincent J. Pottier, *ibid.*, p. 7.

11 *Gazette*, 18 December 1914.

12 See *inter alia* notes taken from MacRae's correspondence in the Law School files, newspaper clippings kept by Horace Read in a book marked Cuttings, and Judge R.H. Murray's 'Canada's First Law School Passes its Half-Century Milestone,' in *Port and Province*, December 1933, p. 23.

13 'Comity and the Capacity of Companies,' 36 *Canadian Law Times* 98 (1916).

14 *Gazette*, 5 March, 5 April, 27 October 1915; and 22 December 1916.

15 Minutes of Board of Governors, 9 July 1881.

16 *Ansul*, January 1976, pp. 5-6.

17 Saint John *Telegraph-Journal*, 12 February 1963.

18 5 *Proceedings of Canadian Bar Association* 16-18 (1920).

19 For the comparative tables see 4 *Proceedings of Canadian Bar Association* 201-24 (1919); the Dalhousie Law School curriculum of 1918-19 is set out on p. 219.

20 Letter dated 15 January 1920.

21 The Standard Curriculum and the Report of the Sub-Committee will be found at pp. 250-7 of 5 *Proceedings of Canadian Bar Association* (1920) and the debate at the plenary session at pp. 16-54 of the same volume; see also letter from MacRae to MacKenzie, 12 September 1923.

22 MacRae, 'Legal Education in Canada,' 1 *Canadian Bar Review* 671, 675 (1923).

23 Letter from MacRae to Mr Justice Harris, 2 July 1915.

24 *Alumni News*, January 1938. The quotation in the first part of the sentence is from Dean Sidney Smith, *Halifax Herald*, 28 October 1933.

25 Professor H.A. Smith of McGill in an address to the Association of American Law Schools on 31 December 1921; 'Legal Education in Canada,' 4 *American Law School Review* 734, 736.

26 F.M. Covert, *Ansul*, January 1976, p. 42.

27 *Ibid.*, p. 41, and J.G. Hackett at p. 20. For full biographical details of John Read see *Ansul*, April 1969 and May 1974.

28 Frank E. Archibald, *Mostly Maritimers* (Windsor, NS, 1972), pp. 11-14; letter from Smith to MacRae 8 October 1920; letter from MacRae to A.S. MacKenzie 15 December 1920.

29 Russell had something to say about it in an address to the Canadian Bar Association in 1918: 'Legal Education,' 3 *Proceedings of Canadian Bar Association* 118.

30 J.T. Hebert, 'An Unsolicited Report on Legal Education in Canada,' 41 *Canadian Law Times* 593, 600 (1921).

31 'Some Phases of American Legal Education,' 1 *Canadian Bar Review* 646, 653-4 (1923).

32 See Horace Read's draft volume on MacRae and 'Interview with Dean Read [John Read],' *Ansul*, May 1974.

33 Arthur E. Sutherland, *The Law at Harvard* (Cambridge, Mass: Harvard University Press, 1967), pp. 179-80.

34 *Gazette*, May 1922.

35 'Interview with Dean Read [John Read],' *Ansul*, May 1974. See also Calendar 1886-87 and 6 *Osgoode Hall Law Journal* 180.

36 MacRae 'Legal Education in Canada,' 1 *Canadian Bar Review* 671, at p. 671 (1923)

37 Information derived from Law School Calendars for 1924-25 and succeeding years, supplemented by the writer's personal knowledge.

38 Letter to President MacKenzie, 12 April 1913.

39 Letter to Professor Ira MacKay of the McGill Law School, 26 September 1921. For a more extended and detailed criticism, see John Read's 'Memorandum Re Proposed Changes in the Affiliated Courses' in Faculty Minutes, 12 November 1921.

40 Brian D. Bucknall *et al.*, 'Pedants, Practitioners and Prophets: Legal Education at Osgoode Hall to 1957,' 6 *Osgoode Hall Law Journal* 141, 186 (1968).

41 *Ibid.*, p. 193.

42 The title 'Evidence' in the first edition of *Canadian Encyclopaedic Digest* (Ontario ed.), Volume 4 (1928). This title is 470 pages long and makes copious reference to Wigmore and Thayer, the leading American writers on the subject; it was, and rightly, much admired in its time, particularly because it introduced Wigmore to the working members of the profession in Ontario.

43 Letters from Sidney Smith to Horace Read, 1 March 1954 and 7 July 1954.

44 William S. Learned and Kenneth C.M. Sills, *Education in the Maritime Provinces of Canada* (New York: Carnegie Foundation for the Advancement of Teaching, 1922), p. 18.

45 8 *Proceedings of Canadian Bar Association* 101 (1923).

46 See Reed, *Present-Day Law Schools* (note 8), pp. 358-9; article in 6 *Osgoode Hall Law Journal* (note 40), p. 186; and 'Quill' [Horace Read] in an article from the *Gazette* reproduced in the *Morning Chronicle*, 9 November 1922.

47 Professor H.A. Smith of McGill in 8 *Proceedings of Canadian Bar Association* 100 (1923).

48 Reed, *Present-Day Law Schools* (note 8), p. 331.

49 *Alumni News*, September 1921.

II DALHOUSIE'S LITTLE LAW SCHOOL
SECTION THREE 1920-1933: THE GOLDEN AGE

1 N.A.M. MacKenzie, 'The Things I Remember,' Address at Dalhousie Convocation, 12 August 1953.
2 11 *Canadian Bar Review* 392, 394 (1933).
3 Letter, 3 February 1929.
4 Letter, 27 March 1929.
5 Letter, 31 December 1919.
6 In 'Fifty Years of Legal Education at Dalhousie' (note 2), at 394. The information contained in this paragraph is drawn from the reminiscences in *Ansul*, January 1976, and from 'Weldon Tradition' articles on Keiller MacKay and John Read in other *Ansuls*.
7 *Gazette*, September 1913, p. 31.
8 R. St J. Macdonald, 'An Historical Introduction to the Teaching of International Law in Canada,' 1974 *Canadian Yearbook of International Law* 67, at pp. 94-5.
9 Charles Morse, 'The Teaching of Law,' 4 *Canadian Bar Review* 483, 487 (1926).
10 See Calendar 1927-28; an unpublished section of an interview with John Read (1973); F.M. Covert in *Ansul*, January 1976, p. 41; and letter from F.M. Covert to Dean R. St J. Macdonald, 8 July 1974.
11 Letter from A.S. MacKenzie to MacRae, 12 October 1923.
12 A Conversation with Dean Read, *Ansul*, May 1974.
13 *Gazette*, 19 March 1925.
14 M.M. McIntyre took his place for that one year. McIntyre, a native of Sackville, New Brunswick, had just graduated from the Harvard Law School. In later years he became Dean of the Alberta Law School and still later a member of the original faculty of the Law School at the University of British Columbia.
15 Letter to George Wilson, 25 January 1929, and letter to Horace Read, 6 May 1929.
16 Letter from Sidney Smith to the President, 27 March 1929, and letter from the President to Smith, 10 April 1929.
17 Denne Burchell in *Ansul*, January 1976, p. 87.
18 Laskin, *The British Tradition in Canadian Law* (London, 1968), 84.
19 The full-dress article is the one by John Read to which we have so often referred: 'Fifty Years of Legal Education at Dalhousie.' This and the three editorial notes will be found at pp. 392, 402, 628, and 690 of the volume.
20 For a record, some of it detailed, of distinguished graduates as of 1933 see two articles by Sidney Smith, *Gazette* 17 February 1932, and *Halifax Herald*, 28 October 1933. See also an article by Charles Morse in *Gazette*, 26 November 1929.
21 The three quotations are, taking them in order, from: an article by Charles Morse in *Gazette*, 26 November 1929; an article by Vincent MacDonald in *Alumni News*, January 1938, entitled 'Dalhousie Law Tradition'; and an unsigned (but, according to Horace Read, written by Sidney Smith) article in *Gazette*, 22 February 1933, entitled 'The Law School's Birthday.'
22 'The Law School's Birthday.'

23 See *Halifax Herald* and *Halifax Chronicle*, 28, 30, 31 October 1933, and *Gazette*, 2 November 1933, for information relating to the fiftieth anniversary celebrations.
24 *Gazette* 14 January 1930.
25 *Ibid.*, 27 October 1932.

II DALHOUSIE'S LITTLE LAW SCHOOL
SECTION FOUR 1933-1945: THE GREAT DEPRESSION
AND THE SECOND WORLD WAR

1 'Report of the Benchers' Special Committee on Legal Education,' 13 *Canadian Bar Review* 347, 355 (1935).
2 Letter from J. McG. Stewart to Colonel Laurie, Chairman of the Board, 19 March 1945.
3 Letter from Sidney Smith to Horace Read, 19 February 1954.
4 Read and MacDonald, *Cases and Other Materials on Legislation*, University Case Book Series (Brooklyn: Foundation Press, 1948).
5 *Gazette*, 12 October 1934.
6 *Parliamentary Powers of English Government Departments* (Cambridge, Mass: Harvard University Press, 1933).
7 12 *Canadian Bar Review* 545, 601 (1934).
8 See the following letters: MacDonald to Stanley, 10 October 1935; Stanley to MacDonald, 11 October 1935; Stanley to MacDonald, 10 October 1934; and MacDonald to various graduates, 18 and 19 November 1935.
9 See, for example, letter from MacDonald to Stanley, 9 April 1935, and Memorandum of December 1938.
10 See MacDonald, 'Judicial Interpretation of the Canadian Constitution,' 1 *University of Toronto Law Journal* 260 (1935); MacDonald, 'The Canadian Constitution Seventy Years After,' 15 *Canadian Bar Review* 401 (1937); and an editorial in the *Winnipeg Free Press* reproduced in the *Halifax Herald*, 17 July 1937.
11 'The Lawyer – Citizen in the New World,' 21 *Canadian Bar Review* 777, 781 (1943).
12 Letter from Bennett to Stanley, 29 March 1943.
13 Letter from J. McG. Stewart to Colonel Laurie, 19 March 1945.
14 per Peter O Hearn, *Ansul*, January 1976, p. 78.
15 *Torts in the Conflict of Laws* (Ann Arbor: University of Michigan Press, 1942).
16 See Nova Scotia Laws 1933, c.36, Law School Calendar 1934-35, and Reed, *Present-Day Law Schools in the United States and Canada*, pp. 349-59. The 'American observer' is Reed, at p. 359.
17 The passages in quotation marks are (shamelessly) lifted from John Willis, *Ansul*, January 1976, p. 65; some of the wording has been slightly altered.
18 'Judicial Interpretation of the Canadian Constitution,' 1 *University of Toronto Law Journal* 260 (1935).
19 'Statute Interpretation in a Nutshell,' 18 *Canadian Bar Review* 1 (1938), and *Canadian Boards at Work* (Toronto: Macmillan, 1941).
20 28 *Canadian Bar Review* 267.

III CHANGING: 1945-1966

1 *There Stands Dalhousie* (published for the Dalhousie Alumni Association in 1976 by Josten's National School Services Ltd., Winnipeg), p. 104.
2 [1964] *Canadian Bar Papers* 112.
3 'Professional Aspects of Legal Education,' 28 *Canadian Bar Review* 160, 162 (1950).
4 Read, 'The Public Responsibilities of the Academic Law Teacher in Canada,' 39 *Canadian Bar Review* 232, 246-7 (1961).
5 The main sources of the information contained in this paragraph are: Laskin, *The British Tradition in Canadian Law*, pp. 83-6; Bucknall *et al.*, 'Pedants, Practitioners and Prophets: Legal Education at Osgoode Hall to 1957,' 6 *Osgoode Hall Law Journal* 141, 221-8 (1968); and statements made to the writer by the late Dean Wright (the writer was one of Wright's colleagues from 1944 to 1952). The Wright side of the great debate is well stated in C.A. Wright, 'Should the Profession Control Legal Education?,' 3 *Journal of Legal Education* 1 (1950); the Bencher side is equally well stated in R.M. Willes Chitty, 'Legal Education,' 3 *Chitty's Law Journal* 89 (1953).
6 G.F. Curtis, 'Trends in Legal Education,' 4 *Canadian Bar Journal* 21, 26 (1961).
7 See *ibid.*, pp. 26-7, and Cohen, 'Condition of Legal Education in Canada; Fifteen Years Later' (note 2), p. 121.
8 Trends (note 6), p. 25.
9 The information in this paragraph is derived from Lederman, The Association of Canadian Law Teachers,' 30 *Canadian Bar Review* 608 (1952), from various documents found in Horace Read's files, and from the writer's own knowledge.
10 The generalizations, which are the writer's, were inspired in part by: Cohen, 'Condition,' Read, 'Public Responsibilities,' Curtis, 'Trends,' and R.I. Cheffins, 'Canadian–U.S. Legal Education Compared,' 8 *Canadian Bar Journal* 170 (1965).
11 The quotations – and the information – in this paragraph are from 'The Post-War Years, 1945-1963, President's Convocation Address, May 16, 1963,' a pamphlet published by Dalhousie University in 1963.
12 See reminiscences of G.V.V. Nicholls in *Ansul*, December 1977, and letter from W.R. Lederman to Lady Dunn, 9 July 1958.
13 Letter to Colonel Laurie, 20 September 1945.
14 Letter to Lady Dunn, 23 July 1958.
15 'Classification in Private International Law,' 29 *Canadian Bar Review* 3-33 and 168-84 (1951); 'The Independence of the Judiciary,' 34 *Canadian Bar Review* 769-809 and 1139-79 (1956).
16 *Treaties and Federal Constitutions* (Washington DC: Public Affairs Press, 1955); 'Sovereign Immunities from Jurisdiction of the Courts,' 36 *Canadian Bar Review* 145 (1958).
17 For an appreciation and short life of Sir James Dunn by Lord Beaverbrook, see *Alumni News*, December 1958, pp. 20-5. See also Beaverbrook, *Courage: The Story of Sir James Dunn* (Fredericton, NB, 1961); pp. 47-57 give the story of his days at the Law School.

18 This account of the coming of the Angus L. money and the Dunn money is based princi-
pally on material which will be found at the end of Horace Read's volume on Vincent
MacDonald and in the early pages of Horace Read's volume on Horace Read.

19 See *Gazette*, 15 October 1948, and end of Horace Read's draft volume on MacDonald.

20 *Ansul*, January 1976, p. 22.

21 *Halifax Chronicle-Herald*, 3 July 1964.

22 Among the many sources on which this section is based are: Dean Read's reports to the
President in President's Reports 1950-54, 1955-59, and 1959-63; Read's volume on
Horace Read, 1950-64; and the reminiscences in *Ansul*, December 1977.

23 President's Report 1955-59, p. 50, and President's Report 1959-63, p. 43.

24 For 1950-54, 1955-59, and 1959-63.

25 The passages in quotation marks are from Read's remarks as recorded in minutes of staff
meetings, 21 September 1960, and from Read's Report to the President in President's
Report 1950-54, p. 69.

26 *Hearsay*, May 1976, p. 11.

27 'What is the Problem Method?' 40 *Canadian Bar Review* 200 (1962).

28 Reminiscences, *Ansul*, December 1977, p. 76.

IV IN THE WELDON BUILDING: 1966-1976

1 Frederick H. Zemans and Lester Brickman, *Clinical Legal Education and Legal Aid –
The Canadian Experience*, Bulletin of the Council on Legal Education for Professional
Responsibility Inc. (New York), Volume VI, no. 13 (May 1974), p. 5.

2 On the history and activities of the Clinic see Harvey Savage, 'The Dalhousie Legal Aid
Service,' 2 *Dalhousie Law Journal* 505 (1975). See also David R. Lowry, 'A Plea for
Clinical Law,' 50 *Canadian Bar Review* 183 (1972).

3 In an article by an Australian law teacher in 2 *Dalhousie Law Journal* 3 (1975).

4 Faculty minutes, 22 January and 26 May 1926.

5 For a full description of Marine and Environmental Law at the School in 1975-76 see the
first issue of *Hearsay*, January 1976.

6 For a full description of the Continuing Legal Education program up to the end of 1975
see *ibid*.

7 See I.M. Christie, 'The Law School Curriculum,' *ibid*., May 1976, for a valuable survey of
the present curriculum by an ex-chairman of the curriculum committee. For a comprehensive survey of the situation right across Canada see John P.S. McLaren, 'Curriculum
Development in the Law Schools of Common Law Canada,' which will be found in a
collection of lithographed materials prepared for University of British Columbia Faculty
of Law, Conference on Legal Education, 22-23 November 1974. The discrepancy between
Professor Christie's date of 1968 and my date of 1969 is explained by the fact that Faculty
Council's decision to move to an optional curriculum was made at the end of the academic
year 1968-69, viz. at the end of April 1969; he calls it 1968, I call it 1969. In any event, the
new optional curriculum did not come into effect until the beginning of the academic year
1969-70, viz. in September 1969.

8 *Ibid*.

APPENDIX V HOW THE DALHOUSIE LLB DEGREE BECAME 'PORTABLE'

1 The main source for the story of how the School's LLB degree became portable is the exhaustive play-by-play account given by Horace Read in his first draft of this history; that account was backed up by a number of mimeographed unpublished documents submitted to the Conference of Governing Bodies of the Legal Profession in Canada. Supplementary published sources include: Vincent MacDonald, 'Professional Aspects of Legal Education,' 28 *Canadian Bar Review* 160, 165-6 (1950); Brian D. Bucknall *et al.*, 'Pedants, Practitioners and Prophets: Legal Education at Osgoode Hall to 1957,' 6 *Osgoode Hall Law Journal* 141, 219-20, and 226-8 (1968); and Dalhousie University, President's Report 1950-54, pp. 75-6, and President's Report, 1955-59, p. 74.

2 *Gazette*, 24 January 1947.

3 *Ansul*, January 1976, p. 84.

4 Vincent MacDonald, 'Professional Aspects of Legal Education,' 28 *Canadian Bar Review* 160, 165-6 (1950).

5 Toronto *Globe and Mail*, 16 October 1952.

INDEX